Norman Handy was born in Beckenham in the southeast of England. He went to Clare House School and secondary school at a mixed boarding school in Cranbrook, Kent. Later, he studied Law for Accountants, Business Economics and Accountancy at Southampton University.

Even during his studies, he travelled as often as he could, cycling down La Loire Valley and behind the Iron Curtain. After leaving university, he lived and worked abroad, ending up on a date plantation.

He returned to the United Kingdom and, after working in a riding school, followed a career in the financial services sector based in London, including periods working aboard in Europe, the Middle East and Asia. He published his first book in 2017.

Norman Handy

WHITE TO BLACK

AUSTIN MACAULEY PUBLISHERS™
LONDON * CAMBRIDGE * NEW YORK * SHARJAH

Copyright © Norman Handy 2024

The right of Norman Handy to be identified as the author of this work has been asserted by the author in accordance with sections 77 and 78 of the Copyright, Designs and Patents Act 1988.

All rights reserved. No part of this publication may be reproduced, stored in a retrieval system, or transmitted in any form or by any means, electronic, mechanical, photocopying, recording or otherwise, without the prior permission of the publishers.

Any person who commits any unauthorised act in relation to this publication may be liable to criminal prosecution and civil claims for damages.

All of the events in this memoir are true to the best of the author's memory. The views expressed in this memoir are solely those of the author.

A CIP catalogue record for this title is available from the British Library.

ISBN 9781035865635 (Paperback)
ISBN 9781035865642 (ePub e-book)

www.austinmacauley.com

First Published 2024
Austin Macauley Publishers Ltd®
1 Canada Square
Canary Wharf
London
E14 5AA

Table of Contents

Chapter 1: Travelling North	7
Chapter 2: Murmansk, City of Monuments	15
Chapter 3: Over the Border to Norway	24
Chapter 4: Petrozavodsk	29
Chapter 5: The Moscow Canal	41
Chapter 6: Moscow Visit	50
Chapter 7: The Golden Ring	57
Chapter 8: Nizhy Novgorod	68
Chapter 9: The Khanate of Kazan	80
Chapter 10: Ulyanovsk, Lenin's Birth Place	88
Chapter 11: Samara	96
Chapter 12: Saratov	103
Chapter 13: Volgograd	109
Chapter 14: Astrakhan and Caviar	119
Chapter 15: Volga-Don Canal to Rostov-on-Don	127
Chapter 16: Krasnodar	135
Chapter 17: Circassian Genocide	144
Chapter 18: Sochi	149
Chapter 19: Hero City Novorossiysk	157
Chapter 20: Russian Wineries	167
Chapter 21: Crimea	176
Chapter 22: Sevastopol	187
Recipes	192

Chapter 1
Travelling North

I was sitting in my train compartment with a couple opposite me, Katia and Anatoli, and a fourth person on my left, Sasha. We had made our introductions, and I had discovered that none of them spoke English. I didn't know enough Russian to have a proper conversation, but I knew enough to get by with the four most important areas of interaction. These are greetings to appear polite, numbers to bargain in markets and tell the time, directions to where you want to go and lastly food, so that I could read a menu and order what I wanted. The fifth essential area wasn't relevant here, which was all the questions about whether there was Wi-Fi, how to connect to the internet and the passwords.

I was sitting next to the window on the right-hand side of the train, facing the direction of travel as it headed north. I had been very specific about my requirements for my pre-booked seat, as I wanted to see the morning sun and benefit from its warming glow. And later in the day, I didn't want the glare of the evening sunset, as it might obscure my view and any photo opportunities. As it happened this early in the season, it would not be a problem due to the overcast and clouded skies. It was a 29-hour journey, covering 1,300 kilometres, so I had plenty of time to look out of the window.

I was taking a train from St Petersburg northwards to Murmansk, a major port and city on the northern coast of the country overlooking the Barents Sea, part of the Arctic Ocean. The city is located well within the Arctic Circle, over 2,300 kilometres from the North Pole, but it is not the most northerly city. That accolade goes to Norilsk, 1,400 kilometres from the pole. The nearest point on the mainland to the pole is Cape Chelyusk, 1,300 kilometres away, although there is a Russian island that is 400 kilometres further north.

I had caught a taxi from my hotel on the corner of Nevsky Prospekt and Sadovaya. It was a short drive out from the centre of the city and over the Neva River to the Ladozsky Station. My train duly came up on the board, and I went to Platform 3 Track 10 and waited for it to arrive. My ticket indicated that I was on carriage No. 1, berth 17.

We were soon out of the urban area and passing through a forest of largely silver birch and pine trees. There were a few dachas with small vegetable gardens nestled in the trees, but other than those few signs of human habitation, it was a never-ending forest. My compartment was a second-class compartment for four passengers, and we sat on the lower two berths. The top two berths folded back and their undersides were headrests during the day. There were other options such as first class, a private compartment, but this was expensive. The third-class compartments were for six people but were cramped. Beyond this was Economy, an open carriage with bunk beds stacked three high with space between for just one person to stand. There were no seats; you were expected to either lie on your bed or stand in the corridor.

We crossed several major rivers. Each bridge was set high above the water to allow navigation of ships underneath. I was looking out for the major Neva River, which links St Petersburg with Lake Lagoda, and ultimately via rivers and canals, with the White Sea in the Arctic, to Moscow and down the Volga. Each time we crossed, I looked for river traffic to give me a clue, but there was none. The route crossed it, but which river was the one, I was not sure until I checked a map later; and the first major river crossing was over the Neva.

The railway travels along the southern shore of Lake Lagoda then crosses the Neva River and passes up the west side of Lake Oneda. It was the fifth or sixth major river crossing at Lodeynoe Pole, which the Svir River. And whilst I knew the route on the map, all I saw was a forest. For most of the river crossings, the two railway tracks would peel apart and go up separate embankments to cross their own dedicated bridges. Traffic going from St Petersburg travelling north was on the right-hand tracks, and the traffic going south came towards us on the left-hand tracks.

After Lodeynoe Pole, there was a delay. Engineers were working on one of the bridges, replacing the track bed. Therefore, all traffic had to use just one bridge with inevitable delays. We made up the lost time not by travelling faster, but at each subsequent stop, we would not wait the allocated time for the stop but set off again as soon as everyone had embarked or disembarked.

A train table was posted in the corridor of the train. Trains run on Moscow time throughout the country, but I was spared this additional mathematical and geographical problem as this trip was all within the same time zone. Also, unlike previous trips, the timetable was in both Russian Cyrillic and Latin script, which somewhat spoiled the fun, as I struggled with the unusual letters and tried to mouth the name of a Russian town that I had never heard of. I often got it right, but there were times when I mispronounced the Russian version of the name.

At Podporoshe, there was a large derelict industrial complex. There was a 3-minute scheduled wait, but the train came to a halt and almost without waiting it pulled away again. Tickets have to be booked, and the authorities knew that no one was getting on or off and, therefore, no need to wait at all but they still had to stop. The only losers were the smokers who had hoped to get a quick puff whilst passengers got on or off. This was where we crossed the Svir River.

By the time we reached the town of Svir, we were back on schedule. This was to be a 34-minute stop, where we were going to change locomotives. We were met by an army of hawkers wearing thick coats, hats and gloves against the cold, selling their wares on the platform. There were soft drinks, beer and ice cream in coolers, sweet pastries, smoked fish, sweets, home-grown vegetables from allotments and lots of soft fruits, including green and red gooseberries, black and red currants, some fruits I didn't recognise and blackberries except these ones were yellow. I bought myself some lovely-tasting fresh strawberries but was appalled at the price. I should have checked before I bought them but should have realised that they would have travelled a long way to reach here in spring.

Everyone got to stretch their legs, the smokers have a chance to indulge in their habit and you can stock up on snacks if you didn't bring enough for yourself or just want something to pass the time. On my first railway trips in Russia more than a decade before, the hawkers were usually old women making a little extra, but now there was a whole range of ages and sexes represented as if it had become some people's full-time jobs.

There were more trees than you could shake a stick at. The green of the forest was contrasted by the white bark of the birch trees and the light brown bark of the pine trees. The only other flora of note were occasional patches of giant hogweed growing in the cleared area between the track and the forest. There were clearings in the forest where no trees grew, just grass, reeds and the occasional alder. These were low-lying areas subject to flooding or high water tables. Trees don't like this as their roots are either frozen solid in winter or drowned in summer.

The view of the forest was occasionally interrupted by freight trains heading south. These were inevitably a mixture of cement wagons, grain carriers, ore wagons, empty car carriers and covered wagons that could have anything inside them. Unusually, I saw no containers. But somewhere to the north were some major industrial complexes, and there seemed to be freight trains passing us every 10 minutes.

I saw what I would have called beaver dams if I was in North America, but beavers aren't endemic to the area. I also didn't see any pointed stumps typical of the way that beavers chew down trees. More likely, these dams may have been created when a broken branch got caught, which trapped the next one, and so on until a natural dam developed.

At Lavda, we had another 11-minute unscheduled delay. Engineers were working on the line, and we had to wait for traffic going south to clear the bottleneck. The provodnista came in and gave me a box containing cutlery, a piece of cake and a bottle of water. She asked me something, but I didn't understand. The others weren't in the compartment, so I couldn't take a cue from them. It must have been about food, as she had just given me cutlery…I tried various guesses, such as how much, I want it in 15 minutes, or I'll have fish, but I was asked the same question again and again until she gave up with the stupid Englishman who didn't understand her and she walked off.

Sasha had returned, and we were joined in the compartment by the middle-aged couple, Katia and Anatoli, clutching their cutlery boxes. The couple didn't seem interested in talking to me or Sasha. They left their boxes on the small table under the window and rummaged in their bags.

Sasha tried to make a conversation but only got monosyllabic answers, and he gave up, slumped in the corner at the other end of my berth, closed his eyes and went to sleep. Meanwhile, Katia got out a Kindle, and Anatoli opened a 200-page A4-size book of puzzles and crosswords. He turned to page one and pulled out a pen to start filling in the boxes.

A waiter from the restaurant car came in and dropped four polystyrene trays plus some rolls and sauce sachets on the table. I assumed that it was for us. I sat at the little table and opened the boxes. There was a choice of chicken and rice or beef and beans. I am a pescatarian at home, but I am less particular when travelling by necessity. I was hungry, so I chose the beef.

Anatoli complained to the waiter that he hadn't ordered this, and he checked a list with compartment numbers and food orders. I realised that I might have been wrong about the meal being complimentary, and a mistake might have been made. Sasha was asleep, and I didn't understand the exchange between the waiter and Anatoli. The waiter left but didn't take the food with him, and the couple didn't touch it…it just lurked there on the table for the rest of the afternoon. I asked Anatoli about the food, but I didn't understand his answer in Russian, so I just left it to sort itself out in due course.

The toilets were a long way from my previous encounters with facilities on Russian trains. Instead of falling straight onto the tracks below, they were like aircraft toilets and operated with a vacuum into a holding tank. There were two buttons and two instructions, but they didn't align with each other. There were two instructions above each other and then two buttons, side by side, one red and one green. I picked out a few words that I recognised, such as 'push', 'button', 'red', 'green' and 'provodnista', but I couldn't remember the Russian for 'flush' which I must have seen in aircraft toilets, but it escaped me.

I didn't want to upset the provodnista, as she rules the carriage and you depend on her for so much, especially as I hadn't gotten off to a good start with her. The set of instructions, including 'red' and 'provodnista' I guessed was to summon help, so I pushed the green button and was rewarded with the satisfying whooshing sound of the bowl emptying and avoided upsetting the provodnista.

The toilet also had a plentiful supply of water, soap, toilet paper and paper hand towels, and the facilities were regularly cleaned by a cleaner who seemed to hoover the corridor and compartments three times a day, clean the toilets and refill the dispensers. There were still improvements to be made, such as having hot water and supplying a plug. The basins are such that there is not even a hole for another tap and nowhere to fix a plug on a chain.

We approached Petrozavodsk along a cliff above the town. We could look down on the city spread along the shoreline of the lake through the trees. As we came into the station, we passed a large black 0-10-0 steam locomotive with some parts picked out in red or white. Thousands of these locomotives must have been made since most large stations seem to have one on display. This was part of the American Lend-Lease programme during the Second World War to move goods around the vast expanse of the country.

I had just enough time to walk back down the platform and take a photo. The stop was scheduled for 30 minutes, but we were behind schedule again and would be moving on as soon as possible. However, there was a lot of parcel freight and post to load and unload, which took time. A lot of the bags had China Post stencilled on the front, but I doubt that there really is that much post being sent from China to Pedrozavodsk. It is probably just the bags that are being reused.

A man in rail livery was coming along the side of the train. He carried a small hammer on the end of a long handle. He was alternatively tapping the axle hub and the wheel. The axle hub gave off a low, dull thud sound, and the wheels gave off a high-pitched singing sound, meaning both were sound. I first saw this on Dr Zhivago and have only seen it happen in Russia. But I note that the modern railway worker counterpart of the man in the film also carried a hand-held infrared heat sensor as a backup to the hammer and sound test.

There was a military post to the north of the town with a huge amount of hardware parked in neat rows. I resisted the urge to take a photo, but that also cost me a photo of a bridge as I didn't have my camera in hand as we crossed.

It was 6 pm and time for an evening meal. No one had come around with more cutlery or to take our meal orders, so I went to the restaurant. I thought that I had just negotiated passing the provodnista's cabin and got to the next carriage without any challenge when around the corner came Elena, my provodnista, whose name I knew from the badge that she wore on her lapel. I had made a point to remember her name, just in case. I greeted her by name, but she still stood in my way and asked where I was going in a very stern voice. I smiled and said that I was going to the restaurant. She smiled in return and stepped aside. Wow! I thought to myself…being pleasant to her work, and so she's not so bad after all.

I passed the first-class compartments, and they were a lot nicer. The corridor had fabric curtains, the carpets had a deeper pile and it was quiet…no children or noisy televisions, and they had control of the temperatures in their compartments, either cool air-conditioning for the summer or heating for the winter. More often than not, as I walked past some of the open doors, I got a blast of hot air.

I sat facing the direction of travel, but there would be no photo opportunities as the glare from the glazing would be too strong and it was already dark outside. We arrived in Medvezhya Gora just as I sat down, and like at Petrozavodsk, I caught glimpses of the town and the lake through the trees, lit by street lights and lamps along the promenade along the shore.

It was quite a varied menu, but the restaurant music was too loud. I ordered the borscht, followed by veal risotto 'Pajarsid' with brown bread, grilled vegetables and a bottle of Sibirskaya Korona. I had ordered a veal risotto from the English version of the menu, but I doubted that I would get veal risotto

'Pajarsid' as the Russian version of the menu said it was chicken and the Russian list of ingredients also said that it was chicken.

My first course came, but I got white bread, not brown as I had ordered, and a Baltika beer. I finished it anyway and then ordered a Sibirskaya Korona. She repeated just Korona, so I repeated it just to make sure that she had gotten it right. She was also asking me whether it was good, and I was nodding my head and then realising that whilst I had been ordering the right beer, she had been pointing at the empty bread plate and that I had just ordered more bread by nodding. Lucky for me, I was hungry, but I did get the right beer this time. And the main course was chicken and not veal, but I somehow expected that anyway.

I got back to the compartment at 8 pm to find all three of my travelling companions in bed; two were asleep, and Katia was still reading. The food boxes had gone, so I never found out what the deal was. I made my bed, but it was too hot for me with the heater working overtime, and it was too early to go to bed. I nudged the thermostat down, and I stood in the cooler corridor for 2 hours whilst the temperature dropped.

The clouds had thinned, and there was a bright three-quarter moon that rose and cast eerie shadows over the countryside as we passed. However, it didn't rise very high and was often obscured by trees. It wasn't the usual white, but it was a wonderful golden yellow.

I tiptoed into the compartment and went to bed as quietly as I could to be considerate to the others. It was still too hot for me to sleep comfortably. I was not sure whether I had any sleep or whether I had just dozed for hours when Anatoli and Katia got up and packed. Then it dawned on me that this was why they had gone to bed so early, as they were getting off at Belomersk in the early hours of the morning. Sasha seemed to spend most of his time asleep, whether it was day or night and didn't even stir.

I was awake early, before the sun rose, and with the unaccustomed noise of the train. There was a lot of door rattling noise from the tracks and people talking in the corridor. It is difficult to brake or pick up speed quietly when there are sixteen carriages and the train weighs several hundred tons, so there will inevitably be some buffer noise as well. Sasha was awake, so I folded away my bedding and made myself tea. Every carriage has a samovar, a heated metal container traditionally used to heat water at the end of every carriage, for travellers to make themselves a hot drink. Their use has spread throughout neighbouring countries, and the hot water is now used for drinks and food, such as pot noodles, which are very popular in Mongolia and China.

There were clear skies, and the sun was shining. In the sun, it was warming markedly, but in the shade, it was still cool. It seemed our carriage had been set to a temperature of around 24–25°C, as it rarely wavered. Other carriages I noted as I went to the restaurant car somewhere near the centre of the train were registering 23°C or 21°C…still hotter than comfort for me but still cooler.

Chapter 2
Murmansk, City of Monuments

We stopped briefly in Kola after which the peninsula is called and the next stop was Murmansk. The city straddles a small fjord, Kola Bay, an estuarine inlet of the Barents Sea. It was the last city founded in the Russian empire in 1915. The First World War requirements to link Russia with the allies by sea led to the construction of the railroad from Petrozavodsk, the previous northernmost terminus of the railway, to the ice-free port at Murmansk. The city is just 108 kilometres away as the crow flies from the border with Norway and 182 kilometres from the Finnish border. It boasts to have the northernmost trolleybus system in the world and is the largest city north of the Arctic Circle although the population has been shrinking in recent years.

We arrived dead on time at 11.55 am. Sasha warned me that it would be cold outside. I was still too hot and looking forward to being cooler so I didn't bother with an extra layer. I stepped out of the carriage and immediately changed my mind about the extra layer as it was cold on the platform and there was a chill wind. I opened my rucksack and pulled out a thick fleece.

Standing by the door was the provosnista. I said goodbye and wished Elena a farewell and good luck for the future…unfortunately in Russian. Why, unfortunately? As I was saying it she looked over my shoulder and nodded towards someone in that direction. Then an official in plain clothes introduced himself to me as an immigration officer. He spoke in good English and showed me his ID. It definitely had his name on the pass but since I had never seen one before, I had no idea whether it was genuine or not but Elena seemed to know who he was.

He was young and not confrontational and in plain clothes but he did ask me a few questions…including did I speak Russian. I replied 'No' to his raised eyebrows having stood right next to the provodnista whilst I said goodbye to her in Russian. I then added that I only knew a few well-rehearsed and useful phrases. He quizzed me on my itinerary which he obviously knew but I had that feeling that why ask if you know unless you want me to know that they know?

My first brush with the Eastern block was in Finland trying to get into Russia several decades before. I had been followed by some either very gormless gooks or an attempt to frighten me. I saw them following me and ultimately came face to face with both of them in a nearby tourist attraction castle.

On my first trip through the Iron Curtain to East Germany. I watched it again. I had been to visit Schwerin in East Germany but had decided that I would catch an earlier train than on my schedule advised to the authorities and would spend some time in another town én route, Bad Kleinen. I got off my train and I was the only person to be called aside by the only official there and asked for my passport and visa details by an officer in English. I passed that test but was I now a watched man?

Of all the masses of people getting off the plane in St Petersburg, I was walking past an immigration x-ray machine like everyone else without anyone getting stopped and heard first some raised voices and later some shouting and I was confronted by an armed security guard who beckoned me back towards the scanner. I had a range of medications, crampons, ice-axes, camping gas gadgets, knives and all sorts of paraphernalia so I wasn't best pleased about being stopped although it could all be explained. They seemed uninterested in the stuff and let me carry on.

But Sasha was right, it was cold outside but luckily it was just a couple of hundred metres to the Azimut Hotel, a modern seventeen-storey business hotel. It opened in 1984 and was the tallest building north of the Arctic Circle. There was hot water, and plugs in the basins, it wasn't too hot inside and the rooms were spacious.

I went to a local supermarket and got some food and drink and retired to my hotel room. I did some research on where to go tomorrow and went to bed early.

Breakfast in the hotel was at 7 am and I left the hotel for a long walk up a slope and out of town to Lake Semyonovskoye and overlooking it, the Military Monument to the Residents of Murmansk. This shows some pictures of the devastation of the town by German raids on the port and in complete contrast overlooks a lake with ducks swimming peacefully on the lake with its unruffled surface.

Then I took a walk up to the top of the hill which brought me to the Alyosha Monument, the Monument of the Defenders of the Soviet Arctic during the Great Patriotic War. This is a large stone depiction of a soldier, 35.5 metres high, looking west over the bay of Murmansk and towards where the battle lines were facing the Germans and Finns. There is an eternal flame at the base. Other cities that have received the Hero of the Soviet Union are also remembered along the base of the monument.

The city of Murmansk, located on the Kola Peninsula close to the Norwegian and Finnish borders, was a strategically important seaport and industrial city. It was the only Soviet port on the northern coast that did not freeze in the winter and was vital for the transport of supplies to the south.

German forces, including 800 Finns under German command, launched an offensive against Murmansk on 29th June 1941. More than 180,000 grenades and inflammable shells were fired on the city itself. Fierce Soviet resistance in the tundra and several Soviet counter-attacks made an Axis breakthrough impossible. Axis forces discontinued their attacks in late October 1941, having failed to take Murmansk or to cut off the Karelian railway line. Murmansk was awarded the title 'Hero City' in 1985.

I walked down the hill and around the base and I found myself in front of the Monument to the Waiting Women. Its most distinctive feature was a young woman looking out to sea with her left hand raised as if waving goodbye to a loved one. There are a number of padlocks that lovers have left attached to the railings around the monument.

I retraced my steps and stopped when I reached Lake Semyonovkoye. There was a beach being created here so that people could relax in the brief summer. However, work had been delayed as a one-ton bomb from the Second World War had been discovered and work had been delayed whilst it was dealt with.

I continued around the edge of the lake past the Oceanarium housed in a large white domed building to the amusement park not because I wanted to visit the amusements themselves but to see the Semyon the Cat Monument. The story goes that the cat was lost on a trip with his family to Moscow in 1987. But in an act of faithfulness, the cat made its way home and 6 years later returned to the owner's apartment in Murmansk. An amazing story but true.

In a park opposite the Military Monument to the Residents of Murmansk is the Saviour of the Waters church. It is a golden-domed, whitewashed Orthodox church. It is a traditionally designed church but was only built in 2002 and funded by public donations as a memorial to the sailors who died in the Kursk submarine disaster. This was a nuclear-powered submarine that suffered an explosion on board and sunk to the seabed and the 118 crew lost their lives.

There is also a centenary memorial to the victims of the Armenian Genocide committed by Muslim Ottoman troops against Orthodox Armenians during the First World War whilst Russia and the Turkish Ottoman Empire were at war with each other.

The starting date is conventionally held to be 24th April 1915, the day that Ottoman authorities rounded up, arrested, and deported from Constantinople (now Istanbul) to the region of Ankara 235 to 270 Armenian intellectuals and community leaders, the majority of whom were eventually murdered. The Ottoman authorities had already started taking action against Greek and Assyrian communities the previous year and now it was the turn of the Armenians to suffer.

The Muslim Ottomans had always regarded their fellow non-Muslim fellow countrymen as second-class citizens. The Armenians were Orthodox Christians and had more in common with the Russians with whom the Ottomans were fighting. There were large Armenian populations on both sides of the battle lines. This led the Ottomans to fear a rebellion and an internal revolt.

The initial deportations and murders were followed by the wholesale killing of the able-bodied Armenian male population through massacre and subjection of army conscripts to forced labour. Then the women, children, the elderly, and the infirm were forced on death marches leading to the Syrian Desert driven forward by soldiers. The deportees were deprived of food and water and subjected to periodic robbery, rape, massacre and starvation. The actual numbers are disputed but it is estimated that 1.5 million people were killed.

Just a hundred metres away down the hill is the Memorial Complex to the Soldiers and Seamen who died in Peacetime. It is a nine-storey brick-built octagonal tower with alternate storeys built of red and white bricks in the form of a lighthouse. At its base is a piece of wreckage from the Kursk to remember the sailors who perished.

I walked back towards the centre of the city and passed the Monument to the Arctic Convoys, an open area of grey slabs to represent the sea and in the centre, half of a globe with the countries picked out and showing the routes of convoys from Europe and along the Arctic coast of Russia to Murmansk and Arkhangelsk on the far side of the White Sea.

Nearby is the Regional Museum, an imposing four-storey building with a grand portico entrance with sets of double Corinthian columns running the full height of the building. Inside is a wealth of local artefacts from the indigenous people, local fauna and flora, early Arctic exploration, geology and the Second World War. Unfortunately, everything was in Russian so I had to do a lot of guessing but they did have a stuffed beaver although with a narrower tail than the North American beaver…so those piles of branches that I had seen from the train may have been beaver dams after all.

To one side of the museum is the Monument to the Yermak Icebreaker. It is an anchor resting against some rocks and a three-storey high mosaic depicting the icebreaker cutting through a sea of ice. It was the first icebreaker ever built with a strengthened bow and hull to break through thick ice. She was launched in 1898.

On the next corner is a Memorial to Anatoly Bredov who was killed in action aged just 21 in 1944. He was awarded the Hero of the Soviet Union and the Order of Lenin. He and his colleague were surrounded by Germans and his colleague was seriously wounded. Bredov allowed the Germans to approach and when close enough he detonated his grenade and killed all the Germans and himself. His colleague lay injured for two days until Russian troops found them and he was able to retell the story of Bredov's heroic deed.

I made my way through extensive marshalling yards and took a little time to watch the trains being shunted back and forth. Some of it was an enforced wait as the level crossing barriers were down and up to let trains pass. I say down and up as the single bar came down but also steel bollards rose out of the road that were robust enough to stop a tank. Russians are impatient drivers and would drive on even if the lights were flashing and the bar was coming down. The bollards deter any fearless driver and make it safe for the railway staff to shunt wagons back and forth.

Down on the dockside is the Memorial to the Dockworkers who lost their lives in the Great Patriotic War 1941–1945. The names of sixty workers are recorded but considering that the port was under attack for nearly 4 years, they seemed to have had a charmed life if only 60 were killed. In reality, many of their jobs were undertaken by conscripted soldiers.

Opposite is the Lenin Icebreaker, the first nuclear-powered icebreaker to be built and launched in 1957. It was decommissioned in 1999 and converted into a museum. We were taken on a tour of the officer's mess and the seamen's mess, the engine room, the nuclear plant and control room and finally the bridge. It didn't seem to take long and it was all over in just under an hour.

I made no way through the marshalling yards, through the railway station and past a 0-10-0 black locomotive with bits picked out in red which most stations exhibit to a park. The little bit of green space in the centre of the city hosts the Memorial to the Victims of the Intervention 1918–1920. The Bolsheviks had staged a successful coup in October 1917 and had signed the punitive Brest Litovsk peace treaty with Germany in March 1918.

All Imperial Russian commitments made to the allies were ignored and eleven new states emerged from the former Imperial Russian empire in Eastern Europe including Estonia, Latvia, Lithuania and Ukraine and several new states in former Russian Asia. However, the Bolsheviks were not unopposed and various factions took up arms against the Bolsheviks such as monarchists, conservatives, and forces loyal to the former government. The anti-Communist forces were collectively known as the White Army.

With an agreed peace on the Eastern Front, German troops that had been fighting there were transferred to the Western Front and Germany launched a major offensive. Therefore the allies supported those various factions against the Bolsheviks who were seen to be a hostile government and even landed troops in Russia with the ultimate aim of getting the Russians to rejoin the war. Meanwhile, the Red Army was defending the revolution against the White Armies during the civil war.

The Memorial to the Victims of the Intervention 1918–1920 is a curious memorial. The plague is fixed to a waist-high column. Surrounding it is a viewing platform up a flight of steps which double back on themselves to reach the top viewing platform above the short column. It is located in the centre of a park surrounded by trees so there is nothing to view from the top. The irony is that it is also painted white, the colour associated with the opposition forces.

And there is a connection between this monument and a village near my home town. In the parish church of the village of Southwater is a Commonwealth War Grave in the corner of the cemetery. It was only after the Falklands War in 1982 that families of the deceased had the option to repatriate their fallen loved ones. Up until then, soldiers were buried near where they fell. The gravestone recorded that this was the grave of Private Harry Bennett, aged 25, of the Royal Sussex Rifles who had a depot in nearby Horsham. The other curious fact is the date of death that intrigued me as it was recorded as 3rd May 1919, six months after the end of the war in Europe.

At the start of the First World War, one battalion of the Royal Sussex Rifles was stationed in India and served there throughout the war. Another battalion was stationed in Egypt fought the Ottoman forces in Palestine and participated in the Gallipoli campaign. These troops were evacuated from Gallipoli on 9th January 1916 and joined their comrades in France. However, at the end of the war in Europe, some troops were sent to Murmansk to support the White Army. Private Harry Bennett was injured and repatriated to England but died of his wounds.

I was making my way to the Museum of Murmansk Shipping which is in a beautiful traditional building but it was closed. But I did get to see the Monument to the Twin Cities which is a cross with the names of the ten cities with which it is twinned plus a large map of the world to show where the twin cities were in relation to each other.

Although now there are 12 cities which are twinned with Murmansk, I was surprised that I had visited half of them, namely Rovaniemi, the home of Santa Claus and the first city to be twinned with Murmansk in Finland in 1962. The other cities that I had visited were Luleå, Sweden (1972), Tromsø, Norway (1972), Groningen, Netherlands (1989), Akureyri, Iceland (1994), which is incidentally one of my top three countries to visit and lastly, Harbin, China (2015), which in complete contrast is one of the worst countries that I have ever visited.

I had not bothered to count the number of countries that I had visited until I met several Australian and New Zealanders who would drop into the conversation the number of countries that they had visited. For Europeans with 50 countries on the continent all within a 4 hour flight, it is easy to notch up quite a few. Australia and New Zealand are so far from anywhere else and so expensive to reach that they are proud of the numbers that they have visited.

There are 195 countries in the world according to membership of the UN, 193 countries with two non-members with observer status, the Vatican and Palestine. I met a fellow traveller in Africa, Noah, whose aim was to visit all the countries in the world. We all have a reason to travel but that wasn't one of mine but out of interest I had counted up the number of countries that I had visited and it was more than half of the total. The ones that remain are off the beaten track and difficult to get to such as small island nations and those that are politically unstable or at war.

And as a link between the 195 countries and British army involvement overseas, there is a fascinating book titled 'All the countries we have ever invaded', sub-titled 'and the few we never got round to' by Stuart Laycock which is an A to Z of those countries and a brief history of British military operations in them and British forces have operated in more than 80% of them. I shouldn't really be surprised as we have a long naval tradition, and have been involved in two world wars and countless colonial conflicts and clashes with other empires.

Around a corner was the Monument to St Cyril and St Methodius, both 9th-century Byzantine Christian theologians who influenced the cultural development of all Slavs. They were brothers born in Thessalonica and Methodius lived 815–885 and Cyril, born Constantine lived 826–869. In 862, Prince Rastislav of Great Moravia requested that Emperor Michael III and Patriarch Photius send missionaries to and evangelise his Slavic subjects and the two brothers set off.

The languages that the Slavs spoke had never been written down and due to the different sounds that made up words, the Latin script was insufficient but there was a need to write the language down to preach to and educate his new flock. Cyril was an educated man so he invented a whole new alphabet which became known as Cyrillic. He used a mixture of symbols from the Latin, Greek and Hebrew alphabets plus some that he invented himself.

Therefore when reading Russian some symbols are familiar to most people but have different sounds associated with them once you know that the text is Russian. But Cyril was inconsistent in his application of his new alphabet and there are many false friends. The Russian letters A, E, K and M have the same sound as in Latin but a Russian H is a Latin N and similarly the P is sounded as an R and C as an S. The Russian ф comes from Greek and is an F sound whilst the ш comes from the Hebrew letter shin and is a 'sh' sound. And care is required as the very similar щ letter, the same letter but with a tail is a shch sound.

Other Russian letters seem to be unique such as Д sounds as a Latin D, the Russian Ь which is a symbol to soften the preceding letter and И sounds as an 'E' as the 'i' in 'police'. These don't seem to have any obvious link to other alphabets and were invented by Cyril. Technically, for those in the know, Cyril created the Glagolitic alphabet and it was Naum, a follower of Methodius who created the Cyrillic alphabet but Cyril still gets all the praise.

In the nearby park was a statue of Sergei Kirov, a leading Bolshevik and Communist leader until murdered in 1934, but no connection to Murmansk as far as I am aware. But just to his left was the Monument to the Codfish, a steel representation of a cod with steel reinforcing rods bent into the shapes of waves crashing over a rock. Considering the coat of arms of the city had a cod on its shield which is such an important part of the city's economy, this was much more significant to the city.

I went down Lenin Boulevard past a statue of the man himself to see the rather plain Monument to the Soldiers of Law and Order and further along, three life-size guards in military uniform being the Monument to the Border Guards of the Arctic. The last monument was the Monument to the 6th Heroic Komsomol Battery which is an artillery piece set on a plinth two storeys high. They were fighting the advancing Germans during the Second World War but for this battle, they had no infantry or tank support but held out against German attacks for a week until all 71 of them had been killed.

Part of this is due to the stoicism of the Russian character but also partly due to the vicious military police. Many people will recognise the scene from the 2001 film Enemy at the Gates, starring Joseph Fiennes, Jude Law and Bob Hoskins when the attacking Russians are overwhelmed by German firepower and retreat only to be shot by their own side for retreating.

Chapter 3
Over the Border to Norway

The next morning, I was picked up by my driver, Vladimir, with Vadim, my interpreter for both Russian and Norwegian and his wife and my guide, Mila. We drove out of the city and over the new bridge onto the left bank of the river. We stopped at Minkino where there is a monument to the armed forces. There are several SAM missiles including one of the type that shot down Gary Powers, the US pilot of a U2 spy plane shot down over Russian territory in 1960. There was also allegedly a Yak fighter although on close inspection even to the untrained eye, you can see that the fuselage and the wings are from different types of aircraft.

There is a monument to the various batteries who provided anti-aircraft cover for the docks against enemy bombers including one to the Women who Operated the Batteries. Then we were back on the road and stopped much further on at the Valley of Glory Monument. This is located at the point of the furthest advance that the German forces achieved against the target of Murmansk. This is a point overlooking the Zapadnaya Litsa River (renamed and translated as Western Face).

All the names of those killed during the conflict are recorded here in stone. There are memorials, a statue, a tank plus two maps, carved into polished red granite, of the German advance in June to September 1941 and the Russian counter-attacks in October 1944 that liberated the whole area plus Kirkenes in northern Norway. The Germans had invaded Russia in Operation Barbarossa on 22nd June 1941. The advance here started a week later on 29th June code-named Operation Silver Fox. They had planned to cover the 220 kilometres between Kirkenes and Murmansk in just two weeks but after three months of fighting, they were 90 kilometres short of their target and would never regain the initiative.

The taiga turned to tundra as the trees became more stunted and eventually disappeared to be replaced with just grass and small bushes. Some of the lower areas were just marsh and the deeper folds in the ground contained lakes. There were still patches of snow in sheltered areas which had yet to be melted by the strengthening spring sunshine. The area has been heavily glaciated by ice sheets so much of the scenery is smooth rounded hills.

We stopped at Titovka. It is an odd place. We had seen very little traffic but this place was a hive of activity. It has cabins to rent which look like old wagons from a freight train and are converted into cosy little nests. There is also camping for the very hardy or those on a budget but for comfort's sake, this is not a place to try camping unless you can afford an upgrade if the weather turns bad.

There are opportunities to go quad biking or just hire a quad in order to get yourself and your fishing gear to some of the best fishing places in the area. You can go hunting or choose from plenty of other outdoor activities. It is also a cafe stop and a small cafe selling simple food. It has several chiller cabinets, one for food, one for soft drinks and three for beer so you can tell where visitors' priorities lie. I had had breakfast at the hotel but I still had a cod pie with my coffee, something like a Russian version of a Cornish pastie. I wondered whether Sasha was here. He was a mechanic from Moscow and he had taken a week off work to go fishing somewhere outside Murmansk and this would seem to be an ideal spot.

There is a monument to the fallen with a bell on top of a long pole and you are encouraged to ring it to remember the fallen. Next to it is a wartime mobile communications hut on wheels which has been converted to a museum. That is a rather grandiose title to call a museum as it is more of a caravan which houses some artefacts that some amateur historians have gathered together. There is a soundtrack of a battle in progress with maps and pictures on the walls and a pile of rusty items that have been found locally lying across the floor and on tables against the wall.

We passed a lake and there was a range of military vehicles including amphibious vehicles, several tanks, artillery and howitzers pointing to the far shore of the lake. It was a marine training ground and they were undertaking manoeuvres with the use of live ammunition. There were several booms of artillery firing, the air was full of the smell of cordite and there was the rumble of heavy diesel motors that propelled the tanks and APVs across the range.

Next came a camp named Sputnik. This was where Yuri Gagarin spent some of his early career. In an interview on television, one of the girls who remembered him at the base said that he was always going to be either in prison or in space. Luckily for him, the authorities found a use for his particular character.

There is another base nearby simply called '19kms'. Besides the military bases, which I don't mind mentioning as the authorities would not put sensitive bases next to main public highways, I still observed the 'no photos' rule, in the town of Zapolyarny. This a nickel mine owned and operated by Norilsk, a giant Russian mining company that also operates a nickel mine in Russia's most northerly city of the same name.

It was immersed in controversy when it was allowed to dump tailings into a local fjord. The company mines and processes ore here but it is a much smaller operation than it used to be and consequently the town has the feel of a ghost town with empty, derelict or run-down buildings everywhere. It is uneconomic to run but is operated on a caretaker basis so that if prices suddenly improve, it can ramp up production quickly.

Then the road surface suddenly changed and it had a smooth surface, gentle bends and gradients running along embankments and through cuttings as if someone had degreed that this bit of road needed to be upgraded. There were still road works but someone somewhere obviously thinks that it is a good investment.

We crossed the border with surprising ease. On the Norwegian side, there are also significant road improvements with a new bridge and a tunnel being built through a hill to allow traffic to bypass the centre of a small local community. In no time at all we were in Kirkenes. It was a lot smaller than I had imagined, with fewer than 3,000 people in the town and perhaps a similar number in the immediate area.

During the occupation of Norway by Nazi Germany, Kirkenes was the nearest base for the German Kriegsmarine and the Luftwaffe's Jagdgeschwader 5 to the front at Murmansk. Kirkenes is second after Malta on a list of European towns experiencing the most air-raid alarms and attacks, with more than 1,000 alarms and 320 air attacks. The town was liberated by the Red Army on 25th October 1944 when the German Wehrmacht was pushed out and fled back to the main theatre of operations to protect the motherland. But before they left the area, they destroyed most of the remaining infrastructure. Only 13 houses survived the war so there was no outstanding architecture or old buildings to be seen.

The present church was built in 1959 and compared to the lavish ornate and gilded creations that I had seen elsewhere, this was a plain church. The cemetery covered a large area but only contained a few gravestones but none of the magnificent funeral architecture associated with the late nineteenth century. I had read in my guide that passenger cruise ships and Russians came here to shop but the town centre was a very functional couple of shops for locals with a few extras. Norway is too expensive for Russians and cruise ship passengers can find more interesting baubles elsewhere.

I bought a few museum tickets to different museums and a couple of coffees but that was about all I spent. Petrol is expensive so my driver had filled up on the Russian side of the border. My guides and driver had brought their food and when my hotel heard that I was going to Kirkenes for the day, they had provided me with a packed lunch at no extra charge. However, we all scored on duty-free as the Russians think it is cheap and the Norwegians think it is so cheap that they often go to Russia just to shop. But the quality isn't the same so other than the duty-free there is not much to entice anybody.

The port is fairly functional and there is not much to see of interest. There are several colourful Norwegian houses that are common in Norwegian communities but little else. The local museum is interesting but only fills an hour even if you read every information sign. I had wanted to see Andersgrotta which is a bomb shelter that can accommodate 600 people. I had lived in Guernsey and had seen the tunnels that the Germans had built in the granite in both Guernsey and Jersey. Unfortunately Andersgrotta is only open at 12.30 on certain days or for pre-booked groups of ten or more and as it was closed on the day that I visited, so I didn't see it.

There are some large mines nearby and there are ore transfer shipment points in the harbour but they are not visible to the passing tourist as a lot of the infrastructure is underground. It is the terminus for the 8.5-kilometre-long railway line between Kirkenes and the Bjørnevatn mine at Sør-Varanger. This is a single-track railway used solely to haul 20 daily iron ore trains from the Bjørnevatn Mine to the port at Kirkenes. Construction started in 1907 and it became operational in 1910. It was the world's most northerly railway until 2010, when the Obskaya-Bovanenkovo Line was constructed by Gazprom and later extended to the Karskaya making it 572 kilometres long and more than 200 kilometres further north than the terminus in Kirkenes.

We drove west along a fjord for the views which are more dramatic than Russian fjords as they have greater height whereas Russian fjords have been rounded off by glaciation and are much flatter. I stopped at a waterfall and then it was the long drive back to the Azimut Hotel in Murmansk.

I went to the local supermarket but I still didn't understand the rules about buying alcohol in supermarkets, and again, I was refused. I recognise that there is a problem with alcoholism in Russia and that the restrictions on buying alcohol were meant to benefit society but once you know the rules, the local population can work around them. I was still ignorant and had another dry evening in my hotel room.

I went for a long walk to find the Northern Naval Fleet Museum and failed. I found the right roundabout, the correct turn, the right piece of open space after a supermarket but it wasn't there. I walked about…I had nothing but time to spare, walking in ever larger concentric patterns but I didn't find it. It wasn't where Trip Advisor or Google said it should be.

I couldn't remember the Russian name of the museum but I did remember the big, 'bolsh' as in Bolshoi Ballet and Bolsheviks, plus building and blue, the colour of the building from a picture in my guidebook.

I tried asking a few of the locals. They must have thought that I was mad. I tried asking for a museum. When I got the inevitable shake of the head, I tried saying it was a big, blue building. I was directed to a lot of big blue buildings and none were the right one. I rather regret that I didn't take any photos as I would have had the largest collection of photos of blue buildings in Murmansk of any photographer in the world.

I found a large overgrown space in the right place but no building. The last entry on the internet had said that it was very dilapidated but it had probably fallen down or had been pulled down or relocated. I walked around until I found myself standing in front of the memorial to the 6th Heroic Komsomol Battery at the far end of Lenin Prospect. I knew where I was and gave up my search for this non-existent museum to return to my hotel.

Chapter 4
Petrozavodsk

I returned to the hotel, picked up my bags and went to the railway station. I left Murmansk at 19.20 and was due to arrive in Kem at 6.35 am. Most people prefer to fly or drive so the train was not particularly busy. I had a compartment to myself for the whole night and I set my alarm clock for half an hour before arrival. I need not have worried as the provodnista came and knocked on the door an hour before the scheduled arrival time to make sure that I was awake.

I got off the train in Kem and it was foggy and cold. I was met by my guide who introduced herself as Polina, a charming young local girl. We got into her car and she drove from the station to Papinsaari for a traditional breakfast. There were 'oladushky', local pancakes with condensed milk, porridge, bread, cheese and sausage.

The city of Kem was first mentioned in records in 1450 when the Novgorod 'posadnik' or lord of the manor, Marfa Boretskaya donated it to the Solovetsky Monastery. A wooden fort was erected there in 1657 and the city's wooden cathedral was erected between 1711 and 1717.

After breakfast, it was time to board the ferry for the 2 hour journey to Solovetsky Island. It was cold and damp and there were lumps of ice floating on the surface of the water which the small craft nudged to either side as we motored towards the island. It had been an unusually long and cold winter and there were still some patches of snow on the ground and ice on the lake. I had been to Moscow every April for several consecutive years for work as I was attending the Russian Insurance Conference sponsored by the All Russian Finance Ministry.

Spring in Russia is a very short affair and in the space of a couple of weeks it can change from deepest winter to hot summer but the changeover can be early or late. Being a regular visitor in April I had experienced both ends of the spectrum; warm, bright and sunny weather suitable for wearing just a shirt and freezing conditions, howling winds and snow requiring a thick jumper under an equally thick coat plus gloves, scarf and hat. It would be common to see people wearing balaclavas with just their eyes exposed.

We got off the boat and took a taxi around the lake to my hotel which overlooked the monastery. We went to visit the Marine Museum first, housed in a small shed but it was closed. Some of the exhibits on the grounds outside were on open display such as a reconstruction of Peter the Great's sailing boat, the Saint Peter. Other exhibits in the open include a minesweeping decoy and a traditional boat of the local Paumori people, a small sub-tribe belonging to the Sámi people who are the local population who inhabit this area of Russia and also parts of Norway, Finland and Sweden.

Then Polina took me to meet our local guide for our tour of the monastery. We visited the Church of the Transfiguration, the two bells standing outside, the Church of St Nicholas, the refectory and then the monks' cells, often three or four to a cell. We saw the chapel which had escaped a major fire in 1933 and then had a walk along the tops of the walls and a visit to two of the towers before visiting the cells and the granary, which had a special heating system to keep the grain dry.

Starting in 1923 and lasting up to 1939, the monastery and the island were one of the first labour camps created by the Bolsheviks, a forerunner of the infamous gulags. Polina took me to one of the former barracks which has been refurbished and made into the Museum of the Repression. Opposite the museum were other buildings of the same design, other former barracks now converted to other uses. One was now occupied as a shop and the rest were private houses.

Going back towards the hotel, we passed the Maritime Museum which now was open. Inside they had a typical local fishing vessel on display, a model of the St Peter, the Peter the Great ship that he had built to a European design and unlike any locally built ships. There were various maritime-related artefacts, plus pictures of the recreation of St Peter by local craftsmen. It was built in 2003 and every year it undertakes a recreation of one of the journeys that it made when it was new in 1693.

There was a suggestion that I might want to have a rest but I was keen to see more as I might only come this way once in my life. The next activity therefore was to hire some mountain bikes for a ride into the forest. I paid for the hire of two bikes and we headed into the forest. We cycled over rough tracks through the forest to reach the Sekirno-Ascension Minor Monastery. This was an extension of the main monastery but it was used to punish erring monks. It sits high on a cliff overlooking the White Sea.

The church itself is rectangular and two storeys high, whitewashed, with a central octagonal tower of one extra, smaller storey protruding from the top with an onion dome above. Inside are some beautiful paintings and an abundance of gold leaf. There are a few other buildings on site but they are not open to the public. There is a long flight of steps down to the shore but I wasn't tempted.

That evening, we went for a meal in a local hotel and I ordered fish and a bottle of Georgian sauvignon blanc. Georgia is over three thousand kilometres away but it was the nearest that I could get for a local wine. It was much sweeter than I am used to or preferred.

On our way back to our hotel after the meal, we passed a gentleman on his iPad. Polina leant over and said that she was sure that it was Vladimir Medinsky, the Minister of Culture. We had to go back and check. It was him and she introduced herself and me. He spoke excellent English and we had a brief chat. We posed for photos and left him to continue checking his emails.

The next morning, we caught a local ferry from the small port in front of the monastery for the 40-minute rides to Bolshoy Zayatsky. We had a guide with us who introduced himself as Alexei. He was very knowledgeable and informative but spoke in Russian but Polina did a simultaneous translation.

We took a boardwalk across the delicate tundra which was interspersed with patches of tigra as we were right on the transition between the two ecosystems. There are fourteen labyrinths on the island and our route would take us past three of them. They take the form of concentric swirls with some having just one route to the centre and some having two routes. They are made from stones which form the ridges and over the centuries, they have become covered with grass and ground-hugging plants and now appear as concentric ridges of plants.

No one is sure how old they are for certain but they are between 2000 and 3000 years old. There is even less agreement on their use or who made them. There are also piles of stones standing in neat cones. These are called sanctuaries but again little is known for certain. Some had bones and implements buried under them and some had nothing underneath.

Arriving back at the pier, before boarding our boat back to the main island, we had a look at the bakery, the main building and St Andrews Church. During the Repression, this was used as a place for pregnant inmates but the altar has since been restored as a church. There was paper and a pencil near the entrance for visitors to write the name of a loved one for the priest to say a prayer for them for their health or the soul of a departed loved one.

It was then back to the main island. On our way from the pier to the hotel, there was a gathering of dignitaries outside the entrance of the monastery including Vladimir Medinsky whom we had met the night before and Oriel Orlov, the governor of Archangelsk. Polina asked one of the armed but plainclothes security detail holding people back about what was happening. The Patriarch of Moscow and All Russ (an old reference to Russia), Kiril was expected shortly.

We were rewarded with a cavalcade of three vehicles which turned in a 180-degree arc outside the entrance and the Patriarch got out with a number of other dignitaries. The group from the vehicles were met by a welcoming committee and together they went into the Church of the Transfiguration. Then there was a short blessing followed by a procession. There were more ceremonies but I had seen enough so we went to have some pelmeni, similar to ravioli at the hotel for lunch before a transfer to the main ferry back to Kem.

There was some time to kill in Kem. We walked around the city until it was time for an evening meal. I had a fish salad in a local restaurant as we waited for the 20.55 train to take us to Petrozavodsk. The only issue for me was that it arrived in Petrozavodsk at 04.22.

Polina had a compartment further down the carriage and I shared a compartment with a middle-aged couple. They were Yuri and his wife Galina and we soon got chatting about travelling, they had been to see the wildlife and volcanoes of Kamchatka in Russia's Far East. They showed me a lot of pictures of their adventure, the scenery was wild and spectacular and despite it being summer when they visited, there was still snow on the ground. I had just added another location to my bucket list of places to go and see.

I was woken by the provodnista half an hour before the train was due to arrive in Petrozavodsk. I got dressed and gathered my things together as quietly as I could so as not to disturb the other occupants and tiptoed out of the compartment. It was sleeting but we were met by a driver to take me to the Frigate Hotel overlooking the Lake Onega and I crashed for what was left of the night. This was Polina's home town so after dropping me off at the hotel, the driver took her home.

I wasn't going to be staying in Petrozavodsk that evening but in a traditional Karelian village 100 kilometres west of the regional capital at a village called

Kinerma. It is just one of a total of twenty villages in the western Russia region that have the designation of Best Historical Villages and are part of the BTV organisation. Polina returned to the hotel at 10.30 am and together we took a car from Petrozavodsk to Kinerma. This was where I was going to stay in a traditional, historical building.

We passed through a lot of unbroken forest. There are many animals in the forests but from the train and the road, I would be very lucky to see any of them. There is the four-kilogram Wooden Goose or Cock, also called the Deaf Bird as it makes a lot of noise as a mating call in the spring and so is easy for hunters to locate.

There is also the wolverine, one of the top three deadliest animals due to its temperament and attitude. There are flying squirrels, brown bears, beluga or white whales, moose and one of the only three types of freshwater seals (the other two are in Lake Lagoda and Lake Baikel). There are beavers, unpopular with woodmen as they change the water table and gnaw at the trees. There are also lynxes, eagles, and wolves who have a bounty on their heads.

In the winter, wolves can come and take farm animals and have recently started to visit communities and attack their pet dogs. Local hunters use the Karelian Bear Dog for its quick reflexes and fearless nature which have made it very popular for hunting aggressive games, including bears, moose, wild boar and Spitz pointer dogs who point out the game. In 2015, there were an estimated 250 wolves but the government likes to keep them under control. In the year that I passed through, their numbers had swelled to 500 and the bounty per wolf had tripled, increasing from 3,000rbl to 10,000rbl.

It sounds a lot in dollar terms but they are not easy to kill. Several hunters are needed to work together to find and trap the animals so that they can be killed but the wolves are clever and can be elusive. It is not a living but it can be an encouragement to a community whose livestock and pets are threatened by a pack that has moved into their community.

We arrived at Kimerna village along a rough track. It was a traditional village and the houses were all made of wood, from rounds of timber slotted together. The building that I was going to sleep in was an old farmer's house with attached barns for animals and implements consisting of two storeys with more rooms under the eaves.

Inside it was much as the family would have lived in it a hundred years ago. There were planed timber floors, round timber walls, planed timber ceilings and a brick-built hearth in the centre of the residential area so that it could warm several rooms at the same time and be used for cooking. It was spacious with a kitchen table that could seat eight people.

There were traditional outside WCs consisting of a small shed over a hole but the guest houses had been modernised for guests with running water and a toilet flushing into a cesspit.

Polina introduced me to my host for the next few days, Kalmikova who runs the house stays in the village. I had ordered a banya, the Russian equivalent of a sauna. Kalmikova's two children, Igor and his younger brother Ivan, had lit the fire in the banya earlier in the afternoon and the inside of the banya was hot and ready for a sauna. It takes a while to heat up, hence the need to order it in advance.

The banya was a separate building at the bottom of the garden. This is a traditional black banya, meaning that there is no chimney above the fire. The fire is lit and the smoke fills the room but there may be a small hole in the roof to allow the smoke to escape or sometimes, the door is opened to allow smoke to escape. It is called a black banya as everything inside is black from the smoke and soot of the fire, but surprisingly, it is not dirty inside.

A banya typically has three rooms, an entrance and changing room, a washing room and the hot banya itself. I had the place to myself so I stripped off, washed and entered the banya. Outside of the building was a tub full of water that was constantly refilled from a hose connected to the local stream. This was the frigidarium area where after getting sweaty and hot in the banya, you could cool down with cold water before re-entering the banya for another session.

I had been told that there were few people about, and the banya was secluded from the rest of the village; therefore, it was alright to be naked and pour cold water over yourself on the porch before re-entering the banya. Initially, it felt a bit pervy to stand naked on the porch but just as I had been told, there was no one about and as it was an accepted local practice, I alternated between the hot banya and the outside cold porch. It was just a shame that there was no one else to chat with as that is part of the fun of sharing a banya.

After my banya, Polina and I walked across the village to have supper cooked by Kalmikova in her new farmhouse. It was new but built in the traditional style out of round tree trunks. The meal was goulash, kvass, a black drink made from bread, salad and a courgette-like vegetable followed by pancakes and apple jam.

After the meal, I said to Polina that I had finished in the banya and that she was free to use it so I went to bed and she went to the banya. I had a great night and I woke up feeling very refreshed after my black banya.

At 9.00 am after breakfast, Igor, the youngest son of Kalmikova's children knocked on the door of my building. He was dressed in traditional peasant clothing to take me on a tour of the village and our first stop was the small church. A soldier returning to the village more than two centuries before had a dream to search for an icon and he found it in a nearby field. He brought it to the village and told everybody about it.

The village decided to build a small chapel to house the icon. There was a great storm and the building was burnt to the ground and people thought that the icon was destroyed. However, it was found in a nearby field and hence it was a miracle. The village constructed a new building which is the building that can be seen today which was built in the 1760s. The oldest surviving house in the village is also of the same age.

More than 150 years later, the Communist authorities degreed that the building was to be destroyed. The demolition team started by demolishing the bell tower but it fell over and the bells made such a noise that the workers were all frightened and feared that it was a bad omen. They stopped demolishing the building and so it has survived.

The building had a hole in the roof but the locals were not allowed to repair it so it fell into disrepair. However, during the Great Patriotic War, the area was occupied by the Finnish army and they helped the villagers to repair the roof and to preserve the icon.

The original icon was moved to Petrozavodsk for safekeeping but in 1979 the building was broken into by vandals and all but two of the altar icons were stolen. The panels seen today in the altar are the two original surviving panels and the rest are replacements.

In the same building that I had stayed in is the village museum. There used to be 168 people living in the village. It is an unusual location as most villages are situated next to a lake but there is no lake here. There was a collective farm here during the Communist era but there was a lack of mains electricity which meant that the authorities believed the village would be unviable and support for the collective farm was withdrawn. This effectively meant that the collective farm was bankrupt and people started to move to the city and now only five people live here all year round. The other houses are used in the summer by their owners or are used to house guests but otherwise, the village is empty.

Then after the tour around the village with Igor, I had a cooking master class led by Kalmikova on how to cook traditional Karelian pies. The ingredients are water, salt, a little white wheat flour and rye flour. We needed to mix together the ingredients and knead and roll the mixture into an oblong shape. The filling that we were going to use was boiled millet which I spread across the oblong. Then I pinched the edges and they were ready for the oven. A beaten egg was used to glaze the surface. Kalmikova's pies were a regular oval shape whereas mine were a little irregular.

After the cooking lesson, it was time to get back to Petrozavodsk for a tour of the city. The city was founded in 1703, by Prince Menshikov who called it Petrovskaya Sloboda at the behest of Tsar Peter the Great. This was during the Great Northern War 1700–1721 with Sweden and the tsar needed a new iron foundry to manufacture cannons and anchors for the Baltic Fleet. At first, the foundry used the name Shuysky Zavod (literally, factory at the Shuya River), but a decade later it became Petrovsky Zavod. It changed its name again in 1777 to its current Petrozavodsk. The original factory closed in 1734 but foreign industrialists ran a copper smelting operation nearby.

The industry revived in 1773 when Tsarina Katherine the Great established a new iron foundry upstream on the Lososinka River, designed to provide cannons for the ongoing Russo-Turkish Wars. This foundry was named Alexandrovsky, after St Alexander Nevsky, the celebrated Russian hero, prince and saint. He lived between 1221 and 1263 and served as Prince of Novgorod three times during his life, Grand Prince of Kyiv 1236–52 and Grand Prince of Vladimir 1252–63 during some of the most difficult times in medieval Russian history. He was the grandson of Vsevolod the Big Nest but became famous due to his repeated victories against German and Swedish invaders although he still paid tribute to the Golden Horde. He was to become a saint in 1547 and St Alexander Nevsky is the patron saint of the region.

The factory was reorganised, modernised and expanded under the supervision of Charles Gascoigne in 1787–96. He was a British industrialist, a partner and manager of the Carron Company ironworks. He declined the first invitation but Tsarina Katherine the Great's advisors said that he was the best man for the job and she increased her offer until he couldn't refuse. The road where the factory was sited was called English Street until it was renamed Karl Marx Prospect by the communists.

The city museum details the story of the foundry including segments of the first railway built in Russia in 1788 made in cast iron to move heavy parts of cannons around the factory. Some claim that this was the first railway in the world. There are also displays of petroglyphs, and geological specimens from the area including granites, marbles and other minerals.

There is a promenade running along the shore of Lake Onega completed in 1993. Lake Onega is the second-largest lake in Europe. It is 245 kilometres long by 90 kilometres wide. Its surface elevation is 33 metres above sea level and its deepest section is 127 metres. It is drained by the Svir River which flows into Lake Ladoga, Europe's largest lake. Lake Ladoga has a lot of islands but Lake Onega has more than 1,350 islands.

The lake is also the start of the White Sea-Baltic Canal, often abbreviated to the White Sea Canal. It was built between 1931 and 1933 and opened four months early. It was feted as one of the achievements of the First Five-Year Plan. Until 1961, it was called the Stalin White Sea-Baltic Canal. It was built with Gulag labour provided by 127,000 inmates. Official sources indicate that 12,000 died in the process, but historical research suggests that as an alternative and perhaps more accurate figure is that 25,000 died to achieve the Five-Year Plan's remarkable success of opening the canal four months ahead of schedule.

However, it wasn't such a remarkable success from the shipping viewpoint. It had been planned to have a depth of 5.4 metres which would have allowed for ocean-going ships up to 3,000 dead weight tonnage which typically have a draft depth of 4.6 metres. Its actual depth due to cost issues and political interference, saw a completed draft depth of only 3.5 metres which equates to a vessel with a dead weight cargo limit of 600 tonnes. The canal starts at Povenets on Lake Onega after which there are seven locks close together, referred to as the 'Stairs of Povenets'.

The canal crosses Lake Vygozero and after 227 kilometres it reaches Belomorsk on the White Sea. Shipping can cross the White Sea to reach the major port of Arkhangelsk and access the Atlantic Ocean around the coast of Norway and the Arctic Ocean. Ultimately from here, shipping can also reach the estuaries of the major rivers that empty into the Arctic Ocean from Siberia. The northern shipping routes are only open in summer due to icing in winter, although the summer shipping season nowadays is extended by Russian ice breakers that can escort ships in convoy during the late spring and early autumn.

Along the promenade are various granites and marbles from Karelia on display plus various avant-garde sculptures which were presented to the city by its twin cities around the world. They have official names but they also have local nicknames.

In one of the parks along the promenade is The Wedding House used for functions. Set a little further back from the shore is the opera house, built in 1950s in traditional style and a modern opera house stands opposite. The cathedral seen in many old photos of the city was demolished by the communists and the one standing there today is a reproduction.

I met Polina again at 10.30 am and she accompanied me to the ferry port and she handed me my ticket. I was taking a hydrofoil to Kizhi Island, a UNESCO-designated site. The hydrofoil usually takes an hour and a half ride to see the large unique wooden cathedral and open-air museum. I was booked on a hydrofoil named Meteor. One of its sister ships was called Comet. They all have the same company livery of bright green so are easy to identify. I thanked Polina for all her help and boarded the boat. However, the journey took a little longer as the ice floating in the lake meant that speed restrictions applied and the hydrofoil could not go at its usual speed.

I met my local guide for the island, Victoria and despite the island being no more than six kilometres long and no wider than two kilometres, we got a bus to the Restoration Centre. There are several tours on offer but the winter church was undergoing some minor renovation and the giant summer church was undergoing major reconstruction.

The church seen today was built in the eighteenth century but had suffered from the harsh climate. It was built with donations from the local community. This was one of the areas within Russia that was free and not subject to feudal serfdom. As long as they paid their taxes they were not subject to the various restrictions placed on serfs. They were not rich but they were free and had more than sufficient agricultural surplus so were able to accumulate wealth. This also made them independent-minded and hence the building is very different from other Russian Orthodox churches with 22 domes with no ecclesiastical link, only ascetic and architectural.

This freedom also led to a revolt lasting 2 years starting in 1769. The local governor ordered the peasants to assist in the development of the ore mining and iron plants being developed in Petrozavodsk during harvest time. The peasants ignored the order so that they could gather their harvests so that they could survive the harsh winter. The conflicting priorities meant that relations between the authorities and the local population deteriorated and led to civil unrest and ultimately to the Kizhi Uprising. It was eventually put down by the army when they arrived with cannons. Some of the fit and able-bodied rebels were forcibly conscripted into the army whilst the leaders and some other influential followers were exiled to Siberia.

In the original building, no nails were used, it is all held together with just joints, wedges and wooden pins. The buildings are roofed with shingles, brown where they are new or have been partially covered by another shingle that protected them from the sun and silver or grey where they have been exposed to sun and rain.

An internal metal frame has been constructed to take the weight of the church and the timbers are being removed in sections for refurbishment. Original wood is treated and reused wherever possible. Some sections of timber have to be replaced but some timbers are so bad that they have to be replaced in their totality. An exact copy has to be produced so that it fits with all the other pieces.

The new wood has to be matched with the old. Recent climate warming means that trees grow faster so there are fewer tree rings per foot of timber than the original piece of timber. Therefore they will flex at different rates. A similarly old piece of timber needs to be found with the same number of tree rings to ensure that both flex at the same rate. The whole section of the church is reassembled in the workshop to ensure that it is correct and then it is stored until the builders are ready to reposition it on the preserved structure.

I walked along the length of the island passing Vasiliev's Village, the highest point on the island and Yanka Village. There are carefully preserved houses on the outside but the insides have been modernised and these are used for staff accommodation. Then I came to the summer church missing levels four and five. The very top is in place but it was missing most of its lower domes.

Next door to it behind the same perimeter wall is the winter church, which is complete and visitors can see most of it. There are several other buildings to see and the atmosphere is added to by the crops growing in the vegetable gardens next to the houses, the haystacks in the fields and traditional fencing around some of the fields.

There are other traditional buildings on the site, mainly farmhouses, with similar construction to the house that I had visited and slept in in Kinerma. The barns were attached to the residential building so that the farmer did not have to go outside in the winter. The hay was stored in a barn and the animals were in another area, but both connected to the house.

Chapter 5
The Moscow Canal

I had chosen to travel further south by boat and I was expecting to be picked up at the pier that served Kizhi Island. I was relaxing in the café in the warmth and calm of the café out of the biting cold wind having a cup of coffee. The café looked out over the lake but there were no big ships at the pier and none to be seen steaming towards the island. I was getting apprehensive.

There were 15 minutes to go before the arranged pick-up time and still there was no big ship in sight. I went down to the pier and wandered through the thin crowd of people milling about. I was relieved when I found a member of staff wearing the uniform of the ship that I was due to travel on with the company logo on the back, the name of the ship embroidered over the heart and a little name tag pinned to the lapel. I introduced myself and explained that I was due to join the ship and she went off to find her supervisor.

I was indeed expected and I was ticked off the list of passengers and asked to board a boat. I was naturally intrigued as to where the cruise ship was and I got an explanation although some of the details I gleaned from my fellow passengers later.

The original schedule was for the ship to depart St Petersburg and sail up the Svir River and across Lake Onega to Kizhi Island. Then the ship would steam back across Lake Onega and back to the canal to continue its journey to Moscow. The cold late spring meant that there was a lot of floating ice which meant that there were speed restrictions in force, especially at the locks. The ice would collect in the locks but care is required as if the ship pushed too much ice into the narrow confines of the lock, it might damage the hull, the lock gates or the sides of the locks. On some of the narrower sections of the canal or the river, if there was a lot of ice being pushed to the sides, it would scour and erode the banks and require dredging to maintain the depth.

The ship had been behind schedule and rather than traverse the lake, the captain had decided to drop off the passengers near where the river exits the lake to take a coach to Petrozavodsk and then a local boat to Kizhi Island. The ship would miss out crossing and re-crossing the lake and traverse several more locks to gain time going up the narrow river. The passengers who had visited Kizhi Island would be bused back from Petrozavodsk after their visit and catch the ship up.

It was a 2 hour journey to travel back to Petrozavodsk where a coach was waiting to drive us around the lake to reach the ship. The ship can take hundreds of passengers but when those who had wanted to visit Kizhi heard about the long transfer, many of them backed out so I joined the other passengers on just one coach. It was a 4-hour journey to reach the ship in the dark. The usual dinner time had passed but those of us who visited Kizhi were treated to a modest and informal buffet.

I got the opportunity to chat with some of the other passengers. There were a multitude of nationalities but most people spoke English. Some of my fellow passengers retreated to the bar but I had had a long day and I went to my cabin.

We were travelling along the Volga-Baltic Waterway. After Peter the Great had fought Sweden and gained territory on the Baltic, he made Saint Petersburg his capital in 1712. There was a pressing need to improve transport from the hinterland of Russia to the Baltic Sea and the first canal was completed in 1709. An expansion of these early canals was the Mariinsk Canal System which was completed in 1810 and is an outstanding technical achievement for the early nineteenth-century canal builders.

The new canal linked St Petersburg with Rybinsk on the Volga. This system was upgraded over the centuries but the Volga-Baltic Waterway was a major improvement and follows a similar course as the Mariinsk Canal System which was completed in the 1960. This canal links Lake Onega with Cherepovets on the Rybinsk Reservoir created by a massive dam at Rybinsk and the canal link is 368 kilometres long.

In the morning, we were crossing Lake Beloye and entered another section of a man-made canal. All along the canal and across some of the open stretches of water, there were buoys in the water to ensure that ships stayed in the navigation lanes where the depth was assured and where it was dredged when necessary. Some of the water is not sufficiently deep for the average draft of ships using the canal so these buoys are essential for safe navigation.

We moored at the wharf at Goritsy, which is a small settlement with several single-storey wooden buildings and not much else. Judging by the number of traders and small shacks selling tourist trinkets, I guess that most of the village income was closely linked to the selling of souvenirs to the considerable number of tourists that flock here in the summer but there were only a few determined stall traders braving the cold.

A coach was due to pick us up but it hadn't arrived as the monastery was just three kilometres up the road, the fitter amongst us started out walking. A little later we had arrived at the entrance of the largest monastery of the Russian North, the Kirillo-Belozersky Monastery. It was founded in 1397 on the shores of Lake Siverskoye by St Cyril or Kirill of Beloozero, the nearby town which is thirty kilometres to the north which today is called Belozersk on the shores of Lake Beloye. The monastery is built of brick and the walls are whitewashed; although the weather had been harsh to the whitewash and had peeled in places and needed another coat, the dilapidated appearance only added to its charm.

A wall surrounds the whole monastery up to seven metres thick. It was built between 1654 and 1680 and incorporated part of the original citadel that stood on the site and later resisted the Polish-Lithuanian army during the Times of Troubles. There are eight large towers and several smaller ones, each built to a unique design. The landward walls on the inside are three storeys high with cloisters running along the two upper storeys.

Inside the walls, there are eleven churches and two priories plus many other buildings that the monastery would need. There are large enclosed spaces and areas of grass so there is plenty to see or just sit around in the sun on a nice day. I just had to visit all the buildings open to the public and took great delight in walking through the museum. The Bolsheviks converted the premises to a museum but the monks have now returned and visitors may be lucky enough to see some of them in their distinctive robes. Today part of the monastery is still a museum and there are many ecclesiastical and historic exhibits on view. After collecting the last of the passengers, we cast off from Goritsy and continued along the canal. We entered the Sheksna River and negotiated the locks at Sheksna, named after the river.

Every day a small group of people would be invited onto the bridge. That afternoon I had my invitation and we gathered at the allotted spot and were then led through some areas reserved for the crew to reach the bridge. The bridge was largely as you would expect it to be with lots of glass giving magnificent views. There were loads of dials and screens monitoring all sorts of things like engine revolutions, speed, depth, radar, air-conditioning and the like.

During the night, we continued to follow the Sheksna River through a couple of locks and past Cherepovets to enter the Rybinsk Reservoir and the city of Rybinsk over 130 kilometres away across the reservoir. This is also called the Rybinsk Sea as at the time of its construction it was the largest man-made body of water in the world. Construction on the dam started in 1935 and filling the reservoir started in 1941 but it was 1947 before the reservoir was full and it started producing its designed output of 346MW of power.

Numerous communities affected by the rising water levels were moved involving the relocation of 150,000 people. The historic town of Mologa and 663 villages were flooded. In recent years, the project has been increasingly viewed as a typical example of Stalinism for its disregard for the interests of the local people affected by the construction of the dam. There are the spires of flooded churches pointing skyward from the water's surface but I had missed those earlier as we passed them during the night. The Rybinsk Reservoir is the northernmost point of the Volga.

The Volga is Europe's longest river with the largest catchment basin at more than 1.35 million square kilometres. The Volga rises in the Valdai Hills 225 metres above sea level northwest of Moscow and about 320 kilometres southeast of St Petersburg. It takes a long arc north and east before turning south. It flows for 3,530 kilometres before reaching the Caspian Sea where it has produced an extensive delta. Eleven of the largest twenty largest Russian cities lie on its banks. Some are widely recognised and some are unknown in the west. They are in order going downstream, Tver, Yaroslavl, Nizhny Novgorod, Cheboksary, Kazan, Toyatti, Ulyanovsk, Samara, Saratov, Volgograd and Astrakhan.

The route to Moscow was off our starboard bow but we were taking a detour to descend the locks at Rybinsk and to visit Yaroslavl. The city of Yaroslavl was founded at the confluence of the Volga and the Kotorosl Rivers by a prince of Kievan Rus called Yaroslav the Wise during his rule of the Principality of Rostov from 988 to 1010. However, the city was not mentioned in official records until 1071 when there was unrest there due to famine. It was the capital of the independent Principality of Yaroslavl from 1218 until it was incorporated into the Grand Duchy of Moscow in 1463. During the Polish occupation of Moscow, it was the country's de facto capital in 1612. From its earliest beginnings, it has always been a major trading centre and in 1860 Yaroslavl was connected with Moscow by telegraph and in 1870 it was connected with Moscow by railway.

It has had its darker days. The city staged a counter-revolution against the Bolsheviks known as the Yaroslavl Rebellion which lasted from 6th to 21st July 1918 when the Red Army regained control having killed hundreds of people and destroyed hundreds of buildings. In the Second World War or the Great Patriotic War, as it is known locally, it escaped occupation by the Germans; however, as it was a major industrial centre and one of the few bridge crossings over the Volga it suffered repeated bombing raids. Today it is a vibrant friendly city stretching more than 25 kilometres along the banks of the Volga.

We were picked up by a coach from our moorings and driven into the centre of the city. We visited the Assumption Cathedral, which is a beautiful building. It has plain white walls with a complex grey roof line topped with five large golden domes over the main area and another golden dome above the entrance. It appears well preserved but this building was rebuilt in its current form in 2010. It is surrounded by carefully manicured gardens that also stretch along a promontory formed by the Kotorosl River before it finally joins the Volga, known as the Strelka Fountains. It has a flower bed planted to portray the symbol of the town, a bear walking upright carrying an axe over its shoulder with the date of the founding of the city in 1002. In the gardens around the cathedral is a memorial to the fallen in the Great Patriotic War, made of granite with an eternal flame.

At the other end of the gardens is the Church of Elijah. This was built between 1647 and 1650. It has white walls and a green roof topped with five onion domes, also in green with two separate towers. But its real masterpiece is the ornate, bright, colourful and intricate decorations on the inside where every surface has been embellished. It is one of the best examples created by the masters of this art.

Next to the river is the Governor's Garden Museum with the building set out as it would have been for the governor more than a century ago. It has staff in period costumes and we were entertained with music and a dance show in the ballroom. There is a large garden on one side with views up and down the river and across to the other side.

There was some spare time in which some people headed to the nearest restaurant whilst I wandered through the streets gazing at the buildings, the churches and little chapels such as the Adoration Chapel in a park near the centre. I found the nineteenth-century old market with its long arcade with Ionic columns plus a lot of unlisted but fascinating old buildings before a speedy self-guided walk through the magnificent Spaso-Preobrazhensky Monastery, behind its high whitewashed walls. Then it was a brisk walk back to return to the pick-up point for the coach back to the ship.

There is always so much to see and so little time. Some people didn't really seem interested in any of the culture and history. It was as if they just wanted to be able to say that they had been there. After the main attraction, they would find a coffee shop or a restaurant. Some of these people were the same people who were always late and delayed the departure of the coach. One may be forgiven if there is an unexpected problem but habitually being late is just rude.

Whatever time that they had been given to be at the pick-up point, you could be sure that they would turn up 10–15 minutes late, whilst everyone else had made the effort to be back in time. They were the same people who would be queueing for the restaurant on board 15 minutes before the meal time. Breakfast would be served between 7 am and 8:30 am. They would be there before seven a.m. but still be late for a nine a.m. coach departure. The coach was waiting to leave Yaroslavl to take us back to the ship with everyone on board except those same two couples who were always late.

There was noticeably more traffic on the Volga River than on the Baltic-Volga Canal and due to the greater depth, the ships were larger. There were all sorts of vessels such as bulk carriers with cargoes of ore or aggregate. There were ships with hatches over their holds so there was no guessing what they carried. I also noted that I had not seen any container ships unless the containers were hidden below decks under the hatches. There were purpose-built gas and chemical tankers with a mass of pipework on their decks and the tops of pressurised tankers poking over the gunwales. Some ships seemed to be very low in the water with very little freeboard. I didn't check the Plimsoll line on every boat but on canals, there is less chance of high waves, compared to the open sea.

At the end of the day, we got back on board and cruised up the Volga. It was the early evening as we passed Rybinsk and its dam and passed through the locks to the Rybinsk Reservoir built at the confluence of the Volga and Sheksna Rivers. The city was founded in 1071 and had been an important transport and trading city for centuries. It has changed names several times from Rybinsk to Shcherbakov named after Alexander Shcherbakov, First Secretary of the Moscow Regional Party Committee and a founding member of the Soviet Writers' Union, along with Maxim Gorky in 1946, back to Rybinsk in 1957, then to Andropov named after Yuri Andropov, head of the KGB and Soviet leader who crushed the Prague Spring and invaded Afghanistan in 1984, and back to Rybinsk in 1989.

There was only a short passage across the bottom section of the Rybinsk Reservoir before we re-entered the Volga and continued upstream. In the morning, we moored at the wharf opposite Uglich. The city is very attractive from the water with its many colourful churches and spires, with its older buildings and the Kremlin on the river bank. It is a short walk to the sights that we had stopped to see.

Uglich was founded in 1148 and has a wealth of history. Being on the borders of Moscovy and trade routes it was often attacked and plundered by enemy armies on their way to attacking Moscow. It's one big piece of history that occurred in 1591. After Ivan the Terrible's death, his son Dmitri was exiled here in 1584. On 15th May 1591, the 10-year-old child was found in the palace grounds with his throat slit.

The tsar's chief adviser Boris Godunov was suspected but investigators concluded that his death was an accident. I find it hard to believe that any accident could have resulted in a child's throat being slit and there must have been a cover-up of massive proportions which seems more probable. Many people refused to believe that he was dead and this led to several false Dimitri's arising during the Time of Troubles before the Romanovs became tsars. There is a story that the bell used to announce Dimitri's death had its clapper removed and it was exiled to Siberia for telling such grave news. The coat of arms of Uglich features the Tsarevich holding a knife in his hand.

We walked from the mooring through the town past several beautiful buildings such as the Hotel Uspenskaya. This is a pink building whose upper floor is the hotel and the ground floor consists of an arched arcade with shops. On the opposite corner is an ornate green building which is the Governor's Mansion, formerly the Yevreinov Mansion whose construction was started in 1892.

Just beyond the centre of the town in the grounds of the Kremlin on the shores of the river, stands the Palace of the Tsarevich. It is one of the oldest buildings in the town built in 1480. It is surprisingly quite a plain two-storey building built of red brick, although there is decorative brickwork under the eaves at the gable ends. Despite the plainness of three of the sides of the building, the entrance on the first floor is accessed up a stairway with thick pillars holding up the roof over the stairs with tall pointed roofs above the first steps, above the bend in the stairs and above the door.

Near the river is the Church of St Dmitri on the Blood. The Romanov family built this and did much to promote Dimitri's ascension to a saint. It is a beautiful red and white building with green roofs and five blue onion domes with gold decorations. On the other side of the Palace of the Tsarevich is the Cathedral of the Transfiguration of Our Saviour, a yellow and white building with green onion domes, an ornate porch and a separate bell tower.

There was plenty of time as we were due to get our own lunch in the town. I took advantage of the extra time by skipping lunch and walking along many of the roads feasting my eyes on the architecture, and the many fine merchants' houses. The churches, a monastery and even the older wooden secular buildings all had their own charms.

When we had moored in the morning, I had been looking at the shoreline and its array of buildings in the Kremlin. As we cast off we had views of the dam at Uglich just a little further upstream. This raised the river level to allow uninterrupted and deep-water navigation and to also allow the river flow to generate electricity. We entered the locks on the far side of the river from the city. The control room is set on an arch high above the upstream entrance to the lock. The building was constructed of reinforced concrete. However, there was an ominous crack right through the centre of the arch of the control tower.

The construction of the dam also flooded a lot of farmland and communities. Kalyazin was known for its Makaryevsky Monastery, a collection of ecclesiastical buildings. After the completion of the Uglich Hydroelectric Power Station in 1940, the rising waters flooded and submerged both the old town and the monastery. Here, poking out of the waters are the top five tiers of the flooded belfry known as the Kalyazin Bell Tower which is all that can be seen of the former old centre. It is a neoclassical bell tower rising to a height of 74.5 metres over the waters of the Uglich Reservoir. The steeple belfry was built in 1796–1800 as part of the Monastery of St Nicholas. Of its 12 bells, the largest weighed some 1038 poods, equivalent to 17 tons. It was cast in 1895 to commemorate the coronation of Nicholas II of Russia.

When Joseph Stalin ordered the construction of the Uglich Dam in 1939 to form the Uglich Reservoir, the old parts of Kalyazin were submerged under the reservoir's waters but the belfry was left as a landmark towering above the water.

That evening we had a farewell Gala Dinner. The staff had dressed in costume and those in the know had put on their Sunday Best. Formal dinners happen on most trips at least once and so they had packed accordingly. I had been caught out on an earlier river cruise but this time I was prepared. I don't like to lug things around for weeks on end on a long trip that I might only use once or twice at the most. Therefore I had a cardboard crown and some tinsel to make the impression that I was a king. They were cheap, light, small, easy to pack and wasteful but I had no qualms in not bringing them back home when I had had my last formal dinner.

During the evening and the night, we continued up the Volga. At Dubna, there is another dam where the Moscow Canal joins the Volga. River traffic going upstream needs to negotiate the locks next to the dam and then take a tight 90-degree turn to the port to negotiate the entrance to the canal. Then we cruised southwards along the Moscow Canal.

The Moscow Canal connects the Volga River with the Moskva River to the south and is 128 kilometres long. It was built between 1932 and 1937 using Gulag labour under the direction of the Soviet secret police and Matvei Berman, head of the GULAG Soviet prison camp system from 1932 to 1937. Allegedly 22,000 prisoners died during its construction. The Moscow Canal was previously called the Moskva-Volga Canal until 1947. The canal connects to the Moskva River in Tushino (an area in the northwest of Moscow), from which it runs approximately north to meet the Volga River in the town of Dubna, just upstream of the dam of the Ivankovo Reservoir.

Chapter 6
Moscow Visit

Thanks to the Moscow Canal, Moscow has access to five seas, the White Sea, the Baltic Sea, the Caspian Sea, the Sea of Azov and the Black Sea. As such, it is sometimes called the 'port of the five seas'. Apart from transportation, the canal also provides for about half of Moscow's water consumption, and the shores of its numerous reservoirs are used as recreation zones.

We passed through several locks and a set of three locks close together at Dedenevo before entering the Uchinskoye Reservoir formed by the dam just outside Puchkino. The canal cuts through a peninsular stretching into the reservoir before cutting across a narrow neck of land to enter the Pirogovskoye Reservoir on the Klyazma River. We cruised across this reservoir, left the Klyazma River and entered another man-made section of the canal.

I stood on deck in the early morning sun and watched the scenery drift past. Then we left the narrow confines of the canal as we came to the Moscow dock area.

This area is very wide with moorings along both sides. There were other cruise ships moored along the side of the canal. One wharf had several cranes and huge piles of aggregate that had been unloaded ready for the construction industry. I was surprised to see a frigate moored against a wharf but via the network of canals and rivers, ships can reach the Black Sea, the Baltic Sea, the Arctic Sea, the White Sea and the Caspian Sea.

We moored opposite a grandiose building overlooking the canal. There was a park behind it and beyond it was the Leningradskoye Highway about level with Rechnoy Vokzal on the map, the last stop on metro line No. 2 and the second oldest metro line which opened in 1938. Leningradskoye was the same road that Napoleon marched down to enter Moscow in September 1812.

I had a few days to spend visiting various tourist sites in and around Moscow but there were a couple of issues. I have visited Moscow many times, either on business or as a tourist and wherever you are going in this vast country, all trips seem to have a layover in Moscow and have a city tour included in the schedule and I had already seen the major sights several times. Since I had booked two back-to-back cruises, the passengers from St Petersburg had a couple of days visiting Moscow whilst the passengers joining the next leg of the cruise had a couple of days visiting Moscow and the two schedules were identical.

I had noticed that I had a little difficulty integrating into the groups when I had arrived on board after everyone else had had time to settle into their cliques when I had joined after several days of their cruise in Kizhy. Therefore I resolved to forego the tours with the passengers who had started in St Petersburg and join the group who would be starting in Moscow in a couple of days' time and I went to find a hotel on land for a few days. I had had two weeks on the boat and I would have another three weeks én route to Rostov-on-Don so I guessed that I had earned a few days break from cruising.

From my hotel, I walked to the metro at Paveletsky to travel to Tushkinskaya and then caught the No. 151 bus. My aim for the day was to visit the Arkhangelskoye Estate. It can trace its history back to the 16th century. A wooden church named after the Archangel Michael was built here in the 1660s, replaced by a stone one in the 17th century and it is the oldest structure on the estate. But it's the splendour of the palace and its lavish interiors that have the wow factor, for this is an estate that has been home to some of Russia's wealthiest aristocrats, including the Sheremetevs, the Golitsyns, and the Yusupovs.

Early resident Fyodor Sheremetev, whose family name was used to name one of Moscow's airports and the family was once the richest family after the tsar, helped secure Mikhail Romanov's accession to the throne. Later, it belonged to Prince Dmitry Golitsyn, who was a close associate of Peter the Great. It was Dmitry who transformed the place, building a wooden palace and hiring a team of landscapers to create an immaculate French-style formal garden.

However, many believe that Arkhangelskoye's heyday didn't come until the start of the 19th century. Prince Nikolai Yusupov purchased the estate and saw it not as an investment but as a place to house his vast collection of sculptures and paintings. He began a tradition of social gatherings and the estate entertained a who's who of Russian emperors from Alexander I to Nicholas II, as well as notable public figures such as the celebrated poet Alexander Pushkin. If you were a favoured guest, you might be honoured with a personal bust.

Things didn't go so well in 1812 thanks to the war with Napoleon. Though Yusupov's precious works of art were removed and hidden, the palace was still looted. After the war, Yusupov returned and restored the estate to roughly what we see today. Inside, there are impressive works of art and the gardens reflect their formal origins, with walkways, sculptures and manicured shrubs. One of the most unusual buildings on the estate is the Gonzago Theatre and some of the original sets and the stage curtain still survive. But its setting is one of the major draws, with the first view as you approach the main house on the hill still something that takes your breath away.

I was going to have the next three weeks confined to the ship except for any free time that I had and following the guide around the multiple tours that we would have as we stopped at every major city as I cruised down Europe's longest river. Therefore, I felt that I needed some exercise and I set out early from my hotel to walk along the riverfront, through an empty Red Square as it was too early for tourists and worked my way around the Kremlin to Manege Square to Arbatskaya Street. It looked easy on the map on the laptop but the shops don't start until some distance from the Kremlin and the road is called Vozdvizhenka Ulitsa as it leads away from Manege Square which confused me for a while until I reached the Boulevard Ring where Arbatskaya actually starts.

I wasn't actually intending to do any shopping but this was the main shopping street. I had visited it a few years earlier and it was a massive building site. The city has a district heating system using the waste heat from power stations to provide hot water and space heating to the city. On my last trip, there was maintenance being undertaken to the metro system, road works were being undertaken to the road system to put in some underpasses and the hot water pipes had been temporarily diverted into giant pipes above the ground down the centre of the road which took up space so the congestion was awful and pedestrians had to weave their way across pipework and dodge through congested and impatient traffic.

This was a very different experience as the pipes had been buried underground again, the traffic flowed through its new underpasses and the unimpeded shopping experience of Arbataskaya Street had been restored. I met an old fellow Russophile for lunch. Her given birth name was Lisa which co-incidentally in Russian means 'fox' but I knew her as 'Kiska' which in Russian is an endearment term for a pet cat and cat is 'kot' but 'kiska' translates more like 'pussy cat'. But she was no pussy cat, she went to university to study Russian in Moscow and stayed on there and worked as the local correspondent for a major international news organisation. Unknown to me at the time, this was to be the last time that I would see her as she was killed a few months later in an air crash whilst on assignment covering the conflict in Syria.

After lunch, I crossed the Novoarbatsky Bridge along Kutuzovsky Avenue and descended the stairs to walk along the promenade next to the Moskva River through a park and past the Taras Hryhorovych Shevchenko monument. He was a Ukrainian poet, writer, artist, public and political figure, as well as folklorist and ethnographer who lived 1814–1861 and his literary heritage is regarded to be the foundation of modern Ukrainian literature and, to a large extent, the modern Ukrainian language.

When I reached the Third Ring Road Bridge across the Moskva River, I turned away from the river with the intention of cutting across the thin neck of land of one of the meanders in the Moskva River. It was a confusing network of roads, pedestrian crossings plus a lot of heavy traffic so when I reached a railway bridge, I diverted along some back streets to reach the Kievsky Railway Terminal, one of the nine railway terminals in Moscow. As the name suggests, there are regular services to Kiev and there used to be regular services to Belgrade, Zagreb, Varna, Bucharest, Sofia, Niš, Budapest, Prague, Vienna and Venice.

The station was built between 1914 and 1918 in the Byzantine Revival style, which is a beautiful building and especially pronounced is the 51 metres high clock tower at one end. Originally it was named the Bryansk station as this was the first major destination served by the station. It was designed by Ivan Rerberg and Vladimir Shukhov, a brilliant engineer whose work I would come across many times over the next few weeks, and this station is considered an important landmark of architecture and engineering of the time.

The beautiful station building is flanked by a gigantic train shed which is distinguished by its simplicity and constructive boldness. Security is such that only ticket-holding passengers are allowed entry, so I bought the cheapest ticket to the next station in order to gain access to the insides. The platforms are covered by a massive glazed parabolic structure 321 metres long, 47.9 metres wide and 30 metres high weighing over 1,250 tons. Its open-work steel trusses are clearly visible, and they demonstrate the elegance of the grandiose building and cutting-edge engineering.

I could have taken the metro back to the hotel or a direct walk but I needed the exercise and I chose to walk along the embankment along the Moskva River which takes a long meander around the Khamovniki District which is known for its Pushkin Museum, the Cathedral of Christ the Saviour, the Novodevichy Convent and the Luzhniki Stadium at the far end of the meander which was used for the 1980 Olympics.

I signed out of the hotel and made my way back to the ship. I dropped my bags in my cabin and made my way back to the quayside. There were coaches waiting next to the gangplank and we got on to be driven to some fascinating places. Autumn is the time to see the spectacular colours in the nation's parks but this was still springtime and the trees were bare. The exact time the leaves change varies of course from year to year, but usually in the autumn there is a rich colour palette of russets, ochres, golds and oranges around late September to mid-October. However, right now, after a long winter, the trees were bare and only just budding. Some of the statues had been removed or covered to protect them from the winter and the fountains were empty.

The coach stopped at the Novodevichy Convent which was established in 1524 by Vasili III, the Grand Prince of Moscow, in commemoration of his conquest of Smolensk in 1514. The buildings are surrounded by high walls and topped with twelve towers. It is very colourful with white walls and buildings part red and part white, topped with golden domes. The oldest building inside is the five domed Smolensky Cathedral which was rebuilt in the 1550s. Much of the architecture is in the Muscovite Baroque style.

There is a large and impressive six-tiered, octagonal bell tower commissioned by Tsarina Sofia, which towers 72 metres high, making it the second tallest structure in eighteenth-century Moscow after the Ivan the Great Bell Tower in the Kremlin. In 1922 the Bolsheviks closed the convent and converted it into a museum.

Beyond the walls is a park and a lake. It is claimed that this was the place that inspired Tchaikovsky to write the Swan Lake ballet in 1875. Another claim is that it was inspired by a traditional folklore tale called 'The White Duck' which has a similar storyline. As if to emphasise this link, in the park there is a one-metre-high bronze duck followed by nine little ducklings.

The coach then followed the Moskva River along the embankment and dropped everyone on the embankment opposite Red Square for a city tour starting with the Kremlin. I had been here before and had visited many times but each visit included several of the cathedrals within the Kremlin walls but never the same combination. I have now forgotten which cathedrals I have visited and any that I haven't but I have visited so many that I am not worried about missing out on one or two.

I joined the tour to see the cathedrals but since I hadn't kept a record of which ones I had seen and not seen, I was none the wiser after the tour on whether I had actually seen them all. The tour was going on to see the outside of the Bolshoi Ballet, the Metropol Hotel, a magnificent art nouveau building, Detsky Mir, a large children's toy shop and the Lubyanka.

The building was originally built for an insurance company but was taken over by the Cheka, the Bolshevik secret police and became the prison and torture chambers and continued to be used by subsequent replacement organisations such as the OGPU, NKVD, MGB and KGB. I had seen all of these several times so I checked with the guide on the time and place that the coach would take us back to the ship and I slipped away to take a couple of Metros to visit the Bunker 42 Cold War Museum at Taganskaya. The site appears to be a non-descript neoclassical building but this is just a façade to blend into the surroundings and was built to divert attention to the entrance into the bunker. I had checked out opening times and was nearly put off by the cost of the tour but if I wanted to see it, I had to pay the price.

The bunker was constructed in 1955 as a communication and command post for the Soviet Union's nuclear forces in the event of a nuclear attack. There are massive blast doors to protect the facility from a nuclear blast over the city. There are 12 levels going down 60 metres and to get to the bottom, there are 290 steps so it is only for people who are fit enough to descend and climb that many steps. There was an introductory film in the exhibition hall and then a guided tour of the facility.

The bunker was fully equipped with everything needed to survive a nuclear attack with its own air recycling system, food stores, diesel generators, stocks of fuel and a well to provide clean drinking water. Up to 30,000 people could live and work here and be self-sufficient for 90 days without assistance from the outside world. We were treated to a view of Stalin's office with a mannequin of the man sitting behind his desk.

Whilst this room was similar to an office above ground, many of the rooms and corridors seemed unfinished with exposed Metro-type steel panels bolted together or plain steel sheets with rivets sunk deep into the walls and due to its unique nature, I am surprised that I haven't seen it before as a set for a science fiction film. Other areas had been upgraded such as the museum area where there were exhibits including some which were very hands-on and popular with the younger members of the tour group who were posing for photos.

That evening, before dinner on the ship, we had a practice evacuation, putting on our life jackets that were stored in our wardrobes in our cabins, and walking to our allotted lifeboat station. Some of us were encouraged by the crew to climb into the lifeboats, but it seemed to be a voluntary activity and many passengers declined. Given the rather high average age of the clientele, I suspected that a lot of them would need help to get into the boats in a real emergency. We returned our life jackets to our wardrobes and settled down to dinner.

Chapter 7
The Golden Ring

After a couple of days back on board, but spent visiting the sights of Moscow, it was finally the time to depart. We had another day touring Moscow and once everyone was back on board and all were accounted for, the captain weighed anchor and to the sound of some loud military-style music played over the ships sound system, we pulled away from the mooring at Moscow's Northern River Port and headed for the Moscow Canal.

There are eight locks on the canal between Moscow and the Volga but Lock Nos 7 and 8 are upstream of the river port. It was dusk as we steamed along the canal and it got darker as we cruised along the canal through the outskirts of Moscow. I spent some time watching the city lights glide past but as the sun set, it got noticeably colder so I was happy to go inside to the restaurant to warm up.

The ship negotiated several locks during the night and by the next morning, before breakfast, we negotiated Lock No. 1 at Tempy and just six kilometres downstream, we entered the Volga just upstream of Dubna where there is a large dam that creates the Ivankovo Reservoir which produces hydroelectricity.

Dubna is mentioned in Aleksandr Solzhenitsyn's book The Gulag Archipelago as a town built by Gulag prisoners. It is 125 metres above sea level, situated approximately 125 kilometres north of Moscow. The city boasts that it has one of the world's tallest statues of Vladimir Lenin at 25 metres high, built in 1937. The accompanying statue of Joseph Stalin of similar size was demolished in 1961 during the period of de-stalinisation. Another claim to fame, if that is the right term is that when the collective farm system was set up after the revolution, one of the first collective farms was organised in the Dubna area.

The first development at Dubna was a fortress built in the area in 1132 by the order of Yuri Dolgoruki who ruled the Rostov-Suzdal Principality. It existed until 1216 when the fortress was destroyed during the feudal war between the sons of Vsevolod the Big Nest. Many historical figures had interesting names and monikers. Vsevolod earned his 'Big Nest' moniker as he had fourteen children by his wife, Maria Shvarnovna.

As we steamed downstream towards Uglich, we passed the Kalyazin Bell Tower again. We had been sailing along the reservoir formed by The Uglich Hydroelectric Station, a hydroelectric station on the Volga River in Uglich and it is the first of the Volga-Kama Cascade of dams. It began operating on 8th December 1940, making it one of the oldest hydroelectric plants in Russia. The plant has a 120MW capacity and is operated by RusHydro. There is also a hydropower museum located at the hydroelectric plant dedicated to the development of hydropower.

Construction of the dam began in 1935 and the first excavator arrived in January 1936. The plant's design was finally approved on 23rd May 1938 by the Economic Council of the USSR Council of People's Commissars, modelled after the Rybinsk hydroelectric station. Gulag prisoners were used in the construction. Just like the Kalyazin Bell Tower, some of the oldest buildings in the region, including the 15th-century Intercession Monastery in Uglich were flooded by the rising water levels of the reservoir. The first hydroelectric generator went into operation on 8th December 1940, and the second generator began operating on 20th March 1941.

We reached Uglich, descended through the locks on the north side of the dam and steamed along the channel separating ships from the swelling water being discharged from the hydroelectric plant. At the end of the channel, we crossed the main river and moored a little distance downriver of the dam. Uglich was first mentioned in 937 making it more than 200 years older than Moscow although the city was only officially founded in 1148. The defences were developed by Ivan the Terrible on a spit of land between a tributary river and the Volga with a moat across the neck of the peninsular.

Coaches were waiting for us to take us into the centre of the city. I had visited the Kremlin just a few days earlier but even if the same places are visited, it is with another guide and some of the stories are different and some of the rooms visited are different so despite having been on a tour a week earlier, I joined the group for another tour of the Kremlin area, the cathedral of Resurrection, the palace of Tsarevich Dimitri and the church of Dimitri on the Blood.

The group was taken around the Kremlin but it was raining and much of the tour was outside in the rain. The numbers in the group thinned as people left to seek shelter, have a cup of coffee or walk back to the ship. The group also included 14 Chinese, all members of an extended family. Only one of them spoke sufficient English to listen to and understand the stories that the guide was telling us. The others would drift away and take photos of each other standing in front of every church, statue or gate that we stopped at. At the end of every tour, the one person who spoke English would go through everyone's photos and give a brief summary of what the guide had told us in English about the church or fortress.

It was still raining when the tour was over. There was plenty of time before we had to be back on board so there was time to see more of the city but the rain and cold made any further exploration an uphill struggle. The city is known for its fine metalwork and precision watchmaking. As I walked along the arcade of shops, there were noticeably a lot of watch shops mixed in with the souvenir shops.

I walked up the main street and wondered at some of the fine fretwork on the old single-storey houses. I passed the fire station with its tower looking out across the city. When cities when made of wood, the threat of a conflagration of fire spreading through the whole settlement was a major fear hence the fire watch tower. But the rain was unceasing and I turned around to walk back through the local public park with its war memorial and eternal flame back to the ship.

During the evening, the ship set off again to make its way down the Volga to reach the southern stretches of the Rybinsk Reservoir. I had been here just a week before, coming down from Cherepovets on the far north of the Rybinsk Reservoir but we were just crossing the southern section of the reservoir to negotiate the locks to continue our journey down the Volga to Yaroslavl. We moored during the night and woke up for breakfast at the river docks near the centre of Yaroslavl.

Yaroslavl is renowned for its 17th-century churches. It is also an outstanding example of the urban planning reforms introduced by Katherine the Great in 1763. These took the form of implementing roads radiating out from the centre but it also preserved the Spassky Monastery that is one of the oldest in the Upper Volga region.

The city slowly developed and by the 16th century, it was a major trading centre. The expansion of the Russian empire with the capture of Kazan and Astrakhan further down the Volga opened the way for trade across the Caspian to Asia, the Caucasus and southwards to Persia, present-day Iran. Foreign trade developed and English traders chose the city as a safe place to store goods before trading them further down the river. Trade was brisk in cloth, sugar and spices. Other nationalities followed, Germans brought ceramics, armaments and paper.

The French brought wine and fruit. The Dutch came with linen and glass. Yaroslavls exports were leather, fish, flax and works of art.

The first Russian theatre was founded here in 1750 by Fyodor Volkov and in 1786 the city was the first regional city to publish a provincial magazine. My city tour started with the Monastery of Spaso-Preobrazhensky Monastery on the banks of the Kotorosl, now a museum. I had had a brief walk through the site on my previous visit but now I had a knowledgeable guide to walk and talk me through the history of the buildings.

There are several religious buildings and a bell tower with several bells. Its exact date of construction is uncertain but probably started in the late 12th century by Prince Konstantin of Yaroslavl. It was both a religious site and a residence for the princes.

A short walk along the river bank is the Uspenskiy Kafedral'nyy Sobor, the Assumption Cathedral. Although built in a traditional style, it was started in 2005 so as to be completed in 2010 for the city's millennium birthday. In front of the cathedral is an eternal flame.

The memorial was inspired by the story of a worker and his lover. They would be separated by the war and they had a photo taken of themselves and tore it in half with each of them taking a part of the photo of their loved one. The worker joined the army, went to the front and was killed. The torn photo of his lover was found in his pocket. At the same time, his lover was working in an armaments factory and was killed in an air-raid, and again her half of the torn photo was found in her pocket.

After a visit to the eternal flame, there was a walk through the gardens to St Elijah the Prophet's Church which although I had seen the week before, I had not had a chance to see the insides. Then we had time to walk around the centre of the city and I took a walk through the local market, which was once housed in the old market but has since been moved to a modern, functional building and although the colours and sights were interesting, I had hoped to see some of the original architectural wonders. The old market is still standing and is located just around the corner but has been renovated and is now an arcade of upmarket shops.

That afternoon there was a 1 hour optional tour to Rostov Veliky, known in English as Rostov the Great, so called to distinguish it from Rostov-on-Don. It was originally called Sarskoye Gorodishche and was believed to have started as a Viking settlement built to protect the Volga trade route. It was first mentioned in 862 when it was described as an important settlement. By the 10th century, Rostov Veliky had become the capital city of one of the most prominent Russian principalities. It became the see of one of the first bishoprics in Russia in 988. In the 14th century, the bishopric became an archbishopric but it was on the front line and was frequently attacked by Mongols, the last sa^{ck}ing occurring in 1408 led by Edigu. In 1474, the principality was incorporated into Muscovy.

The city is the alleged birthplace of Alyosha Popovich, a legendary medieval knight and folk hero. The city has an incredible Kremlin, said to be the finest outside Moscow. It has several ornate churches and cathedrals and is noted for its enamels. It has a massive bell tower and its bells are famous, each with its own name the largest bell, cast in 1688, weighs 32 tons. It is also one of the famous cities of the Golden Ring.

The Golden Ring is a collection of ancient cities that surround Moscow with lots of history, monasteries, kremlins, cathedrals, icons and UNESCO-designated sites. The term was coined by Soviet historian and essayist Yuri Bychkov, who published a series of essays on several cities in the newspaper Sovetskaya Kultura in November-December 1967 under the heading 'Golden Ring'. There isn't a definitive list of these cities but there are the principle eight cities such as Sergiev Posad, Rostov Veliky, Pereyaslavl Zalessky, Yaroslavl, Kostroma, Ivanovo, Plyos and Suzdal. Several other cities also consider themselves part of the Golden Ring such as Vladimir, Rybinsk, and Uglich.

These ancient towns, which also played a significant role in the formation of the Russian Orthodox Church, preserve the memory of the most important and significant events in Russian history. The towns have been called 'open-air museums' and feature unique monuments of Russian architecture from the 12th to 18th centuries. These towns are among the most picturesque in Russia and have preserved many traditions and the culture of ancient Russia to this day although old and have many similar sites, they are all unique.

The only city in the Moscow Region to be included in the Golden Ring is Sergiev Posad, about 75 kilometres northeast of the city on the road to Yaroslavl. Its top destination is the UNESCO-protected Troitse-Sergieva Lavra monastery which was founded in 1337 by St Sergius of Radonezh. He was declared the patron saint of the Russian state in 1422. His numerous followers founded more than 400 cloisters all over Russia, including the celebrated Solovetsky, Kirillov, and Simonov monasteries. The Lavra is now one of the most important religious sites in Russia and St Sergius is one of the most revered native Russian saints.

Pereslavl-Zalesskiy is the birthplace of Alexander Nevsky, The city also has links with Peter the Great who had a 24-foot boat, the Fortuna, on nearby Lake Pleshcheyevo which was the start of the Russian Navy and is on display in a museum on the Veskovo Estate.

Ivanovo is both the youngest and the most industrial of all Golden Ring cities. Previously the city was known as Ivanovo-Voznesensk after the two former villages which merged to form the new city in 1871. It is forever connected with its once-booming textile trade which led to the city being known as Bride City and Russian Manchester.

Suzdal is often referred to as an open-air museum for the number of old buildings that have been preserved and the lack of industrialisation. Vladimir was the former capital of medieval Russia and is a very historically important city. It is somewhat more industrial than its neighbour of Ivanovo but its Golden Gates, St Demetrius' Cathedral and the Dormition Cathedral are UNESCO-protected and masterpieces of ancient Russian architecture.

After touring the Kremlin and its cathedrals, the next stop was the Spaso-Yakovlevsky Monastery, or the Monastery of St Jacob Saviour on the outskirts of Rostov Veliky which overlooks Lake Nero. The monastery was founded in the 14th century by St Iakov of Rostov. The earliest building is the Cathedral of Conception of St Anna, (the Zachatievsky Cathedral), constructed in 1686 and the other large building is the Saviour Transfiguration Cathedral, built in the same century.

We left Rostov Veliky and it was dark by the time we got back to the ship. It was late so we went straight to the restaurant for the evening meal. During the meal, the captain cast off and we headed down the river. It wasn't very far from Yaroslavl to our next stop at Kostrama, just 85 kilometres downstream. Sometime during the night, we docked at Kostrama so we were moored when it was time for breakfast.

Kostroma is memorable for its picturesque landscapes, monuments of culture, a lot of history and folk art. The area had produced many literary, artistic and philosophical giants and its modern industries include metal forging. The city was first mentioned in chronicles in 1213 and the name is thought to be either from the Finnish word 'kostrum' meaning fortress or it is from the local Khorovod word for a traditional Slavonic dance. Some historians put the founding of the city much earlier as 1152. The city shares the same name as the East Slavic goddess Kostroma.

It was a wooden city which meant that it was always subject to conflagrations caused by fire. There is a fire station with a tower in the centre of the city, which was used as a fire lookout point. But in 1237, Mongol-Tartars attacked and destroyed the city. However, it was destroyed several times by fire, sometimes by enemy armies and sometimes by nature. A fire in 1413 is claimed to have destroyed 30 churches but this is a sign of how large the city had grown to be able to afford to build 30 churches.

There were coaches waiting on the road opposite the river port to take us the short distance from the port, up the river bank to the centre of the city set high up on the bank overlooking the river. On our way to the centre, we passed the statue of Ivan the Long Arm Yuri, or in Russian known as Yuri Dolgorukiy who was a Rurikid prince, the dynasty that ruled Russia before the Romanovs. He got the moniker of 'Long Arm' not because he had long arms but was instrumental in expanding and consolidating control over an area then on the fringes of the empire.

Yuri was an ancestor of Vsevolod the Big Nest and died in 1157 but he played a key role in the transition of political power from Kiev to Suzdal in 1121. In 1108, Yuri was sent by his father to govern the vast Vladimir-Suzdal province in the north-east of Kievan Rus. He founded many fortresses and towns in the area such as Ksniatin in 1134, Pereslavl-Zalesski and Yuriev-Polski in 1152 and Dmitrov in 1154. The establishment of Tver, Kostroma, and Vologda are also popularly assigned to Yuri. In 1156, Yuri fortified Moscow with wooden walls and a moat and is often referred to as the founder of Moscow.

Like many towns of Eastern Rus, Kostroma was sacked by the Mongols in 1238. It was at that time a small principality, under the leadership of Prince Vasily the Drunkard, a younger brother of the famous Alexander Nevsky. Upon inheriting the grand ducal title in 1271, Vasily and his descendants ruled Kostroma for another half a century, until the town was bought by Ivan I of Moscow.

As one of the northernmost towns of the Grand Duchy of Moscow, Kostroma served the grand dukes as a place of retreat when enemies besieged Moscow which happened several times such as in 1382, 1408 and 1433. But it wasn't always a safe place and the city was looted by Novgorod pirates in 1375.

The growth of the city in the 16th century may be attributed to the establishment of trade connections with English and Dutch merchants and the Muscovy Company through the northern port of Archangel. Boris Godunov ordered the Ipatiev Monastery in Kostrama and the Epiphany monastery in Moscow to be rebuilt in stone. The construction works were finished just in time for the city to witness some of the most dramatic events of the Time of Troubles and it was here that Mikhail Romanov was offered the crown as tsar of Russia in 1612. Kostroma was twice ravaged by the Poles and it took a six-month siege to expel them from the Ipatiev Monastery.

We reached the site of the former Kremlin which was made into a park by the Soviets who also destroyed the cathedral in 1934. But in the centre of the park is a large building site and nearing completion was the replacement cathedral. It is being built using reinforced concrete but the design and the finish will be traditional and indistinguishable from a traditional cathedral to the untrained eye.

In the park, there is a statue of Lenin but this one is unusual. Lenin is in the typical position that he is depicted in most statues, his coat billowing, leaning forward with his right hand outstretched. The unusual feature is the plinth on which he stands. It was originally built to support a statue of the tsar in time for the 300-year anniversary of the Romanov dynasty. However, the First World War interrupted the project and although the plinth was finished, it never supported a statue of the tsar and it was used to support a statue of Lenin instead. So it is a mixture of architectural styles with an Imperial plinth and a Bolshevik Lenin.

We walked along an arcade of shops towards the central market. On one corner is the Memorial to the Kostroma Veterans of the First World War. Of the estimated military and civilian deaths total of 18,000,000 some 3,300,000 were Russian.

Across the road is the main open market. In the centre of the side nearest the Volga stands a statue of Ivan Susanin. Whilst Mikhail Romanov was fighting the Poles, it was Ivan Susanin who lured Polish troops into some marshes on a ruse and despite being captured and tortured, he refused to reveal the whereabouts of Mikhail Romanov and so gave him time to muster his forces and continue the fight against the Poles.

The open market was a kaleidoscope of colours. There were clothes, fruits, vegetables, all sorts of fish both fresh, dried and frozen and a wide range of cheeses. Being on a cruise ship, and being fed well three times a day, I really didn't want to eat any more but I did buy a plastic cup of berries. I had no idea what they were but the different colours made them attractive. However, I should have tasted them before I bought them as they were very tart and not to my taste. I donated them to the receptionist back on board the ship and her eyes lit up. She came from southern Russia and these northern berries are very expensive there so it was a treat for her.

It is understandable why the Romanov tsars regarded Kostroma as their special protectorate. The Ipatievsky monastery has a palace inside built by the Romanovs. The city was visited by many of them, including Nicholas II, the last Russian tsar. The monastery had been founded in the early 14th century by a Tatar prince, an ancestor of the Godunov family. The Romanovs had the magnificent Trinity Cathedral rebuilt in 1652, known for the beauty of its frescoes and iconostasis.

At the far side of the market was the central square with several municipal buildings and the fire station with its central tower dominating the skyline, used as a fire watch. Town status was granted to Kostroma in 1719 but in 1773, Kostroma was devastated by a great fire. Afterwards, the city was rebuilt with streets radiating from a central point on top of the river on a plan said to have been introduced by Katherine the Great. She was responsible for the extensive modernisation of several cities and introduced legislative reforms. It is said that she opened her fan and laid it on the table to demonstrate her instructions to her architects to build roads radiating out from the centre. It is one of the best-preserved examples of 18th-century town planning, and the city retains some elegant structures in a provincial neoclassical style. These include the governor's palace, the fire tower, a rotunda on the Volga embankment, and an arcaded central market.

The coaches picked us up and ferried us from the centre across the bridge over the Kostrama River. From the bridge, we had a marvellous view of the Ipatiev Monastery on the banks of the river.

The Ipatiev Monastery, sometimes translated into English as Hypatian Monastery, was founded around 1330 by a Tatar convert, Prince Chet, whose male-line descendants include Solomonia Saburova and Tsar Boris Godunov, and it is dedicated to St Hypatios of Gangra. The Ipatievsky monastery survives mostly intact, with its 16th-century walls, towers, belfry and the 17th-century cathedral.

Our guide took us around the main cathedral but after that, we were left to explore by ourselves, to walk through the buildings and view the collection of icons in the museum. It is a functioning monastery so we caught glimpses of monks in their cassocks as they walked through the grounds. Off to the right of the entrance is the Romanov Hall where the Romanovs lived and is now a museum.

In Russia, domes are known as onion-shaped domes or helmet-shaped domes. Helmet-shaped domes date back to the pre-Mongolian period and were replaced by what is now called onion-shaped domes. It is said that this new form of dome was thought to allow the snow to slide down from them.

Their numbers are very important. One dome represents Christ or one God, three domes symbolise the Holy Trinity of the Father, Son and Holy Spirit. Five domes are to honour the Saviour and the four Evangelists, Matthew, Mark, Luke and John. Seven domes represent the Seven Sacraments. Nine domes designate the nine ranks of angels whilst thirteen cupolas represent the Saviour and the twelve Apostles. Thirty-three domes mark Christ's age on the earth.

The colours of Russian domes are also significant and although the colours of the cupolas are not strictly assigned, they are often chosen according to the interpretation of the church symbolism. The most typical colour is gold, symbolising the celestial glory, the sun and daylight and is used to decorate the cupolas of main cathedrals and churches. However, modern or renovated church domes are not covered with gold but an oxide of titanium which has the same colour but is cheaper and more robust.

Churches consecrated to the Mother of God are decorated with blue cupolas with golden stars. If a church has green or silver domes, it means that they are consecrated to saints. Finally, in monasteries, churches can be topped with black cupolas, the symbol of monkhood.

During the Time of Troubles in Russia, the Ipatiev Monastery was occupied by the supporters of False Dmitriy II in the spring of 1609. In September of that same year, the monastery was captured by the Muscovite army after a long siege. The Time of Troubles ended when the Polish-Lithuanian invasion army was finally repulsed in 1612 and on 14th March 1613, Mikhail Romanov became the next Russian tsar ending the long period of interregnum during which there were many pretenders, opponents and opportunists after the death of Tsar Feodor in 1598.

Most of the monastery buildings date from the 16th and 17th centuries. The Trinity Cathedral is famous for its elaborately painted interior. The Church of the Nativity of the Mother of God was rebuilt by the celebrated Konstantin Thon at the request of Tsar Nicholas I to celebrate the 250th anniversary of the House of Romanov. The Soviet authorities demolished it in 1932, but it was rebuilt in 2013. The main entrance was also designed by Konstantin Thon.

The Ipatiev Monastery was disbanded after the October Revolution in 1917. It had been a part of the historical and architectural preservation, but recently the authorities decided to return it to the Russian Orthodox Church despite strong opposition from museum officials but it is now both a functioning monastery and a museum.

After the tour of the monastery, I walked anticlockwise around the outside of the monastery walls to reach the Museum of Wooden Architecture, created in 1958. It is a collection of wooden churches, peasant dwellings, middle-class buildings and merchant dwellings. There are also two churches, three windmills and various other village buildings.

Many of the old wooden structures were transported to the site under the monastery walls from distant districts of the Kostroma Oblast. It was right up my street as I adore the skills of the craftsmen who created these buildings and of course the insight into the way of life of people in those times. For some of the group, it was just another group of boring buildings and they were just taking photos of each other or drinking coffee in the café but for me, there was not enough time to enjoy the museum.

There is a long straight street overlooking a lake with various buildings along it from simple peasant's buildings through wealthier farmer's buildings with barns and storage areas. There were also several buildings representing the middle classes such as merchants who had within their homes rooms for servants and storage areas for products. Some of the warehouse areas housed a variety of sleighs and agricultural implements.

Off to one side was a path that led into the forest but it seemed that few visitors bothered to walk that far as it was deserted and the path was overgrown. At the end of the path were some more buildings. There was a little church and three windmills. One was a simple farmer's affair to mill grain for his family, and a larger one but both standing on a central pillar made out of a single tree trunk. The third one was a tower four storeys high rising from the centre of a large warehouse. Time was running out and I needed to get back to the ship so it was a fast walk along the far side of the lake and past another church nestling in the trees to board the coach to get back to the ship.

Chapter 8
Nizhy Novgorod

The next stop was Pylos just 60 kilometres downstream or 75 kilometres by road. We left Kostrama in the dark and sometime after midnight, I was awoken as the ship gently nudged the wharf as the captain berthed the ship. I generally prefer to travel during daylight hours as I get to see something but for long stretches of the river between the urban centres along the Volga, the scenery was unchanging.

Sometimes crossing a reservoir, the banks were some distance away from the main shipping lane. Since passing through the last locks, the river is confined between high banks covered in trees. From the ship, there were no views out across the countryside, just long lines of tree-covered steep banks rising up away from the water's edge. Occasionally there was a ravine or a valley where a small stream had cut into the bank. A rough track might wind its way down to the water's edge to give access to fishermen. At the bottom of a track, I would often see a Ulianov or a 4 x 4 Lada parked next to a row of boats. But I was surprised that there was little development along the shore overlooking the river.

Pylos was founded in the 12th century and some years later a fortress was built here. However, the fortress was destroyed in 1238 by Mongols and the town was abandoned. Another town was established in 1410 by Prince Basil of Moscow but it never prospered. Today it is one of the smallest towns in Russia with a population of just 2,500 but it has nine churches, five museums, a theatre and a handful of multi-coloured traditional houses.

We had breakfast overlooking the main road that ran alongside the river bank but other than a group of Japanese photographers, there was very little activity. I had read up on Pylos but there was little of interest for me so I planned to just walk about the town. I used my laptop to find a map and tried to memorise the road plan of the town and set off after breakfast in some light rain. We were moored somewhere downstream of the middle of the promenade along the waterfront.

I walked upstream first. The promenade is about three kilometres long and there is a row of old houses facing the river with sometimes another street behind that before the steep banks cut by the river restrict further development near the river and other buildings have to be built on the plateau stretching away from the top of the river bank. The centre of the promenade is where a small river has cut down through the river bank. There is a long thin pond formed by the causeway over the mouth of the river that the promenade takes. Beyond this is the old main centre of the centre.

There were few people about and even fewer cars. There were many wooden buildings for which the town is famous. It was like walking through another museum of wooden architecture. Some of the buildings were dilapidated or abandoned. One had been damaged by fire, the insides gutted and the roof just a tumble of beams but many of the rounds of timber that formed the walls had been scorched but were still standing. It was like looking at the charred skeleton of a house and would remain so until the workmen arrived to demolish the remains.

Another house leant at a crazy angle with builder's wire fencing around it to keep people away from the unstable structure. The road along the waterfront had once been tarmac but there were more holes, puddles and muddy bits than tarmac. The side streets were just gravel and sand and added to the feeling of quirky but fashionable deterioration.

Many of the old buildings had a small information board outside with details of the original owner, when it was built, its name, what it was used for and adding to the feeling that it was a museum. The upstream end of the promenade is hemmed in by the river on one side and the steep banks of a cliff on the landward side. It ends at some imposing gates of a new hotel, Villa Fortecia.

I returned to the centre of the town. There was a modest run-down covered arcade for traders but it was empty. Across the square was the municipal red brick-built two-storey building. It had some decorative brickwork but had escaped any maintenance or refurbishment and looked old and grey with some missing windows, crumbling bricks and the roof needed attention if it was to survive another winter.

On the opposite side of the square was the small, 18th-century wooden church and on another side was a larger traditional but well-preserved brick church, Voskresenskaya Tserkov, recently painted white and yellow with golden onion domes. The road from the old centre follows a steep cleft in the cliffs overlooking the river with tight bends to reach the plateau high above the river.

You can follow the road inland but there is also a long series of steps up to the top of the cliff to the right that effectively makes a shortcut to the top but it is not for the faint-hearted as they are steep and I lost count after counting over a hundred.

At the top of the stairs, the plateau is flat and easy to walk after the exertions of a long climb. In the trees off to one side of Karl Marx Street is a war memorial to those who perished in the Great Patriotic War, 1941–1945. It is a modest affair with a sprinkling of faded floral tributes and wreaths. There are more than two hundred names on the monument which is about a tenth of the population and might explain why the place is deserted and so few people about. Many of one generation plus others were drafted into the forces and died whilst others moved to the cities to work in factories for the war effort. Conditions might have been bad but once you have moved to a big city, a small rural community loses its attractions and many of the survivors did not return and contributed to the decline.

I walked through the forest in a large arc and past a few dachas and farm buildings. I came across another church, the Holy Trinity Church more by luck than judgement. I find all Russian Orthodox churches fascinating pieces of architecture and even if I have seen dozens, I will still look around the outside and peer inside if the door is unlocked and there is no service being held.

I walked a little further and came to the site of the original Kremlin. It is a good defensive position with the Volga in front and a cliff between the site and the river. On the southern side, a tributary has cut a deep valley and on the opposite side is the cleft that the steep road takes from the riverfront to the plateau. Only a narrow neck of land with a ditch separates the site from the plateau so it is an excellent defensive position.

There are some great views over the town and along the river but little remains of the original Kremlin. There is the Church of the Assumption built in 1699. And the doors were locked. There was a large white building, three storeys high now used as a museum but closed to the public as it was a Monday, part of the international conspiracy whereby many museums around the world close on a Monday.

I took a shortcut down a gully interestingly called Musey Svadby meaning Wedding Museum although there were no buildings on it until the very last lowest short section with just a handful of residential buildings. I crossed the small river and made my way up the far side of the valley to find a small, old, wooden old church, set high on the top of the cliffs overlooking the town and the river. This is the Church of the Resurrection. It was locked but it had some great views and a large cemetery with traditional Russian wooden crosses marking graves.

There was also an incongruous bronze sculpture of a painter and his easel. It probably had a great storey but without a guide or an information board, I was none the wiser. The town was popular with painters and poets and one of the most well-known was Isaak Levitan, Russia's most celebrated landscape painter. According to folklore, he first saw Plyos from the river and on a whim decided to visit the town. He visited Plyos with his student and mistress, Sophia Kuvshinnikova for three summers in a row from 1888. Given the great views of the scenery and the historical link, if I was a betting man, I would suggest that the bronze statue is of him.

I made my way back to the waterfront and the ship, ignoring the souvenir sellers and art museums and art galleries. I passed the Church of St Barbarians to walk along to the other end of the promenade. There was a private beach, and some nice houses and then the road and promenade ended at the gates to a newly built and large private residence.

We left Pylos in the dark after dinner. I slept for a while until I felt sudden movement as the engine noise changed and the boat was making a tight turn. We had arrived at the point where the Volga is joined by the Reka Unzha and the smaller Reka Nemda which is the same place where the Gorky Reservoir begins, the large lake that is trapped behind a giant dam adjacent to the town of Zaborovo nearly 100 kilometres further downstream. The navigation channel changes from the narrow confines of the river and takes a 90-degree turn to starboard into the wide reservoir which is up to 16 kilometres wide.

We had been sheltered by the trees and steep banks but out in the middle of the large expanse of the reservoir, there was a strong wind coming from the southwest and it rocked the boat. At dawn, the wind was followed by sleet blown against the sides of the ship and the windows.

We reached the hydroelectric dam of Gorky Hydroelectric Station, now renamed the Nizhny Novgorod Hydroelectric Station although the city of Nizhny Novgorod is 50 kilometres further downstream. It was built in 1955 between the towns of Zavolzhye on the west bank and Gorodets on the east bank, and the reservoir took 2 years to fill.

We had reached the two pairs of locks earlier than anticipated. We had a timed slot and there was other traffic with earlier timed slots so we could not proceed. For optimal efficiency, boats are given slots and paired up with other boats so as many boats as possible can use the locks at the same time. Only one tug pushing the giant barges can use the lock at any one time but cruise ships are shorter and the locks can take two if the cruise ships are staggered, one at the front to the right and one behind to the left.

As we were too early, the captain turned around and steamed back up the reservoir to fill in time before our slot. We were doing the equivalent of what planes do at airports, we were being held in a holding pattern. I had breakfast looking out the window going back the same way that I had come just half an hour before.

Out turn came and we approached Lock No. 14. We entered the outer basin, protected by breakwaters studded with navigation aids and lights. Ahead of us were twin locks with a massive control tower sitting between the two locks on the upstream side. Above it was a bridge with long approaches on pylons to get the road over the largest ships that might use the locks.

Ahead of us was the Alexander Pushkin, another cruise ship, moored on the right-hand side of the lock. We entered slowly and moored against the left-hand side of the lock. The lock gate rose vertically from its hole and was locked in position. Then the water was let out of the chamber and the ships sank until the level of the water in the lock was the same level as the water in the intermediate basin.

The lower lock gates opened and the Alexander Pushkin drove out and headed across the basin towards the next set of locks. When it was safely on its way, we moved forward into the basin. However, we didn't follow but slowed and pulled to one side of the navigation channel and dropped anchor. There was already another ship in the lock ahead so we would have to wait.

There was a splash and the heavy-duty metal chain rattled as the anchor dropped to the bed of the basin. It hit the bottom and released a cloud of gas bubbles and a muddy plume rose to the surface and drifted off to one side. The wind pushed us around and several more links rattled out from the capstan before we were secure.

We waited whilst the locks were emptied and the two ships moved out. Then the lock was refilled and a tug pushing a barge passed us and entered the lock. The delay wasn't on the schedule and I searched out a member of the crew. He confirmed that we would have to wait and would miss our next time slot but couldn't give an explanation, only shrugging and saying 'this is Russia'. He added that we were in the hands of the lock master and he used the word 'vistek', a semi-derogatory term for someone from not around here, such as locals in Cornwall might refer to tourists as 'grockles'. He turned away and descended a companionway to get on with some task below.

We were still more than 2-hour cruising time from the next port, Nizny Novgorod. The scenery had changed and it was flat land through which the river twisted and the navigation channel was marked with buoys to denote the deepest channel, weaving at times from next to one bank and then across the centre of the river to the far bank. Sometimes the banks were just forest but at other times there were wharves and piers, leisure boats and despite the cold, the wind, the rain and it being a weekday, there were people fishing either from the shore or from small boats, rocking back and forth from our wake.

As we passed through Balakha, I happened to be looking in the right direction to see the Fondness Monument. The banks were not so high and beyond was flat land with buildings, largely three-storey identical blocks of flats. On the top of the bank is a large white stone statue of a mother, sitting down cradling a child.

We passed more forests and some farms and reached the suburbs of Nizhy Novgorod. From the bow of the ship, we slowly passed the Nizhy Novgorod Stadium, a huge modern circular structure built next to the river just upstream of where the River Oka joins the Volga.

On the banks of the Oka River, a little way upstream is the Shukhov Tower also known as the Dzerzhinsk High-Voltage Mast and the Shukhov Oka Tower which is the world's only diagrid hyperboloid transmission tower. It was designed by Vladimir Grigoryevich Shukhov who was a Russian engineer polymath, scientist and architect. It is built of thin steel latticework in a cone that tapers towards the top. There were several towers commissioned between 1927 and 1929 to carry power lines across the Oka River, the tallest being 128 metres. The power line was decommissioned when they were rerouted in 1989. A pair of 128-metre towers was left as a monument but only one tower survives today as the other was illegally demolished.

We arrived at the river port of Nizhy Novgorod right beneath the Kremlin a long time behind schedule. We were moored opposite the Chkalov Stairs which connects the Upper Volga and the Lower Volga embankments. It was built by the architects Alexander Yakovlev, Lev Rudnev and Vladimir Munts. The staircase itself was constructed in the late 1940s by German prisoners of war. It is the longest staircase in Russia. The staircase starts from the monument to Chkalov, near St George's Tower of the Kremlin and the end of Minin &

Pozharsky Square, not actually a square but a major thoroughfare on the Upper Volga embankment, and descends down the river bank to the Lower Volga embankment in the form of a figure of eight and consists of 560 steps.

At the bottom of the steps is a boat placed on a red granite plinth high above the embankment. This is a monument to the Kater Geroy meaning 'Boat Hero' installed here in 1985. The boat is about 20 metres long and on its sole main deck, it has a funnel, a small wheelhouse for the captain, a heavy calibre gun at the front and a machine gun mounted at the back and very little else. The Hero worked on the Volga for almost 100 years, starting work for the Finn Company, set up by members of the Nobel family. The boat participated in both the civil war and the Great Patriotic War including working to resupply Soviet forces during the siege of Stalingrad.

Luckily for us, we were not about to climb the Chkalov Steps up to the Kremlin. We walked along the embankment past the Kater Geroy and climbed aboard some coaches to take us to our first stop which was the Rozhdestvenskaya Tserkov, also known as the Christmas Church but a better translation would be the Church of the Nativity. It was built in 1696–1719 on the orders of Grigory Stroganov. It is one of the best examples of the Stroganov Baroque style. It is built of red brick with many features picked out in white, ornamental window surrounds and colourful domes.

In the 1860s, the belltower started to lean, and over the next two decades, it developed a lean of 1.2 metres. In 1887, its upper tiers were dismantled and rebuilt. It has suffered several fires but has been repaired every time. Its biggest threat came from the Bolsheviks who decided to demolish it but the rector of the church, Sergius Veisov, persuaded the authorities to reverse the decision.

Nizhny Novgorod was founded in 1221 by Yuri Vsevolodovich, Prince of Vladimir but was formerly named Gorky from 1932 to 1990. This was a major port and trading city where traders from the Orient, Siberia and Turkistan came to exchange goods.

Originally the name was just Novgorod meaning 'Newtown', but to distinguish it from the other, older and well-known Novgorod to the west, the city was commonly called 'Novgorod of the lower lands'. This land was named 'lower' because it was situated downstream, especially from the point of view of other Russian cities such as Moscow and Vladimir. Later it was transformed into the contemporary name of the city which literally means 'Lower Newtown'.

The city traces its origin from a small Russian wooden hillfort that was founded by Grand Duke Yuri II in 1221 at the confluence of two of the most important rivers in his principality, the Volga and Oka rivers. Its independent existence was threatened by the continuous Mordvin attacks against it. The major attempt made by forces under Purgaz in April 1229 was repulsed, but after the death of Yuri II on 4th March 1238 at the Battle of the Sit River, the Mongols occupied the fortress.

Along with Moscow and Tver, Nizhny Novgorod was among several newly founded towns that escaped Mongol devastation on account of their insignificance but grew into great centres in Russian political life during the period of the Tatar Yoke. With the agreement of the Mongol Khan, Nizhny Novgorod was incorporated into the Vladimir-Suzdal Principality in 1264. After 86 years, its importance further increased when the seat of the powerful Suzdal Principality was moved here from Gorodets in 1350.

Grand Duke Dmitry Konstantinovich (1323–1383) sought to make his capital a rival worthy of Moscow. He built a stone citadel in 1374 and several churches and was a patron of historians. The earliest manuscript of the Russian Primary Chronicle, the Laurentian Codex, was written for him by the local monk Laurentius in 1377.

After the city's incorporation into the Grand Duchy of Moscow in 1392, when Vasily I annexed it into his empire, the local princes took the name Shuisky and settled in Moscow. After the city was burnt by the powerful Crimean Tatar chief Edigu in 1408, Nizhny Novgorod was restored and regarded by the Muscovites primarily as a great stronghold in their wars against the Tatars of Kazan. The enormous red-brick Kremlin, one of the strongest and earliest preserved citadels in Russia, was built in 1508–1511 under the supervision of Peter the Italian. The fortress was strong and large enough to withstand Tatar sieges in 1520 and 1536.

In 1611, the city became a focus for building a force against the Polish-Lithuanian invaders during the Time of Troubles. In 1612, the so-called 'national militia', gathered by a local merchant, Kuzma Minin, and commanded by Dmitry Pozharsky expelled the Polish troops from Moscow, thus putting an end to the Time of Troubles and ultimately establishing the rule of the Romanov dynasty. The main square in front of the Kremlin is named after Minin and Pozharsky, although it is locally known simply as Minin Square. Minin's remains are buried in the citadel. In commemoration of these events, on 21st October 2005, an exact copy of the Red Square statues of Minin and Pozharsky was placed in front of St John the Baptist Church, which is believed to be the place from where the call to the people had been proclaimed.

In the course of the following century, the city prospered commercially and was chosen by the Stroganovs, the wealthiest merchant family in Russia, as a base for their operations. It was one of the French chefs of the Stroganovs who created the well-known Stroganov dishes of either beef or mushrooms in a rich sauce for the head of the family whose rotten teeth couldn't manage to eat slices of traditionally roasted beef. A particular style of architecture and icon painting, known as the Stroganov style, was developed in the town at the turn of the 17th and 18th centuries.

The historical coat of arms of Nizhny Novgorod in 1781 was a red deer with black horns and hooves on a white field. The modern coat of arms from 2006 is the same but with a ribbon of the Order of Lenin and a gold crown.

In 1817, the Makaryev Fair, one of the liveliest in the world, was transferred to Nizhny Novgorod and started to attract millions of visitors annually. It has its origins in Moscovite princes wishing to establish a competitor fair to the fair held in Kazan, the Tatar capital. By the mid-19th century, the city was firmly established as the trade capital of the Russian empire and perhaps half of all Russian exports had the origins of their contracts in this fair. Industries such as flour milling and shipbuilding grew, dominated by Sormovo Iron Works.

Theshipyard was started in 1849 by the Nizhny Novgorod Machine Factory and it is one of the oldest shipyards in Russia and is known for its development of the production of screw schooners. In 1858, the yard produced the first Russian steam dredger.

The company produced steam engines, carriages, steam locomotives, tramcars, bridges, diesel engines, cannons, pontoons, and projectiles. The shipyard produced 489 ships between 1849 and 1918. In 1854, there were just 15 steamships on the Volga, but by 1870, there were 350 and by 1890, there were over a thousand. The city grew as fast as the shipyard and iron works and by 1913, the population of the city had reached 97,000. During the period 1898–1917, the Sormovo Iron Works built 2,164 steam locomotives and another 1,722 by 1951. During the Russian Civil War, the factory produced armoured trains and during the Great Patriotic War, it built T34 tanks.

Other industries gradually developed, and by the start of the 20th century, the city was an industrial hub. Henry Ford helped build a large truck and tractor plant, the Gorkovsky Avtomobilny Zavod translated as the Gorky Automobile Plant commonly shortened to just GAZ in 1929 with production starting in 1932 with 100,000 cars built by 1936. The company was also responsible for producing the Zim with production starting in 1955.

Maxim Gorky was born in Nizhny Novgorod in 1868 although his birth name was Alexey Maximovich Peshkov. He was a writer, a founder of the socialist realism literary method, and a political activist. He was also a five-time nominee for the Nobel Prize in Literature. In his novels, he described the dismal life of the industrial proletariat. When he returned to the Soviet Union in 1932 on the personal invitation of Joseph Stalin, the city was renamed Gorky. The city bore his name until 1990. His childhood home is preserved as a museum, known as the Kashirin House, after Alexey's grandfather who owned the building.

During the Great Patriotic War, from 1941 to 1943, Gorky was subjected to air raids and bombardments by the Nazis. The Germans tried to destroy the city's industry because it was a major supplier of military equipment. These attacks were some of the most sustained attacks in the entire Great Patriotic War.

During much of the Soviet era, the city was closed to foreigners to safeguard the security of the Soviet military research and production facilities, even though it was a popular stopping point for Soviet tourists travelling up and down the Volga in tourist boats. Unusually for a Soviet city of that size, even street maps were not available for sale until the mid-1970s. In 1970, by the Decree of the Presidium of the Supreme Soviet of the USSR, the city was awarded the Order of Lenin. The city remained a closed city until 1990 when its name was changed back from Gorky to Nizhny Novgorod.

Much of the old central part of the city is built in the Russian Revival and Stalin Empire styles. The coaches took us on a circuitous route from the Church of the Nativity around the city with the guide pointing out various buildings and streets and then dropped us off outside the dominating feature of the city skyline which is the Kremlin with its red brick towers and walls built 1500–1511. However, much of the interior of the Kremlin was destroyed by the Bolsheviks and only the Archangel Cathedral built 1624–1631 remains.

Having walked through the main entrance of the Kremlin, the first thing I noted were the rows of military equipment on show. These were all examples of the output from the city's factories. There were lorries, tanks, a Katyushka rocket launcher and several artillery pieces plus a plane and the conning tower of a submarine. The Chinese family stood in front of every piece for a photo.

Meanwhile, the guide started his speech and my attention moved from the military vehicles to the buildings although many of them were modern government offices.

We stopped at the Monument to Prince George Vsevolodovich and Saint Simon of Suzdal, the founders of Nizhny Novgorod. Behind these statues is the Cathedral of the Archangel Michael. A service was being held and so whilst we could enter, we couldn't take photos and couldn't talk. The insides were decorative but without the guide's insights, I could only stare in awe at the artistry and enjoy it but not be any the wiser.

It had been raining for a while and other than the visit to the cathedral, the rest of the visit to the Kremlin was in the open. The size of the group had shrunk as couples and individuals had drifted away to seek shelter from the cold and rain either in the local café or back on the coach.

Our guide walked what was left of the group past the T34 tank on display overlooking the Volga. Next door was the eternal flame to those who had lost their lives. The next statue was two other notable sons of Nizhny Novgorod who were Prince Dmitry Pozharsky and Kuzma Minin.

In the Time of Troubles, Nizhny Novgorod continued to support Moscow and although most of the country was occupied by the Polish-Lithuanian army, Nizhny Novgorod was still free. The mayor of the city, Kuzma Minin, a wealthy local merchant, called on the people to begin a liberation struggle to free Russia from foreign enemies. Donations were made and an army created and Prince Dmitry Pozharsky, a distant relative of the previous tsar whose ancestral estate was 60 kilometres from the city, was appointed as its commander. The army marched towards Moscow. The area under the rule of Prince Pozharsky expanded at the expense of the Polish occupiers and the army grew in strength. On 22nd October 1612, nearly a year after its creation, the army liberated Moscow from the Poles.

The group numbers halved as people got tired of listening to the guide and getting wet and drifted away to find a cafe in the warm and dry or return to the coach and wait. We had another drive around the city with a commentary but it was dark and raining with not a lot to see. We had an opportunity for some free time to walk around the main street. It was here that there were several voices against the proposal. Only two people wanted to go for a walk in the rain down the high street so in true democratic type, there was a landslide vote to return early to the ship.

I was disappointed as I wanted to visit the cable way. In 2012, a cableway connecting Nizhny Novgorod and Bor on the far side of the river was launched. The length of the cableway is 3,660 metres. It has the largest unsupported span in Europe at 861 metres across the Volga. The main purpose is to provide an alternative type of passenger transportation in addition to river taxis, trains and buses. The cable car has also become a popular tourist attraction, thanks to panoramic views from the cabins but I was out voted and went with the coach back to the ship.

Chapter 9
The Khanate of Kazan

We steamed all night across the Cheboksary Reservoir and at breakfast time we were 240 kilometres further down the river passing the city of Cheboksary, the capital city of Chuvashia. There are 1.5 million Chuvashians living in Russia in an area between Cheboksary and central Siberia. The Chuvash name of the capital literally means the 'fortress of the Chuvash' and it was first mentioned in chronicles in 1469. A fortress was built here in 1555 and by 1625 there were 458 soldiers stationed here although the town had only 661 males living there, a far cry from the nearly half a million living there today. About 62% of the population are Chuvash and 34% are ethnic Russian.

The city is the headquarters of the Concern Tractor Plants, Russia's largest tractor and harvester company but as a leading machine building company, it also produces machinery for the industrial, military, agricultural, municipal building and railway sectors making it one of the largest heavy mechanical engineering companies in the world. The city hosts the Chuvash National Museum and Russia's only beer museum but we were only passing through.

We slowed as we reached the next town, Novocheboksarsk where we negotiated Lock No 17. There is a large dam here plus an HEP station which generates 1,404MW of power with electricity cables and pylons marching away in all directions plus a high-level bridge to take traffic across the river.

Below the locks, we were once again on the river with steep banks on either side with a sparse covering of trees. The river was still more than 500 metres wide with buoys to mark the main navigation channel past some islands in the river. The main channel wandered from side to side to avoid shallows.

During the day whilst we steamed, the crew laid on activities. There were announcements over the tannoy on what we would be seeing during the day. There were lectures on Russian culture, cuisine and customs. Some lectures were based on superstitions or history, others were on traditional costumes and their meanings. My favourite series of lectures which I never missed were on improving my Russian-language skills. I am always eager to expand my vocabulary, useful phrases and whatever I might need.

I would be travelling through southern Russia and whilst people may be used to tourists in major centres such as St Petersburg and Moscow, no one would speak a foreign language in small towns there. I used every opportunity to make sure that I had the right phrases and vocabulary so that I could buy bus tickets, ask for and understand directions and work my way through a menu.

We passed under a double railway bridge, two identical bridges built side by side, each carrying a single railway line. The bridges are more than a kilometre long crossing the river on six columns sunk deep into the river bed. We passed several more islands and slowed as we passed under the M7 road bridge. The ship turned into the river port, its upstream side protected from the flow of the river by a breakwater.

The ship moored at the dockside at Kazan not far from the railway station. I had been here before but was just passing through on the train. The train had crossed the river and had made its way slowly past some buildings near the centre to approach the station. From the train, I had caught glimpses of some of the tourist sights, the tops of towers, belfries and cathedrals and from the guidebook I knew that there were some great places to see. However, the train stopped for just an hour and I had had a chance to view some local streets and get some food but I did not have enough time to visit any tourist sites. I made a note of the attractions of the city and vowed to return another time. And this was my return visit.

We were bused from the passenger terminal on the river on a tour of the city to see some of the famous places from the comfort of the coach for an hour before being dropped off at the Kremlin.

Kazan is the capital and largest city of the Republic of Tatarstan with a population of more than 1.2 million making it the sixth most populous city in Russia but the population is outnumbered by the 1.5 million tourists who visit the World Heritage Site of the Kremlin every year. Kazan lies at the confluence of the Volga and Kazanka Rivers, 715 kilometres east of Moscow. Kazan was an important trade and political centre within the Golden Horde and became the capital in 1438 when the original Bulgar fortress Kazan was captured by the ousted Golden Horde Khan Ulugh Muhammad, who killed the local Prince Swan and built a new fortress. The Khanate survived until 1552 when the Khanate and its capital were captured by Ivan the Terrible.

The original city was largely destroyed during Pugachev's Rebellion 1773–1775 which is also called the Peasants' War and the Cossack Rebellion. It began as an organised insurrection of Yaik Cossacks headed by Yemelyan Pugachev, a disaffected ex-lieutenant of the Imperial Russian Army, against a background of profound peasant unrest brought about by Katherine the Great's confirmation of noble's power over serfs, cutting them off from political representation and tying them to their lords. The common serfs' life was already under pressure from famine, crop failures, epidemics, inflation and increased taxes.

After initial success, Pugachev assumed leadership of an alternative government in the name of the assassinated Tsar Peter III and proclaimed an end to serfdom and land reform. At one point, its administration claimed control over most of the territory between the Volga River and the Urals.

Government forces failed to respond effectively to the insurrection at first, failing to recognise its strength and the depth of dissatisfaction and ignoring the army's involvement in the Russo-Ottoman War 1768–1774. One of the most significant events of the insurrection was the Battle of Kazan in July 1774 when the city fell to the rebels and much of the city was burnt. A victory by General Michelsohn at Tsaritsyn, present-day Volgograd defeated the rebels and Pugachev fled but was betrayed by his followers and was captured and executed in Moscow in January 1775.

Kazan was rebuilt during the reign of Katherine the Great using stone and according to a grid pattern plan. Katherine also decreed that mosques could again be built in Kazan, the first being Marjani Mosque. Kazan gradually grew to become a major industrial, cultural and religious centre. Its geographical location at the intersection of major trade routes connecting East and West added to its reputation for its vibrant mix of Oriental and Russian cultures.

After Peter the Great's visit, the city became a centre of shipbuilding for the Caspian fleet. But the city also suffered from several natural disasters such as flooding of low-lying areas and several major fires from 1595 to as late as 1842.

In 1918, Kazan was the capital of the Idel-Ural State but was suppressed by the central Bolshevist government. In the Kazan Operation of August 1918, it was briefly occupied by the Czechoslovak Legion. The Czechoslovak Legion was a volunteer force made up of Czechs, but later 8% of their number were Slovaks, which was created within the Russian army in 1914. They sought to gain allied help in liberating and creating separate homelands for themselves in Bohemia, Moravia and Slovakia territories of the Austro-Hungarian Empire.

They had distinguished themselves during the Kerensky Offensive in July 1917 and had overrun Austro-Hungarian trenches at the Battle of Zborov.

They could recruit soldiers from prisoner of war camps which swelled their numbers from the 40,000 soldiers at the start of 1917. There was always tension between the Bolshevik government and the Czechoslovak Legion. It had been agreed that the Legion would be transferred to France to continue the war against the Central Powers but they suspected that the Bolshevik government would impede their progress under pressure from Germany, with whom the Bolsheviks had signed a treaty to remove Russia from the war and liberate German forces for duty on the Western Front.

Meanwhile, the Bolsheviks feared that this effective fighting force would be anti-Communist. In fact, they were instrumental in supporting the White Army during the ensuing civil war against the Red Army and there were 60,000 soldiers and officers when they were finally evacuated from Vladivostok in 1920.

In 1920, Kazan became the centre of the Tatar Autonomous Soviet Socialist Republic. In the 1920s and 1930s, most of the city's mosques and churches were destroyed. During the Great Patriotic War, many industrial plants and factories in the west were relocated to the east and Kazan, making the city a centre of the military industry, producing tanks and planes which boosted the city's industrial and scientific base and expanded into its current strengths within the mechanical engineering, chemical, petrochemical, light and food sectors. Today it boasts the biggest IT park in Russia and also the biggest technical park in Europe. After the dissolution of the Soviet Union, Kazan again became the centre of Tatar culture and identity.

We were dropped off near the entrance to the Kremlin which was declared a World Heritage Site in 2000. Much of the original Kremlin walls and towers were erected in the 16th and 17th centuries but have been extensively reconstructed after damage and decay.

The entrance is via the Spasskaya Tower built by 16th-century architects Ivan Shiryai and Postnik Yakovlev from Pskov. It was built in five tiers on the instructions of Ivan the Terrible to be similar to the Ivan the Great Belltower in the Kremlin in Moscow. Until the middle of the 19th century, there was a moat with a stone bridge in front of the tower but now filled in.

The entrance is a high arch wide enough for a carriage. The first tier is a large square, two storeys high topped by a squat square tower. On top of this is an octagonal tower and in the 18th century, a ringing clock was installed. Above is another octagonal tower with arches on each face and crowned by a spire which until 1917, had the double-headed coat of arms of the Russian state at its apex but now sports the five-sided Russian star. It was pulled down by the Soviets in 1930 but has since been rebuilt. There is another entrance to the Kremlin to the right, a simple arch created through the walls to ease traffic flow.

The South-Western and South-Eastern Round Towers were built simultaneously with the Spasskaya Tower by the Pskov masters and are a classic example of that style of defensive structures. In the centre of the Kremlin area are two religious buildings, a mosque and just 100 metres away a cathedral. The mosque is the Kul Sharif Mosque which at the time of its reconstruction was the largest mosque in Europe outside Istanbul. It was named after a religious scholar who along with many of his students died protecting the city against Ivan the Terrible in 1552 who demolished the original mosque.

It was rebuilt in 1996 with funding from Saudi Arabia and the United Arab Emirates and isn't a copy of the original but incorporates many traditional features. As an idea of size, it can hold 6,000 worshippers. Mullahs and volunteers read out the Koran over a loudspeaker system 24 hours a day, seven days a week. Visitors can visit the museum, and the library and climb to staircase to view the main floor where services are held. Tatar scholars speculate whether the original building was an inspiration for the construction of St Basil's Cathedral in Red Square with its central cupola, and eight minor domes representing minarets plus its eclectic mix of colours and styles not typical of Russian ecclesiastical architecture at the time.

The name of the Transfiguration Tower comes from the Transfiguration Monastery of the Saviour however one of the original buildings survives. The original tower was built by Postnik and Barma, but it was significantly rebuilt later and it has strong traces of the architectural influence of contemporary Moscow defensive architecture.

The Tainitskaya Tower or Secret Tower at the far end of the site from the main entrance was built in its present form in the 1550s by Postnik Yakovlev. It was named after a secret water source from which it was possible to take water during a siege. The entrance to the tower is in the form of a dog leg, which increases the defence capability of the tower requiring attackers to negotiate a tight bend whilst under fire.

Outside the nearby Cathedral of the Annunciation, we were told that we could take photos without flash provided that there wasn't a service taking place. I opened the door and guess what, there was singing and chanting and service was in progress so no photos were allowed and the local guide couldn't enlighten us with her knowledge. Instead, we went back outside into the rain where she delivered her spiel and told us where to look for the icons, the statues, and the significance of certain things, and then we tiptoed back inside to view all the things that we had just been told about.

The original cathedral was designed by Postnik Yakovlev who was also responsible for designing St Basil's Cathedral in Moscow. The original building was built after Ivan the Terrible captured the city in 1552. It was damaged or destroyed several times in its history but the current version was restored in 1990s. It has five domes, the central dome is gold and the surrounding four domes are blue.

Next door is the famous Leaning Tower of Kazan, one of the few towers that is not situated on the walls of the Kremlin and is an iconic symbol of the city. At over 58 metres high, it is Europe's tallest leaning tower and leaning 1.98 metres out of true, named the Soyembika Tower but the tower's construction date is enshrouded in mystery. Several scholars date its construction to the turn of the 18th century, when tiered towers were exceedingly popular in Russia but legend postulates that the tower was built more than a century earlier by Ivan the Terrible's artisans in just a week's time as he was eager to marry Söyembikä, the local queen. As the legend goes, the Kazan queen Söyembikä looked out across her kingdom and regretted her decision to marry the tsar and threw herself down from the highest tier and hence the name.

The arch in the centre of the tower has black gates and gold trimmings. Beyond it and not open to the public is the president of the Tatarstan Republic's official residence. It is an attractive traditional building but only used for official functions and his offices and actual residence are elsewhere in the city.

Due to our late arrival, it was getting late but the clouds had cleared and gave us a brilliant blue sky sunset and the lights were turned on to illuminate the Kremlin buildings. We moved on to the viewing point, an opportunity to gaze out across the roofs of the old city centre, to marvel at some of the other majestic cathedrals, churches, mosques and other secular buildings or to gawp at the colours of the Ferris wheel on the far shores of the Volga.

We left the Kremlin via another gate and were taken on another tour through the city. By now, it was dark and raining and although the guide's commentary might have inspired us, we couldn't see very much at all. We arrived at our coach park near the main shopping street for an hour's free time to walk about and shop. I hate these moments on any tour as most high streets are very similar with loads of souvenir sellers. On long trips, I don't have money, space and weight allowance to fill up on souvenirs and most just gather dust at home.

There was a rebellion amongst the clients as it was dark and raining and few of the group wanted to go for a walk. Several people expressed a desire to go straight back to the ship. I might only come this way once in my life so I voted for a walk despite the rain and cold.

We reached a compromise and we collectively allowed the few who wanted to go for a walk just 15 minutes rather than the hour promised on the schedule. I walked fast up and back down the main shopping street. There was nothing special about it but until you see it for yourself, you never know what you might be missing. I bought some wine using some of my newly learned Russian phrases.

In a supermarket, you can select what you want and don't need to speak a word. The shop I entered was a traditional shop with cabinets and counters and you told the assistant what you wanted and she would get it out of a cabinet or off a shelf behind her. It wasn't elegant Russian but she understood and I got some bottles of wine, crisps, peanuts and biscuits.

We returned to the ship for the evening meal at 8 pm. We set off sometime during the evening meal to the sound of some loud Russian martial music. The Volga took a tight 90-degree turn at Kazan and finally, we were heading south. The river is wide south of Kazan, often up to eight kilometres wide except for a choke point at Kzyl-Bayrak where it narrows to 1.8 kilometres wide.

Seventy kilometres downstream from Kazan, the Volga is joined by the Kama River, a major tributary. Somewhere along the river south of Kazan we had finally passed the longitude level with Moscow and were heading towards the warmer south. I had travelled south from Murmansk to reach Moscow but had then taken the Moscow Canal northwards again to retrace my steps to travel down the Volga. We had revisited some of the same places along the Volga but at long last the weather was getting warmer.

The width of the river changes as the river flows into a reservoir created by yet another dam further downstream below Ulyanovsk at Tolyatti. There was another tight turn in the navigation channel and I was woken in the night as we left the Volga and entered the reservoir. We were exposed to the wind again and it was a choppy journey as we cruised down the reservoir to steam overnight to Ulyanovsk.

Chapter 10
Ulyanovsk, Lenin's Birth Place

As we approached Ulyanovsk, our next port of call according to the schedule, we passed under two bridges. The first bridge was the Presidential Bridge opened in 2009. It was originally planned to take 9 years to build and although construction started in 1986, work was interrupted by the collapse of the Soviet Union so its completion was delayed. It had been planned and built to add additional capacity as the original Emperor Bridge couldn't cope with the increasing levels of traffic crossing the Volga.

It is a feat of engineering being the second longest bridge in Russia, and at a length of 5,825 metres is the eighth longest bridge in Europe or 12.98 kilometres including the connecting highway sections. It has 25 spans set on columns sunk deep into the river bed and some of the central spans are 221 metres long.

The second bridge that we passed under was the older, original bridge at Ulyanovsk, the Emperor Bridge built 1913–16. It is a box girder-constructed bridge set across concrete pylons standing in the river bed. It is a combined railway and road bridge with the two forms of traffic running side by side but sharing the same pylons.

The bridge also carries high-voltage electricity cables over the river, suspended from metal latticework arms that stretch out horizontally from the top of the box bridge girder sections. The railway section is on the downstream side of the bridge and only visible from the boat as we passed underneath and steamed away from it.

We were early for our timed arrival time so the captain steamed some way along the reservoir before turning around. We slowed and entered the river port protected by a breakwater from the main force of the river current, but we weren't completely free from the current and we gradually drifted, doing a ferry glide from the central channel, facing upstream and slowly moving sideways towards the docks and finally mooring in the passenger river port.

We walked out of the port and onto the waiting coaches. We had a brief tour of the city with various sights being pointed out by our guide. All of the guides that I encountered in every city seemed to think that every building should be pointed out. I was interested in the museums, castles, cathedrals, their architectural aspects and other historical buildings but I never related to their enthusiasm when they pointed out schools, technical training colleges and universities, recited the list of famous people who attended them and whatever other story that may attach to them.

The coaches finally pulled up and stopped outside Lenin's childhood home in the city which together with the house next door has been converted into a museum. His birth name was Vladimir Ilyich Ulyanov and he lived from 22nd April 1870 to 21st January 1924 but better known by his alias Lenin. He was a Russian revolutionary, politician and political theorist. He served as head of government of Soviet Russia from 1917 after the successful Bolshevik October Revolution and of the Soviet Union from 1922 to 1924.

Lenin was born in the city in 1870 but in another house. His father was a prominent public figure as director of education and his mother was a doctor. The couple had six children and had to move home several times as the family grew but his father bought this house. Lenin embraced revolutionary politics after his brother was executed in 1887 for his part in the attempted assassination of Tsar Alexander. His mother had to sell the house and many of the original items in the house were sold or lost.

The house is set up as it was in his youth but only a few items are original, all of the items on display are authentic period pieces to represent the life and times of Lenin's childhood home.

This area of the city is old with all the houses being made of wood and single or two storeys. The authorities have made great efforts to ensure that this modest middle-class house with a large garden is preserved. There are sophisticated fire suppression systems installed with sprinklers inside and outside the building. There are sprinklers set in the grass in front of the building to douse it with water either to suppress a fire inside the house or to keep it cool if there is a fire across the road. There are also fire-break walls built between the museum and the buildings on either side to limit the extent of damage that might occur if there were to be a fire next door.

Several people noticed the sprinkler heads and asked what they were. The guide gave a brief answer but it was not enough for some of the engineers or AC/DC people in the group who wanted to know how it worked. I knew some of the technical details of the system from a former career and I found myself explaining how it worked (or perhaps since this was Russia, how it should work) and answering some of the more technical questions. I was quite surprised to have so many questions as to who is really interested in fire suppression technology. Apparently, there are quite a few enquiring minds out there.

After looking at the house, we had a tour of the small garden. There was the winter kitchen attached to the house and built in brick and the summer kitchen somewhere up the garden path in a separate building. There was a gazebo where the children played and a large number of fruit and nut trees that gave shade during the long hot summers.

We had a little time to regroup outside the museum before we boarded our coaches. I had seen a Ulyanov parked up the road and I wanted a photo of a Ulyanov in Ulyanovsk. Large groups always take time to move and to be ready and as I quickly walked, I felt that I had plenty of time so I legged it up the road. Crossing a side road, parked some way down it were our coaches, waiting for a phone call to return and pick us up. I would see or hear them moving so I was in no danger of being left behind or of delaying our departure. I took my picture of the Ulyanov in Ulyanovsk parked on someone's drive.

The Ulyanov is a nickname for an iconic 4 x 4 van which is built by UAZ in the city. Since 2000 it has been a subsidiary of Sollers JSC. UAZ stands for Ulyanovsky Avtomobilny Zavod, literally Ulyanovsk Automobile Plant. It manufactures off-road vehicles, buses and trucks. The company is best known for the UAZ-450 series utility vehicle, which has seen wide use as a military vehicle in the Eastern Bloc and around the world. The factory started production in 1941 as part of the Soviet war effort and the basis of the factory was the ZIS automotive manufacturer that was relocated from Moscow.

It developed various models but it is the iconic UAZ 450 series which is the most widely recognised model. The vehicle was a sturdy, but not very comfortable vehicle with the ability to overcome virtually any terrain, whilst also providing ease of maintenance. The 450 series reached legendary status, thanks to its reliability and impressive off-road capability. It was originally built exclusively for police and military use but it was made available to the civilian market in the late 1980s. The company produced 51,706 vehicles in 2016.

The vehicles can be seen throughout the country and there are thousands of them everywhere. But they only come in certain colours. Police vehicles are blue, post office vehicles are yellow but the most common colour, more than 80% is military grey. The rest are military green. I searched for another colour, any colour, always ready with my camera but I never saw any other colour.

The grey vans have several nicknames, one of which is 'kozel', Russian for goat as on rough ground they bounce around just like a mountain goat and even on smooth roads the gear transmission is erratic and gear changes can make for a jerky ride. Another nickname is 'buchonka', which is Russian for a small loaf of bread with rounded edges which resemble the shape of the vehicle.

The city isn't only noted for land-based vehicles but it is also the home for Volga-Dnepr Airlines, an international airline that specialises in transporting large, unusual and heavy cargo. It has a large fleet of aircraft including twelve Antonovs An-124, the largest production cargo aircraft in the world capable of carrying 120 tons at an altitude of 10,000 metres over 4,500 kilometres.

Whilst I was taking some time out to take my photo of the Ulyanov, I also noted that there was a fire station complete with a fire lookout tower so the authorities have obviously taken the significance of the Lenin Museum into account when deciding where to locate the local fire station just a couple of hundred metres up the road from the museum.

As a modern city founded in 1648, the empire had already expanded south and eastwards and the threat from nomadic tribes had reduced so there was no need for a large stone Kremlin and the churches and cathedrals were destroyed by the Bolsheviks. There were several large cathedrals but all of them that you pass in the city are modern replicas although seemingly traditional constructions.

During the Soviet period, Ulyanovsk lost much of its historical heritage. All traces of the original wooden fort have disappeared, as have the churches of old Simbirsk but the majority of 19th-century buildings remain in the city. The reconstruction of the Cathedral of the Holy Trinity was considered but has since been cancelled. Therefore the tour took us through the city with the guide pointing out more modern cultural locations such as theatres, universities and museums.

The city is not only divided by the Volga, it is also split by the Reka Svijaga river. The river runs parallel to the Volga sometimes just a kilometre from it but by a strange twist of geography, it flows in the opposite direction, northwards, and only ultimately enters the Volga some 200 kilometres to the north.

The town was founded in 1648 by the boyar Bogdan Khitrovo. It was originally named Sinbirsk but changed to Simbirsk in 1780. A wooden fort was strategically placed on a hill on the west bank of the Volga River. The fort was meant to protect the eastern frontier of the Russian empire from the nomadic tribes and to establish a permanent Imperial presence in the area.

In 1668, Simbirsk withstood a month-long siege by a 20,000-strong army led by rebel Cossack commander Stenka Razin. His real name was Stepan Timofeyevich Razin. He was first noted in records in 1661 when he was part of a diplomatic mission from the Don Cossacks to the Kalmyks. That same year Razin went on a pilgrimage to the great Solovetsky Monastery on the White Sea for the benefit of his soul.

He lost his religious compass and became a bandit and he and his gang of followers looted villages and forced ship trading along the Volga to pay him a tribute. His success brought more notoriety, more followers and more power and his aims turned political and he promoted a Cossack republic. His rebel army rampaged along the banks of the Volga as far downstream as Astrakhan on the Caspian Sea but he was captured in 1671 and executed in Moscow. It was just over a century later that Yemelyan Pugachev was imprisoned here before his final fate of execution.

As the eastern border of the Russian empire was rapidly pushed into Siberia, Simbirsk rapidly lost its strategic importance, but it nonetheless began to develop into an important regional centre. Its population is largely Russian 78%, and the next largest minority are the Tartars at just 10%.

In the summer of 1864, Simbirsk was severely damaged by fire, a constant source of peril for any mainly wooden settlement. However, it was quickly rebuilt and continued to grow. The Holy Trinity Cathedral was constructed in a restrained neoclassical style between 1827 and 1841. The population of Simbirsk reached 26,000 by 1856 and 43,000 by 1897.

In 1924, the city was renamed Ulyanovsk in honour of Vladimir Ulyanov, better known as Lenin, who was born in Simbirsk in 1870. Two other Russian political leaders, Alexander Kerensky 1881–1970, the second Prime Minister of the Russian Provisional Government and Alexander Protopopov, a member of the nobility, a land owner, politician and Minister of the Interior from September 1916 to February 1917 were also born in Simbirsk.

The construction of the Kuybyshev hydroelectric plant was completed in 1957, 200 kilometres downstream of Ulyanovsk which resulted in the flooding of significant tracts of land both north and south of Ulyanovsk and increasing the width of the Volga by up to 35 kilometres in some places. Despite the flooding, some populated neighbourhoods of Ulyanovsk were protected by a flood barrier and remained well below the maximum level of the reservoir. It is estimated that if it was ever to suffer a catastrophic failure, the resulting flood would submerge parts of the city being home to 5% of the city's total population to a depth of as much as 10 metres of water.

During the Soviet period, Ulyanovsk was an important tourist centre, drawing visitors from around the country and foreign visitors because of its revolutionary importance. After the dissolution of the Soviet Union, the tourist importance of Ulyanovsk sharply decreased. In the 1990s, the city went through some hard times involving a slump in production in all sectors, mass unemployment and mass impoverishment. Besides the policy of the regional authorities of that time leaning against the grants and the Soviet system of management has led to a serious crisis of a city infrastructure. It was only in the first decade of the 2000s that the economy started to grow.

Ulyanovsk slowly recovered from these downturns into a regional manufacturing, educational and transportation centre. Now Ulyanovsk is a major, diversified, industrial hub for aircraft and automobile industries.

A railway bridge across the Volga was built in 1912–1916 and two automobile lanes were added to it in 1953–1958, allowing for the city to expand on the Eastern (left) bank of the river and transforming it into a local transport hub.

According to the Ulyanovsk Region Development Corporation, the Ulyanovsk Region is conveniently situated in the centre of the European part of Russia, where east-west and north-south air, rail, car and river routes cross. It has an industrial, transport and business infrastructure and a network of roads and railways which provide a good basis for turning Ulyanovsk into a major transport and logistics hub which provides all forms of transport, river port and passenger terminal, railways with two major passenger and cargo stations, airports and two major bridges over the Volga.

As the ageing Ulyanovsk bridge, the only crossing of the Volga in the 400-kilometre stretches from Kazan to Tolyatti, could no longer cope with the growing needs of the city, the construction of President Bridge, a truss bridge, began in the late 1980s. Completion was delayed significantly due to the catastrophic economic circumstances following the end of the Soviet Union. Its official opening ceremony was on 24th November 2009 by the Russian President Dmitry Medvedev although traffic was using the bridge a few days earlier. The bridge has a total length of 5.5 kilometres, making it one of the longest in Europe.

Among other famous buildings in the city is the house in which writer Ivan Goncharov was born. Ivan Alexandrovich Goncharov was a Russian novelist best known for his novels A Common Story (1847), Oblomov (1859) and The Precipice (1869). He also served in many official capacities, including the position of censor. We had some spare time after the city tour but not enough to find and look around this house. Instead, I went for a walk away from the passenger river port, up the steep bank and around some of the local streets. There was nothing within walking distance that was interesting so it really was just a wander through some streets but keeping a note of where I was and an eye on the time.

We set off to the sound of martial music at dusk to head further downstream. The main river is joined by a major tributary, the Cheremshan River where it forms a long arm of the reservoir. At the top of the arm is the town of Dimitrovgrad situated on the confluence of the Melekesska River with the Bolshoy Cheremshan River. The city was formerly called Melekess and was founded in 1714 as a village for workers of the local distillery. It was known as Melekess until its name was changed in 1972 when it was renamed Dimitrovgrad, celebrating the posthumous 90th birthday of Georgi Dimitrov, the first leader of the Communist People's Republic of Bulgaria.

Six kilometres to the southwest of the city is the country's Federal Nuclear Research Institute. One of their eight atomic reactors provides Dimitrovgrad with district heating. The nuclear research facilities here had been suspected by weather experts as being responsible for the mysterious nuclear cloud over Europe in 2017 but the real source lay further to the east in the Urals.

During the night we sailed past Tolyatti. It was previously known as Stavropol and informally as Stavropol-on-Volga to distinguish it from Stavropol, a large city in southwest Russia until 1964 when it was renamed after Palmiro Togliatti, the longest-serving secretary of the Italian Communist Party. The city was founded in 1737 as a fortress called Stavropol by the Russian statesman Vasily Tatishchev but the city is best known as the home of Russia's largest car manufacturer AvtoVAZ founded in the late 1960s but better known for their products sold under the Lada marque.

The city has some beautiful churches judging by the photos online but there is a catch. The construction of the Kuybyshev Dam and Hydroelectric Station on the Volga River in the 1950s downstream created the Kuybyshev Reservoir. The reservoir was created by the dam of Zhiguli Hydroelectric Station formerly known as the V.I. Lenin Volga Hydroelectric Station located just a short walk downstream from the centre of Tolyatti. It was filled in 1955–1957 which covered the original location of the city and it was completely rebuilt on a new site.

The city also has a great dog story attached to it. In 1995, residents of Tolyatti began noticing a German Shepherd dog at the edge of South Highway, a bypass road in the Auto Factory District of the town which leads to the AvtoVAZ car factory. He was always in the same place, and he rushed at passing cars. Word of the dog spread around the city and the people of the city informally adopted him.

It was discovered that in the summer of 1995, the dog had been riding in a car with a man and a girl. The car had crashed, the girl was killed on the spot, and the man was taken to a hospital where he died a few hours later. However, the dog survived. His name was not known, so people began calling him 'Faithful' or 'Kostya'.

People tried to adopt him and take him into their homes but none succeeded as the dog always escaped and returned to the same spot looking for his master. He would take food from the people but always returned to the same spot. In the snow and rain, in any weather and time of year, he was always in his spot. The dog always waited and ran up to all passing vehicles. Everyone who travelled along that road always saw Kostya running along the roadside or resting quietly on the grass. The citizens became very fond of Kostya and turned his story into a living legend. Stories about the dog were published throughout Russia. For 7 years, Kostya stayed at his post until 2002 when he was nowhere to be seen. A search revealed that he had wandered off and he was found dead in nearby woods.

Chapter 11
Samara

We arrived at Samara at 3 am and dropped anchor in the middle of the river. I was awake and couldn't get back to sleep so I braved the cold and watched a brilliant sunrise in a cloudless sky. We had gone back an hour as Samara is so far east of Moscow and works on SAMT, Samara Time rather than MSK Moscow time. However, just to add to the confusion, the ship's time, the schedules and the time of our tours would all remain on Moscow time.

Samara is named after the Samara River, which probably means 'summer water', signifying that it froze in winter in the local Indo-Iranian language which was spoken here 2000 years ago. It is Russia's ninth largest city with more than 1.1 million people Samara gives its name to the Samara culture, a Neolithic culture of the 5th millennium BC. The city changed its name in 1935 to Kuybyshev 1935 after Valerian Kuybyshev who died that year. He was a Russian revolutionary, Red Army officer and prominent Soviet politician having joined the Bolsheviks in 1904. He was born in Omsk and fermented revolutionary activity in several cities until he moved to Samara in 1917 and rose through the political ranks to become president of the local Soviet during the Russian Civil War he and political commissar in the First and Fourth Red Armies amongst many other positions. He was awarded the Order of the Red Banner and was a principal economic advisor to Stalin. The city retained its name until 1991 when it reverted to Samara.

I watched the shipping along the river and the activity along the embankment, reputed to be the longest in Russia at over five kilometres. We drove along the embankment to a large brewery which produces Zhigulevskoye beer. The original brewery was founded in Samara in 1881 by Austrian count and entrepreneur Alfred von Vacano as the area grew a lot of grain and the water was ideal. It is a large red brick building squeezed into the thin strip of land between the riverfront and the main road and whilst the original red brick brewery still stands, there has been a lot of development of the site along the site with new brewhouses, bottling plants and warehouses.

The original brand was named Viennese Beer, but, according to legend, in 1934 it was renamed Zhiguli to get rid of its bourgeois, Western name. The inspiration for the name was taken from the Zhiguli Mountains which are just across the river. It was a popular beer, allegedly due to both its easy availability and because it was cheap. It could be found extensively throughout the country and at its peak of popularity, it was made in both their own breweries and under licence in more than 700 breweries around the country.

Legend has it that Alexius, Metropolitan of Moscow, later Patron Saint of Samara, visited the site of the city in 1357 and predicted that the town would never be ravaged and that a great town would be erected there. Indeed, the Volga River port of Samara appears on Italian maps of the 14th century, although it did have a bad reputation.

Before 1586, the Samara Bend was a well-known pirate nest that made use of the unique geography of the Samara Bend. In addition to the big bend, the neck of land to the west has a small tributary joining the main river and at Perevoloki it is just two and a half kilometres wide. Lookouts would spot an oncoming boat and quickly cross to the other side of the peninsula where the pirates would organise an attack.

In 1586, Samara started with a fortress built at the confluence of the Volga and Samara Rivers. This fortress was a frontier post protecting the then easternmost boundaries of Russia from forays of nomads and bringing law and order to the region. A local customs office was established in 1600.

As more and more ships pulled into Samara's port, the town turned into a centre for diplomatic and economic links between Russia and the East. But Samara has a chequered history and it also opened its gates and welcomed such peasant war rebels headed by Stepan Razin and Yemelyan Pugachyov, giving them a traditional welcome with offers of bread and salt.

In 1877, during the Russian-Turkish War, a mission from the Samara city government Duma led by Pyotr V. Alabin, presented a banner tailored in Samara pierced with bullets and saturated with the blood of both Russians and Bulgarians who were allies fighting the Ottomans, to Bulgaria, which has become a symbol of Russian-Bulgarian friendship. And due to the cultural connections, it is not so unusual to have Dimitrovgrad just up the river named after a Bulgarian.

The quickening growth of Samara's economy in the late 19th and early 20th centuries was given a boost on 1st January 1851, when it became the centre of Samara Governorate and by then already had an estimated population of 20,000.

This gave a stimulus to the development of the economic, political and cultural life of the community.

The region is a great grain growing area and this assisted the growth of the bread trade, flour milling businesses, the brewery as well as the Kenitser Macaroni Factory. Other industries followed such as ironworks, a confectionery factory and a factory producing matches. The wealthy merchants built a number of magnificent private residences and the city acquired a number of grand administrative buildings. The Trading Houses of the Subbotins, Kurlins, Shikhobalovs and Smirnovs, founders of the flour milling industry and widely known due to Smirnov vodka, were widely known not only across Russia but also internationally wherever Samara's wheat was exported. In its rapid growth, Samara resembled many young North American cities, and contemporaries coined the names 'Russian New Orleans' and 'Russian Chicago' for the city.

By the start of the 20th century, the population exceeded 100,000, and the city was the major trading and industrial centre of the Volga region. During the October Revolution of 1917, Samara was seized by the Bolsheviks. However, on 8th June 1918, with the armed support of the Czechoslovak Legions, the city was taken by the Committee of Members of the Constituent Assembly, or Komuch, who organised a democratic counter-revolution, which at its height governed twelve million people. They fought against the Bolsheviks but on 7th October 1918, the city fell to the advancing Fourth Army of the Red Army.

We moved on from the brewery along Lenina Avenue to the Soyuz Carrier Rocket Monument to commemorate Samara rocket builders. I had wanted to visit Samara for some time ever since visiting the European Space Agency Spaceport at Kourou in French Guyana. People may be aware that they launch Ariane rockets from there but they also launch commercial satellites on Soyuz rockets. Those rockets are made and assembled in Samara, then disassembled and packed into ten containers and shipped out to French Guyana.

I might not be able to visit the production facilities in Samara but I could see the monuments and visit the city. The monument is an actual rocket standing 51 metres high. It was erected on 1st October 2001 as part of the 50th anniversary celebrations of the First Manned Spaceflight performed by Yuri Gagarin.

The Samara space industry developed out of the Great Patriotic War. As a leading industrial centre, Kuybyshev as it was known at the time was already producing aircraft, firearms and ammunition. It received industrial plants from the western areas of Russia which had been evacuated to preserve them and stop them from falling into the hands of the Nazis. Its citizens joined the military forces and its health centres and hospital facilities were turned into base hospitals.

After the war, the defence industry developed rapidly with new facilities built and new products manufactured. Kuybyshev enterprises played a leading role in the development of Soviet domestic aviation and the implementation of the Soviet space program. It was a natural progression to use the skilled workforce to expand from land vehicles into aircraft and ultimately rockets and aerospace vehicles and due to its importance, the city became a closed city.

The launch vehicle Vostok, which delivered the first manned spaceship to orbit, was built at the Samara Progress Plant. Yuri Gagarin was the first man to travel in space on 12th April 12, 1961, and after returning to Earth, he visited the city and addressed the workers who had built the spacecraft. As a dedication to the city's contribution to the development of the aerospace industry, there is the Cosmic Samara Museum and an exhibition of aerospace history in the Samara State Aerospace University.

We stopped in Slavy Square where there is an eternal flame and a large red granite wall where all the names of the fallen of the city are remembered. There is an honour guard of four cadets from the local military training school. Across the square is the Monument of Glory which stands on one side overlooking the Volga to the northwest. The monument is one of the most prominent symbols of Samara. Moscow sculptors Pavel Bondarenko, Oleg Kiryuhin and architect A. Samsonov created it and the opening ceremony took place on 5th November 1971.

The monument itself is a 40-metre column on a pedestal to symbolise a ray of light rising to the sky. On top stands a 13-metre-high man holding wings above his head, all made out of alloy steel so it appears silver and glints in the light. There is an uncanny resemblance of the figure with Yuri Gagarin. The monument is dedicated to the Kuybyshev workers of the aircraft industry. The city's workers built more than 28,000 Ilyushin Il-2 and Ilyushin Il-10 ground-attack aircraft representing 80% of the total wartime production of these aircraft.

There is also an unusual monument of an Ilyushin Il-2 ground-attack aircraft assembled by Kuybyshev workers in late 1942. This particular plane was shot down in 1943 over Karelia, but the heavily wounded pilot, K. Kotlyarovsky, managed to crash land the plane near Lake Oriyarvi. The aircraft was returned to Kuybyshev in 1975 and was placed on a concrete plinth at the intersection of two major roads as a symbol of the deeds of home front servicemen and air force pilots during the Great Patriotic War.

After the outbreak of the Great Patriotic War and Hitler's launch of Operation Barbarossa, the advancing Nazi forces overwhelmed the Russian forces and they fell back. Factories were relocated to the east but as the Nazis continued to advance they threatened Moscow, the capital. As part of the contingency planning, Kuybyshev was chosen to be the alternative capital of the Soviet Union should Moscow fall to the invading Germans.

In October 1941, the Communist Party, various governmental organisations, diplomatic missions of foreign countries, leading cultural establishments and their staff were evacuated to the city. Various buildings were requisitioned and converted to house the influx of government workers, diplomats and others. On 7th November 1941, a special Revolution Day parade was held in the city's Kuybyshev Square to mark the city's role as the wartime national capital. Since 2011, this event has been remembered in an annual military parade organised by the city government.

Opposite the Samara Academic Opera and Ballet Theatre is a large square and off it runs what is today called Ulitsa Shostakovicha. On one side is a large building that was requisitioned to be offices to be used by the ruling government. But what was kept secret at the time was an underground bunker complex built around the back at one end known as 'Stalin's Bunker' but never used.

The bunker was built under the government building and Stalin's office is 39 metres below ground level. After a nondescript entrance and hall, there is a shaft with stairs descending down to a gallery level protected by a thick reinforced concrete roof against bombs. This vertical section of the tunnel uses metro tunnel skeletal plates for the walls so it is basically a metro tunnel on end to get down four storeys from the top level of the bunker and then through gas-proof doors to the technical level which housed all the air-conditioning, air purification plant, pumps, power plant and other essential services. There are in fact two vertical shafts down to the gallery level, built to ensure that there was always an alternative escape route should one be blocked.

Then there is another set of stairs down seven levels. There are ancillary rooms off the circular stairs now used as museum space to display a few artefacts and photographs. At the bottom is a short hallway with Stalin's office off to one side. Around the walls of the room are several false doors and windows, but one door was for his private washroom.

Across the hallway was the conference room with a long table where he would have met his officials sitting at the head of the table and his officials down both sides. Behind them was further desk space with the chairs facing the wall for stenographers and the like so that they would not be sure who was talking and couldn't see any secret documents or maps.

There are no official records that Stalin ever visited Samara. There are some stories that he was seen here and that his double was in Moscow but again no documents have ever been found. Also, it is not certain how the bunker was constructed as no records were kept. Local residents at the time didn't see any construction material arriving or dug-out rock and sand being removed and no noise. When the bunker was finally revealed decades later, local residents had no idea of its existence.

When it was decided to open it as a tourist attraction, some of the former builders were still alive and they were tracked down but they had been sworn to secrecy. They either couldn't remember due to their age or maintained their vow of silence and revealed nothing.

There is a beautiful square opposite a late 19th-century red brick-built theatre with some other beautiful buildings such as a well-maintained wooden building which belonged to a wealthy merchant and several art nouveau-style buildings. Several dignitaries were born or lived in Samara such as Sergei Alexander Schelkunoff, a mathematician and electromagnetism theorist known for his important contributions to antenna theory. Twentieth-century Russian Soviet writer Alexey Tolstoy lived in Samara, and there is a museum dedicated to him. The archaeologist and ethnographer Boris Kuftin was born here as was sociologist and ethnographer Pavel Romanov. But in a flat overlooking the square was where Dmitry Shostakovich lived during the Great Patriotic War. He was evacuated from Leningrad at the same time as the government moved here and finished his Symphony No. 7 there and it had its inaugural performance in the same year. In 1943, he moved to Moscow and in 1945 returned to Leningrad to teach in the conservatory.

Around the corner is the Catholic cathedral built in the late nineteenth century. During Bolshevik times it was used as a kindergarten and a cinema before being refurbished and rededicated and is now a functioning cathedral again. On the corner of the same street is a lovely art nouveau building built by the richest merchant in the city for his beautiful wife. During the war, it was used as the Swedish Embassy. Next door is an interesting wooden building where

Aleksey Tolstoy lived, and besides that, a character from one of his books, the statue of Buratino, the character in The Golden Key, or the Adventures of Buratino published in 1936 based on the 1883 Italian novel, The Adventures of Pinocchio by Carlo Collodi.

By the time we reached Kuybyshev Square, my head was spinning from all the sights seen and the amount of facts that had been thrown at me by the guide. We had some free time to explore the main shopping street or do whatever else that we wanted to do before heading back to the ship to head onwards to Saratov. Some of the details about the square and the buildings before we parted for a while I forget but I do remember that he claimed that it was the largest in Europe. That is like a red rag to a bull for me and I was instantly alert.

Whenever a guide or anyone else claims that the particular sight in front of them is the largest, longest, tallest, oldest and heaviest or whatever, I have to go and check. It was claimed to be 17.5 hectares but there were some provisos since it included some other areas, such as the footprint of buildings built within the square, parks and gardens. It was laid out in 1894 but the Place des Quinconces located in Bordeaux, France claims to be the largest in Europe at 12.6 hectares and was laid out in 1820.

It all depends on how you wish to define 'square', and whether there is a proviso that it is 'open space' or whether it ought to be a hard surface or can in fact include grass spaces. But it is hard to beat Xinghai Square in Dalian, Liaoning Province, China, the name meaning Sea of Stars. This giant open space covers an area of 110 hectares but some areas look like parkland rather than square so it comes back to how you want to define a square. And on that basis, everybody can claim to have the biggest by changing the definition!

Chapter 12
Saratov

A little time after breakfast we passed under the road bridge that connects Saratov with the city on the opposite left bank of the Volga, Engels. The Saratov Bridge across the Volga was formerly the longest bridge in the Soviet Union.

As usual, we had arrived early and the captain steamed some way downriver before slowing and turning about to approach the river port slowly against the current to maintain control. We moored and I went down to climb the gangplank onto land but for some reason, the crew wouldn't let us off the boat. We were due to arrive at 10 am Moscow time and set off on a city tour at 10.30 but we were still an hour early.

The name Saratov may be derived from Sary Tau, meaning 'Yellow Mountain' in the Tatar language but another version of the story of the origin derives from the words Sar Atau, which means 'Boggy Island'. There is no yellow mountain and no boggy island so there is no undisputed origin of the name of the city.

The usual pattern for touring new cities was repeated. There would be some coaches and minibuses waiting in the car park next to the riverport to take us on our tours. Each vehicle had a sheet of A4 in the window with a number on it. We had each been allocated to a group, defined usually by language and each vehicle would have a guide from the boat and a local guide from the city to show them the top tourist sites in their own language. The Germans had several coaches whilst the Poles and Norwegians had a minibus each.

The 'English-speaking' group was a mixture of nationalities and odds and sods. I was the sole English person joined by an Australian and a New Zealander. There was a Dutch couple and an elderly couple from Serbia who had lived in Australia for a few years. The rest of the 20 odd plus group was the extended family from China. Several of them knew some English but only one of them was fluent and confident to speak it.

The sole Chinese girl who spoke English fluently listened to the guide and made notes on her phone and the rest of the party did their own thing which largely consisted of taking photos of each other in front of every statue, church and just about anything that the guide pointed out. Back on board at the end of the day, the sole English speaker would go through the photos and explain what the group had seen.

The numbered coach system usually worked well but there were only six vehicles and none of them had a number 4 in the windscreen. Our coach hadn't turned up. No one was concerned and I was sure that everything was under control but all the others had left on time and we were left standing in a loose group on the tarmac with our guide from the ship talking agitatedly on her phone although she was reassuring us in-between bursts of staccato Russian over her phone that the coach was coming.

Eventually, a coach swerved into the car park at speed and its tyres squealed as the driver spun the steering wheel and burnt rubber to make a tight 360-degree turn and braked hard. The coach was still rocking on its springs as our local guide stepped off the coach to greet us. She introduced herself as Marsha and the driver as Alexandra and we set off.

Our first stop was the Holy Trinity Cathedral just 2 minutes up the road from the passenger port. It was a beautiful church and quite different from other Russian Orthodox churches.

The first wooden Trinity Church, which stood on the site was erected with the blessing of the Bishop of Astrakhan Parthenius in 1674. However, it was not to last as it was burnt to the ground just 10 years later in 1684. It was rebuilt and consecrated in 1695 with the upper church in the name of the Holy Trinity, and the lower winter church in honour of the Assumption of the Mother of God.

The lower church had an innovation of a heating system which was very rare for a provincial building at the end of the 17th century because medieval Russian churches were never equipped with stoves due to fear of fires. Ovens appeared in the upper church of the cathedral only at the end of the 19th century.

It had been eventually rebuilt in brick and stone in a traditional style but extended and the extensions had incorporated the belfry into the main structure. Inside the ceilings are low but the area covered is quite wide with long low graceful arches supporting the floors above. It is also memorable to those who approach from the landward side as the belfry has suffered some subsidence and there is a distinct lean in the tower.

In no time at all we were back on the coach, no doubt trying to make up time after our delayed start for a drive through the city with the guide commenting on multiple sights as we whizzed past. Our route took a weaving pattern through the city centre but not stopping to take in many of the top places to visit although we went past slowly so that we could take photos from the comfort of the coach.

This is some people's idea of 'seeing' a city but personally I like to spend some time in a city to see all of the sights on foot from inside which might take several days. Most cruises only spend a little while in any one city and most of the time is spent eating and drinking on the ship. Coach tours are similar in that they show clients the top two or three sightseeing venues in a city and then move on.

We were on our way to the Victory Park. As we turned off the main road into the park, there was a monument of a YAK 38 jet fighter perched on a plinth, pointing skyward. This aircraft was the Soviet Navy's only operational VTOL strike fighter aircraft in addition to being its first operational carrier-based fixed wing aircraft until it was retired from service in 1991.

The park is situated on a hill overlooking the city and has great views across the urban landscape. There are various military exhibits between the car park and the Cranes Memorial on the top of the hill. There is an armoured train with anti-aircraft guns and a hospital carriage. There is a 24-metre long boat with guns fore and aft that would have patrolled along the Volga. There are artillery pieces and Katyushka rocket launchers. Along another path is a row of tanks of various designs and armoured personal carriers which leads to a collection of more than a dozen exhibits of helicopters, fighters and bombers.

There is an eternal flame to remember the more than 300,000 people who lived in the city and died in the war. The Nazis never got this far and there were no land battles fought nearby but many of the inhabitants went to the front and the fascists bombed the city as it was a major producer of armaments and munitions.

The eternal flame is near the top of the site and the names of the Heroes of the People from the city, those who were awarded more than one decoration for bravery, were recorded on several slabs of granite but I lost count somewhere after 150.

From the eternal flame to the base of the Crane Memorial is a long staircase. There are five landings on the way up, one to represent each year of the war. On each landing is a large block of granite and craved into it is the year and beneath it, the cities where major battles were fought in that year. The list of cities drifts east in 1941 and 1942 as the Nazis advanced and the Russian army fell back, then stabilised and then the great battles of Stalingrad and Kursk, the relief of Leningrad and the advance westward to recapture Russian land and finally the liberation of Kaliningrad, the advance through Poland and the attack on Berlin in 1945.

On the top of the hill is the Crane Memorial, a 40-metre tall tower with a flock of cranes flying southwest around the top to represent the souls of the fallen. It is in a superb position and from the top, there is a commanding view across the city and to the horizon far away.

On the way back to the ship, we went through some of the suburbs of the city. We passed the old cathedral which was closed by the Bolsheviks and the domes removed. It was used as dormitory accommodation for students until the 1990s when it was renovated and refurbished to be once again a fantastic example of traditional Orthodox ecclesiastical architecture although much of it is a replica rather than original.

We had an hour of free time in the city to check out the local market, the conservatory and another traditional church, the fabric of the building preserved as the Bolsheviks converted it to a planetarium before it was reconverted and reconsecrated as a church in the 1990s.

Uvek, a city of the Golden Horde, stood near the site of the modern city of Saratov from the mid-13th century until its destruction by Tamerlane in 1395. Whilst the exact date of the foundation of modern Saratov is unknown, all plausible theories date it to circa 1590, during the reign (1584–1598) of Tsar Fyodor Ivanovich, who constructed several settlements along the Volga River in order to secure the south-eastern boundary of his state. Town status was granted to it in 1708.

By the 1800s, Saratov had grown to become an important shipping port on the Volga. The Ryazan-Ural railroad reached Saratov in 1870. In 1896, the line crossed the Volga and continued its eastward expansion. A unique train ferry, owned by the Ryazan-Ural railroad, provided the connection across the river between the two parts of the railroad for 39 years, before the construction of a railway bridge in 1935.

During January 1915, with the First World War dominating the Russian national agenda, Saratov became the destination for deportation convoys of ethnic Germans, Jews, Hungarians, Austrians and Slavs whose presence closer to the Western Front was perceived as a potential security risk to the state.

During the Great Patriotic War, Saratov was an important railway station on the North-South Volzhskaya Rokada, a specially designated military railroad supplying troops, ammunition and supplies during the siege of Stalingrad to the south in 1942–1943. The city was bombed by German aircraft and the main target was the Kirov oil refinery. The aerial bombardment was so intense that it seriously damaged the installation, destroyed 80% of its plant and destroyed all the fuel stocks.

The city of Saratov played an important role in the history of the Volga Germans. Until 1941, the town of Pokrovsk (present-day Engels across the river), served as the capital of the Volga German Republic. The ethnic German population of the region numbered 800,000 in the early 20th century, and some families had been there for generations. Beginning with Katherine the Great's 1763 Manifesto promising land, freedom from military conscription, religious freedom and no taxes for 5 years, the Russian emperors invited German immigration in the 18th and 19th centuries to encourage agricultural development.

The Volga German community came to include industrialists, scientists, musicians and architects. After the beginning of the German invasion of the Soviet Union in June 1941, the Soviet government forcibly expelled the Volga Germans to Uzbekistan, Siberia and Kazakhstan in September 1941. Only a few ever returned to the Volga region, even after rehabilitation. Others were expelled to Western Europe after the war ended in 1945. Beginning in the 1980s, a large portion of the surviving members of the ethnic German community emigrated from the Soviet Union to Germany.

Reminders of the once prominent place of Germans in the city remain, with the Roman Catholic St Klemens Cathedral (seat of the historic Diocese of Tiraspol) on Nemetskaya Ulitsa meaning 'German Street' being the most notable. The building was designed by Mikhail N. Grudistov, 1839–1914, who also designed the State Bank Building in Saratov which still stands on the corner of Radishchev and Sovetskaya streets but was converted into the children's cinema 'Pioneer' during the Soviet period.

One of the city's most prominent landmarks is the 19th-century neo-Gothic Conservatoroire. When it was built in 1912, the conservatory was Russia's third such institution after those in Moscow and St Petersburg. At the time, Saratov, with a population of 240,000, was the third-largest city in Russia. The main building of the conservatory was built in 1902 by architect Alexander Yulyevich Yagn, and originally it housed a music school. Before the opening of the conservatory in 1912, the building was reconstructed by the architect Semyon Akimovich Kallistratov. When Saratov Conservatory opened in September 1912, it immediately had 1,000 students ready to begin their studies.

Until the end of the Soviet Union in 1991, the Soviet authorities designated Saratov a closed city which was strictly off-limits to all foreigners due to its military importance as the site of a vital facility manufacturing military aircraft. There is a long list of famous people who were born in Saratov or who lived here but one name stands out, Roman Abramovich.

Chapter 13
Volgograd

I awoke as the sound of the engine changed as it was throttled back and the ship started to slow. I dressed and went outside. It was even cooler than the weather forecast had suggested and there was a chill wind blowing. I walked around the deck to stand in the lee of the top deck. The promised clear sunny day was overcast and the temperature was just a handful of degrees above freezing.

We were slowing to enter Lock No. 31. As usual our captain had steamed faster than necessary and had arrived an hour early but there was no other shipping booked so the lock master had agreed to let him through early.

There were signs of a city with heavy industry on the banks, large industrial complexes with tall chimneys and a mass of pipes supported by a lattice of steelwork. Interspersed amongst the trees and ravines down to the river were large blocks of flats. As we progressed downriver, the patches of trees thinned and were replaced by urban sprawl. We were approaching Volgograd which boasts the longest water front although Greater Sochi claims nearly 100 kilometres. Volgograd's waterfront is subject to debate but they still claim that Sochi includes its suburbs in its claim. I checked several guides and guidebooks but they all differ quoting between 70 and 100 kilometres, so until I can find an authoritative source, I can only confirm that it is one of the longest but will refrain from quoting a figure.

We passed under a bridge over the river. It had multiple pairs of pillars sunk into the river bed but only the pillars on the upstream side supported a road bed. The second line of line pillars had been built but the road or rail bed intended to be built had never been completed.

We drifted past the river terminal to make a turn downstream and then slowly made our way upstream against the current to gently glide to our designated mooring. I returned to my cabin to get a coat and a camera so that I would be ready for the city tour.

The noise and vibrations from the engines diminished and then went quiet. I made my way to the disembarkation point but found my way barred by a member of the crew. We were moored but the passenger disembarkation gate was right opposite a mooring point and the gangplank couldn't be deployed. The ship had to be moved just two metres either way to deploy the gangplank and an officer was issuing instructions over a radio but there was obviously a problem co-ordinating the aft and bow mooring lines to allow the ship to move just two metres.

In theory, it was a simple operation but in practice, it required a little more skill than expected. The mooring lines weren't the right length to allow a capstan to pull the boat upstream so they tried to let the current ease the boat downstream but there wasn't enough length on one of the mooring lines. So another one had to be found to be attached to another mooring point to allow the operation to succeed. After what seemed ages, we were finally moored and we were allowed ashore to find our coaches.

Volgograd was originally named Tsaritsyn. Although the city may have originated in 1555, documented evidence of Tsaritsyn at the confluence of the Tsaritsa and Volga rivers dates only from 1589. Grigori Zasekin established the fortress Sary Su, which in the local Tatar language name means 'yellow water' or 'yellow river'. It was planned as part of the defences of the unstable southern border of the empire or tsardom of Russia. The structure stood slightly above the mouth of the Tsaritsa River on the right bank. It soon became the nucleus of a trading settlement.

In 1607, the fortress garrison rebelled against Tsar Vasili Shuisky for six months. Vasili IV, 1552–1612 was Tsar of Russia between 1606 and 1610 during the Time of Troubles after the murder of False Dmitriy I. He was the only member of the House of Shuysky to become Tsar and the last member of the Rurikid dynasty to rule. In 1608, the city acquired its first stone church, St John the Baptist. At the beginning of the 17th century, the garrison consisted of 350 to 400 people.

In 1670, rebel troops of Stepan Razin also known as Stenka Razin, a Cossack leader, led a major uprising against the nobility and tsarist bureaucracy in southern Russia. They captured the fortress and left after a month.

In 1708, another rebel Cossack, Kondraty Bulavin, controlled the fortress. The Bulavin Rebellion, also known as the Astrakhan Revolt, is the name given to a war of Don Cossacks against Imperial Russia between the years 1707 and 1708. The movement was led by Kondraty Bulavin, a democratically elected Ataman or leader of the Don Cossacks. The revolt was triggered by a number of underlying tensions between the Imperial government under Peter I of Russia, the Cossacks and Russian peasants fleeing from serfdom in Russia to gain freedom in the autonomous Don area.

It started with the assassination of Prince Yury Dolgorukov, the leader of the Imperial army's punitive expedition to the Don area, by Don Cossacks under Bulavin's command. The end of the rebellion is associated with Bulavin's death in 1708.

A number of social grievances were prevalent in the peasant population of Russia in the years leading up to the Bulavin Rebellion. Peter the Great's radical reforms designed to westernise old Muscovy in the 18th century were met with widespread discontent. The pious, deeply conservative masses saw his reforms as an affront to their traditional way of life and their Eastern Orthodox faith.

Peter was even equated to the Antichrist and assumed to be an impostor posing as the true tsar. On top of this, Peter's newly formed police state was expanding and this expansion was encroaching upon salt resource sites coveted by the Cossacks for the preservation of their foods. This dispute over land was in one sense an economic issue, but the Cossacks also regarded this as an intrusion upon their semi-autonomous political state. In general, the entire rural Russian atmosphere was in an agitated state, waiting for a catalyst of some kind.

In response to the constraints and fears of living in Peter's police state, large numbers of serfs absconded, abandoning the major urban areas, especially Moscow and the new capital at St Petersburg. Whilst some groups emigrated to Poland or Austria, many chose to avoid the border patrols and instead fled to the rural periphery and the river regions already inhabited by the Cossacks. It was Peter's policy to hunt down and arrest absconders and return them to their lords where they could be counted for taxes, a policy which, by this time, had no statute of limitations. In accordance with this policy, Peter deployed a group of bounty hunters under Yuri Dolgoruki to scout the Cossack regions for fugitive peasants.

Despite the fact that the Cossacks harboured some resentment towards the peasants for overpopulating their region and generally competing for local resources, more deplorable to them was the idea of Petrine agents roaming freely through their territory. They not only refused to give up the fugitive peasants, but on 8th October 1707, a small band of local atamans headed by Kondraty Bulavin ambushed and murdered Dolgoruki and his men in the village of Shulgin on the Aidar River, opening the door to violence and beginning the Bulavin Rebellion.

Little is known about Bulavin personally, but he was born into a Cossack family and would have been old enough to remember Stenka Razin and the revolt of the late 17th century. He developed some combat experience fighting the Kuban and Crimean Tatars in his youth. However, he was never a particularly great military commander, and throughout the rebellion that bears his name, he would forever fall short of becoming an undisputed leader. By 1704, he had risen to the status of Ataman of Bakhmut, a position he held until 1706. It was during this stint that he orchestrated and participated in the destruction of the salt works on the Severski Donets, an act of retaliation for having been evicted by the government as squatters. This conflict was never entirely resolved and was ultimately absorbed into the greater rebellion as it gained momentum. Bulavin was most likely illiterate, but like his contemporary revolutionaries, he possessed a talent for appealing to the people and inciting them to action.

Bulavin's rally cries were simple: the goal was to move against Moscow and destroy the evil influences on the tsar. It is important to note that the rebellion was not against the institution of tsardom but against the figures in power at the time. It was generally believed that Peter was either not who he claimed i.e. the Antichrist sitting in place of the true tsar who was hidden away, or that he was indeed the rightful tsar but was under the control of evil advisers whose destruction would liberate him, and that if given the freedom to act, he would repudiate all of his wicked reforms.

The rebellion suffered from a number of weaknesses. For one, despite all of his rallying, Bulavin never offered a pretender to the throne or suggested a just tsar to replace Peter. This blunder would condemn the rebellion's end goals to ambiguity and would let slip an immeasurable amount of support he might have mustered. Second, Bulavin did not coordinate his efforts with any other pre-existing Muscovite enemies, so despite being heavily engaged in war with Sweden, the military apparatus under Peter was not as divided as it could have been and found the rebellion to be more of a nuisance than a major conflict.

By means of its vastly superior size and efficiency, the regular army was ultimately capable of stamping out the rebellion at all levels. In the end, angered by devastating reversals and Bulavin's tiring claims, factions of his own Cossack followers turned against him. He was found dead on 7th July 1708, having been shot in the head. It is not known whether the wound was self-inflicted or an act of treachery. Following Bulavin's death, the rebellion petered out, with pockets of resistance persisting through 1709, but for all intents and purposes, the conflict was over.

As mentioned, the Bulavin Rebellion bore striking similarities to Razin's Revolt a generation earlier. Both were Cossack rebellions in part, aimed against an imposing governmental institution and driven by animosity for the miserable state of peasant life. They effectively set the stage for the Pugachev Uprising under Katherine the Great.

In response to the uprising, Peter tightened his grip on the Cossack states, causing some 2000 under Ignat Nekrasov to flee to the protection of the Crimean Khanate. Descendants of these Nekrasovites would relocate to Anatolia during the Pugachev Uprising and settle near Constantinople, where their traditional culture would continue to the present day.

In 1717 in the Kuban pogrom, raiders from the Kuban under the command of the Crimean Tatar Bakhti Gerai blockaded the town and enslaved thousands in the area. In August 1774, Yemelyan Pugachev unsuccessfully attempted to storm the city.

In the 19th century, Tsaritsyn became an important river port and commercial centre. The population expanded rapidly, increasing from fewer than 3,000 people in 1807 to about 84,000 in 1900. The first railway reached the town in 1862. The first theatre opened in 1872, and the first cinema in 1907. In 1913, Tsaritsyn got its first tram line, and the city's first electric lights were installed in the city centre.

During the Russian Civil War of 1917–1923, Tsaritsyn came under Soviet control from November 1917. In 1918, White troops under the Ataman of the Don Cossack Host, Pyotr Krasnov, besieged Tsaritsyn. The Reds repulsed three assaults by the Whites. However, in June 1919 the White Armed Forces of South Russia under the command of General Denikin captured Tsaritsyn, which they held until January 1920.

The city was renamed Stalingrad after Joseph Stalin on 10th April 1925. This was officially to and recognise the city and Stalin's role in its defence against the Whites between 1918 and 1920. In 1931, the German settlement colony Old Sarepta (founded in 1765) became a district of Stalingrad. It was renamed Krasnoarmeysky Rayon (or 'Red Army District') and it became the largest area of the city.

Under Stalin, the city became a centre of heavy industry and a transhipment point for rail and river. During the Second World War, German and Axis forces attacked the city, and in 1942 it became the site of one of the pivotal battles of the war. The Battle of Stalingrad had perhaps the greatest casualty figures of any single battle in the history of warfare (estimates are between 1,250,000 and 1,798,619). The battle became a titanic struggle between Hitler and Stalin as both saw it of great propaganda value, each keenly aware of the namesake of the city, and each poured hundreds of thousands of men into the battle.

The battle began on 23rd August 1942, and on the same day, the city suffered heavy aerial bombardment that reduced most of it to rubble. By September, the fighting reached the city centre. The fighting was of unprecedented intensity; the city's central railway station changed hands thirteen times, and the Mamayev Kurgan (one of the highest points of the city) was captured and recaptured eight times.

By early November, the German forces controlled 90% of the city and had cornered the Soviets in two narrow pockets, but they were unable to eliminate the last pockets of Soviet resistance before Soviet forces launched a huge counterattack on 19th November. This led to the encirclement of the German Sixth Army and other Axis units. On 31st January 1943, the Sixth Army's commander, Field Marshal Friedrich Paulus, surrendered, and by 2nd February with the elimination of straggling German troops, the Battle of Stalingrad was over. In 1945, the Soviet Union awarded Stalingrad the title Hero City for its resistance. Great Britain's King George VI awarded the citizens of Stalingrad the jewelled 'Sword of Stalingrad' in recognition of their bravery.

The city was the site of a major offensive and by the time the city was relieved and the enemy driven back, there was little left standing. Our first stop was at one of those pivotal points in the battle. The Pavlov House. It gained its popular name from Sergeant Yakov Pavlov, who commanded the platoon that seized the building. The house no longer exists but there is a modern red brick sculpture of the remains of the house standing on the site. The small group of soldiers were resupplied and held out for 55 days. Its position was strategic as it was just a handful of metres from the flour mill.

This mill was a commercial operation owned by a local Volga German who had a grain and flour milling business. It is several stories high, built of reinforced concrete and faced with several layers of red brick. It was built to last but also had to support the weight of the equipment, the vibrations it made and the weight of the grain and flour. The Nazis repeatedly attacked it but the defenders held firm. The flour mill has been left exactly as it was when the city was relieved. Around the mill were various artillery pieces and tanks, plus some captured German armour and a train used to haul factories to the east and supplies to the west.

Next door to the flour mill is a modern tourist site, the Stalingrad Battle Museum. On the top floor, it houses the largest battle panorama of the Stalingrad Battle. It has a foreground of trenches and reproductions of battle paraphernalia, trenches, dugouts and the like and behind is a painted representation of the battle. It is a collage of various real-life actions that took place on the 26th January 1943 as viewed from the Mamayev Kurgan. Such as a fighter pilot who ran out of ammunition and rammed an enemy fighter, the long line of German prisoners, poorly dressed against the brutal Russian winter, and a soldier whose Molotov cocktail was ignited by a bullet so he ran and threw himself onto an enemy tank and so the panorama unfolds.

On lower floors are museum exhibits of original items associated with the fight. There is also a collection of gifts from around the world such as a bell from Hiroshima and two swords, one presented to Stalin and another presented to the city by George VI.

The process of twinning cities based on mutual experiences was started here in 1945 when Coventry, who had suffered a devastating concentrated air-raid was twinned with Volgograd. Hiroshima followed and other cities joined the twinning process. Today there are streets in Volgograd named Coventry, Hiroshima and later as other twinned cities joined, additional streets were named after them such as Ostrava and Liege.

After the museum, we moved on to Mamayev Kurgan to walk up to the top and to see the changing of the guard. When forces of the German Sixth Army launched their attack against the city centre of Stalingrad on 13th September 1942, Mamayev Kurgan saw particularly fierce fighting between the Nazi attackers and the defending soldiers of the Soviet 62nd Army. Control of the hill became vitally important, as it offered control over the city. To defend it, the Soviets had built strong defensive lines on the slopes of the hill, composed of trenches, barbed wire and minefields. The Nazis pushed forward against the hill, taking heavy casualties. When they finally captured the hill, they started firing on the city centre, as well as on the city's main railway station below the hill. They captured the Volgograd railway station on 14th September 1942.

On the same day, the Soviet 13th Guards Rifle Division commanded by Alexander Rodimtsev arrived in the city from the east side of the river Volga under heavy German artillery fire. The division's 10,000 men immediately rushed into the battle. On 16th September, they recaptured Mamayev Kurgan and kept fighting for the railway station, taking heavy losses. By the following day, almost all of them had died. The Soviets kept reinforcing their units in the city as fast as they could. The Germans assaulted up to twelve times a day, and the Soviets would respond with fierce counter-attacks and resupplied the position under cover of darkness.

The hill changed hands several times. By 27th September, the Nazis had again captured half of Mamayev Kurgan. The Soviets held their own positions on the slopes of the hill, as the 284th Rifle Division defended the key stronghold. The defenders held out until 26th January 1943, when the counterattacking Soviet forces relieved them. The battle of the city ended one week later with a devastating Nazi defeat.

When the battle ended, the soil on the hill had been so thoroughly churned by shellfire and mixed with metal fragments that it contained between 500 and 1,250 splinters of metal per square metre. The earth on the hill had remained black in the winter, as the snow kept melting in the many fires and explosions. In the following spring, the hill would still remain black, as no grass grew on its scorched soil. The hill's formerly steep slopes had become flattened in months of intense shelling and bombardment. Even today, it is possible to find fragments of bone and metal still buried deep throughout the hill.

After the war, the Soviet authorities commissioned the enormous Mamayev Kurgan memorial complex. Vasily Chuikov, who led Soviet forces at Stalingrad, lies buried at Mamayev Kurgan, the first Marshal of the Soviet Union to be buried outside Moscow. Soviet sniper Vasili Zaytsev was also reburied here in 2006. Vasily Grigoryevich Zaytsev, 23rd March 1915–15th December 1991, was a Soviet sniper and a Hero of the Soviet Union during the war. Prior to 10th November 1942, he killed 32 Axis soldiers with a standard-issue rifle. Between 10th November 1942 and 17th December 1942, during the Battle of Stalingrad, he killed 225 enemy soldiers, including 11 snipers.

A feature-length film, Enemy at the Gates (2001), starring Jude Law as Zaytsev, was based on part of William Craig's non-fiction book Enemy at the Gates: The Battle for Stalingrad (1973), which includes a 'snipers' duel' between Zaytsev and a Wehrmacht sniper school director, Major Erwin König.

The monumental memorial was constructed between 1959 and 1967 and is crowned by a huge allegorical statue of the Motherland on the top of the hill. The monument, designed by Yevgeny Vuchetich, has the full name The Motherland Calls! It consists of a concrete sculpture, 52 metres tall, and 85 metres from the feet to the tip of the 27-metre sword, dominating the skyline of the city of Stalingrad, later renamed Volgograd. At 85 metres, it is almost twice the height of the Statue of Liberty in New York.

She is in a striking standing pose taking a step forward, brandishing an 11-metre sword in her right hand and beckoning to unseen followers behind her to follow. It was designed by sculptor Yevgeny Vuchetich and structural engineer Nikolai Nikitin and declared the tallest statue in the world in 1967. It is the tallest statue in Europe and the tallest statue (excluding pedestals) of a woman in the world.

The construction uses concrete, except for the stainless-steel blade of the sword, and is held on its plinth solely by its own weight. The statue is evocative of classical Greek representations of Nike, in particular the flowing drapery, similar to that of the Nike of Samothrace.

We left the car park and walked up a flight of stairs, over a railway track then along an avenue and more steps with huge concrete reliefs of battlefield scenes. There is a single figure near the start of the relief on the left-hand side that represents Vasili Zaytsev.

At the top of this flight of steps is a large pool. On one side are the names of those soldiers who received multiple awards for heroism. On the opposite side are five giant statues in various poses to represent different branches of the military, including the women stretcher bearers who recovered injured soldiers from the battlefield often under fire and often having to carry them over their shoulders.

Up yet more flight of stairs is a large circular hall built into the hillside where an eternal flame burns, guarded by two soldiers. There is a changing of the guard ceremony every hour. The last flight of steps takes you to the base of The Motherland Calls statue.

On returning to the coaches, we had a coach tour of the city, passing a cathedral being built in traditional style to replace the one that was destroyed in the war. We passed the railway station which was rebuilt after the war and the main shopping street. We had a free afternoon and I walked around the city with not much of a plan but eager to get some exercise, fill in some time and see some of the streets that tourists don't usually get to see. I like to see the front of the house but I also like to lift the curtain to see what happens behind the scenes.

Nikita Khrushchev's administration changed the name of the city from Stalingrad to Volgograd as part of his programme of de-stalinisation to reduce the cult of personality following Stalin's death. The action was and remains somewhat controversial, given Stalingrad's importance as a symbol of resistance during the war. During Konstantin Chernenko's brief administration in 1984, proposals were floated to revive its historic name. There remains a strong degree of local support for a reversion but intermittent proposals have yet to be accepted by the Russian government. In 2010, Russian monarchists and leaders of the Orthodox organisations demanded that the city should return to its original name Tsaritsyn, but the authorities rejected their proposal.

More than 50,000 people signed a petition to Vladimir Putin, asking that the city's name be permanently changed to Stalingrad. President Putin has replied that such a move should be preceded by a local referendum and that the Russian authorities will look into how to bring about such a referendum.

The city had already been awarded the title of Hero City in 1965, a rare honour as there are only twelve cities that have been awarded the title. However, on 30th January 2013, the Volgograd City Council passed a measure to use the title 'Hero City Stalingrad' in city statements and celebrations on nine specific dates annually:

2nd February, the end of the Battle of Stalingrad,
23rd February, Defender of the Fatherland Day,
9th May, Victory Day,
22nd June start of Operation Barbarossa, the invasion of Russia,
23rd August, the start of the Battle of Stalingrad,
2nd September, Victory over Japan Day,
19th November, the start of Operation Uranus, which was to surround the German and Romanian armies attacking Stalingrad,
9th December, Day of the Fatherland's Heroes.

Chapter 14
Astrakhan and Caviar

The view from the ship had changed again. The banks were still steep and high in places but the forest had thinned and now it was low stunted trees with patches of grass in-between. Elsewhere there were low river banks, with a wide river winding around bends, splitting either side of sand banks and fluvial islands. According to the map, there was a road near the right-hand riverbank with names of settlements along it but from the river, I saw no settlements and apart from the occasional boat pulled up on the bank or a dilapidated dacha, there was little evidence on any human habitation to be seen from the river.

We had left Volgograd after dark and the bridge across the river was lit up with many different coloured lights that pulsed, flashed and trickled in rainbow colours along the top of the bridge in a beautiful light display.

We had to leave Volgograd as it was a long journey down the Volga to Astrakhan and we needed to get some kilometres under our belts. There are restrictions on navigating at night on the lower reaches so we would have to find a suitable mooring point for the majority of the night.

Early in the morning just before dawn, the main engines revved up, the anchor was pulled up and we were on the move again. It would be a full day sailing without any scheduled stops. On board, there were several cultural activities laid on to keep us amused such as lectures on culture, traditions and costumes.

There was a lecture on Russian cooking with recipes handed out but it didn't make for any photos and there were no demonstrations or tastings. But later in the day there was a traditional tea ceremony, not as elaborate as the Japanese tea ceremony but tea drinking is a big tradition in Russia. The whole family would gather in the late afternoon to drink tea and eat snacks, mostly sweet biscuits, jams on bread but also savoury stuffed bread.

Navigation rules meant that we must reach a suitable anchorage before midnight local time and with three-quarters of an hour before the deadline we pulled off the main navigation channel and dropped anchor with a great amount of noise from the rattling chains. The main engines were turned off and besides the distant hum of the diesel generator in the depths of the ship. It all went quiet. There were a few lights on the bank from scattered farmhouses that I could see from my cabin but otherwise, it was dark.

Had I looked out on the other side of the ship, I would have been able to tell that we had arrived in Astrakhan. It was only when I got on deck that I realised that we had arrived. The bank opposite my cabin was wooded with those few scattered lights but the other bank was bristling with wharves, jetties, cranes, ships moored to the bank, others pulled up onto the shore, grain silos, heaps of sand and gravel, warehouses and all the trappings of a functioning port.

It was a clear, black sky with just a few small clouds and a few stars dimly twinkling but they were extinguished as the sky lightened with the sunrise. The sky changed from black to dark blue, then light blue and finally the first warming rays of the sun lit up the sky in a mass of red, oranges and yellows to the east. The rest of the sky was scattered with a few grey clouds but otherwise graded from light blue to dark blue in the west and finally black, lurking low on the distant horizon as the night raced away from the strengthening rising sun.

There was a mist rising from the water's surface as the light grew stronger. It obscured the bottom half of the Kura River, a tanker from Azerbaijan that was moored a couple of hundred metres downstream of us. It reminded me of another trip that I had made working my way up that river the previous year. This ship was named after that river which provides hydroelectric power to the country, drinking water to Baku and water to irrigate the rich lands of the lower river valley, consequently, it is often just a dribble that reaches the Caspian Sea. Its sister ship, the Aras River, was drifting at its moorings just a few hundred metres further downstream.

As the weak spring sunshine warmed the cool air, the mist dissipated and revealed more than a dozen small boats, each with a fisherman sitting patiently with his rod in the water waiting for a bite. I have never seen the attraction of fishing for a sport. For food or for a business, I can appreciate it but to voluntarily get up hours before sunrise to sit, cramped in a small boat, in the cold, in the dark and especially here which is a major shipping channel with movements of big tugs pushing barges, cruise ships and cargo carriers, it takes a special sort of determination. But Astrakhan is the centre of the caviar industry and it takes its fishing very seriously. Many fishermen get up early to try their luck and hence the navigation rules about sailing at night.

We boarded our coaches and set off for a tour of the city. It was the usual format of driving around some of the major city sights such as churches, universities, statues and bridges such as the Friendship or Armenian Bridge presented to the city by nearby Armenia complete with a fountain although this was still winter, the fountain had been turned off until summer arrives.

Then it was a chance to walk around the Kremlin. We were dropped off outside and walked past the eternal flame in the park opposite, through the entrance gate into the Kremlin grounds. A city existed here for many centuries before it was destroyed in 1396 by Tamerlane. The city was refounded in 1558 after the Khanate here was defeated by Ivan the Terrible and the area was incorporated into the Russian empire.

The entrance tower isn't the original as the first one was built of wood and destroyed by fire. The next two towers were built of brick and stone but started to lean and were pulled down and rebuilt. The one seen today was built in 1906 but also needed some reinforcing to correct a lean.

The Kremlin was built on the top of a hill which has a triangular shape so the Kremlin also has a triangular shape. The walls are thick, several metres and the top battlement is under cover, protected from the rain and snow by a tiled roof, with an open back overlooking the inside of the Kremlin.

Near the entrance is the Assumption Cathedral. It was started in 1699 and took 12 years to build. The upper summer church has a tall roof with the domes of the roof supported by four massive columns. There are tall windows, a giant chandelier and an icon wall reaching the underside of the domes above. The winter church underneath in contrast is dark, with small windows and a low arched ceiling. But despite being a traditional style, there are some modern decorations seen in the lower part of the walls. The years of use by both people attending a service and various other uses when the building was closed by the communists and used as storage meant that much of the decoration was lost and when the building was repaired and refurbished, more modern abstract geometric patterns were used.

There is another church within the grounds, the St Nicholas Church but it was closed for refurbishment and its nearby gate tower, the St Nicholas Church Gate is not open to the public. However, nearby is a small chapel which is the final resting place of St Cyrus, the same St Cyrus who created the Russian alphabet.

The name of the city, Astrakhan, is a corruption of Hashtarkhan, itself a corruption of Haji Tarkhan, a name amply evidenced in the medieval writings. Tarkhan is possibly an aurco-Mongolian title standing for 'great khan', or 'king', whilst haji or hajji is a title given to one who has made the Islamic requisite of pilgrimage to Mecca. Together, they denoted 'the king who has visited Mecca'.

The city has given its name to the pelts from young karakul sheep and to the hats traditionally made from the pelts. Colloquially, the city is known by the short form of just Astra. It is in the Volga Delta, which is rich in sturgeon and exotic plants. This fertile area formerly contained the capitals of Khazaria and the Golden Horde. Astrakhan was first mentioned by travellers in the early 13th century as Xacitarxan. Tamerlane burnt it to the ground in 1395 during his war with the Golden Horde. From 1459 to 1556, Xacitarxan was the capital of the Astrakhan Khanate. The ruins of this medieval settlement were found by archaeologists 12 kilometres upstream from the modern-day city.

Starting in 1324, Ibn Battuta, the famous Muslim traveller, began his pilgrimage from his native city of Tangier, in present-day Morocco to Mecca. He didn't go directly there or back but took a circuitous route that stretched 120,000 kilometres, the equivalent of three times around the globe and took nearly 29 years. During that time Ibn Battuta came into contact with many new cultures which he recorded in his diaries.

One specific country that he passed through on his journey was the Golden Horde ruled by the descendants of Genghis Khan, located on the Volga River in southern Russia, which Battuta refers to as the river Athal. He then claims the Athal is one of the greatest rivers in the world. In the winter, when the weather is very cold, the Muslim Sultan ruler stays in Astrakhan. Sultan Mohammed Öz Beg ordered the people of Astrakhan to lay bundles of hay down on the frozen river to allow them to travel over the ice.

In 1556, the Khanate was conquered by Ivan the Terrible, who had a new Kremlin built on a steep hill overlooking the Volga in 1558. This year is traditionally considered to be the foundation of the modern city. In 1569, during the Russo-Turkish War (1568–1570), Astrakhan was besieged by the Ottoman army, which later had to retreat in disarray. A year later, the Ottoman sultan renounced his claims to Astrakhan, thus opening the entire Volga River to Russian traffic. The Ottoman Empire, though militarily defeated, insisted on safe passage for Muslim pilgrims and traders from Central Asia as well as the destruction of the Russian fort on the Terek River. In the 17th century, the city was developed as a Russian gateway to the Orient. Many merchants from Armenia, Safavid Persia, Mughal India and the Khiva Khanate settled in the town, giving it a cosmopolitan character.

For seventeen months in 1670–1671, Astrakhan was held by Stenka Razin and his Cossacks. Early in the following century, Peter the Great constructed a shipyard here and made Astrakhan the base for his hostilities against Persia, and later in the same century Katherine the Great accorded the city important industrial privileges.

Astrakhan's Kremlin was built from the 1580s to the 1620s from bricks taken from the site of Sarai Berke, another ancient city of the Golden Horde a little way upstream from Astrakhan. Its two impressive cathedrals were consecrated in 1700 and 1710. These were built by masters from Yaroslavl and they retain many traditional features of Russian ecclesiastical architecture, whilst their exterior decoration is definitely baroque.

In March 1919 after a failed workers' revolt against Bolshevik rule, 3,000 to 5,000 people were executed in less than a week by the Cheka under orders from Sergey Kirov. Some victims had stones tied around their necks and were thrown into the Volga.

During Operation Barbarossa, the Nazi invasion of the Soviet Union in 1941, the A-A line running from Astrakhan to Arkhangelsk was to be the eastern limit of Nazi military operation and occupation. The plan was never carried achieved as neither of the two cities nor Moscow was captured. In the autumn of 1942, the region to the west of Astrakhan became one of the easternmost points in the Soviet Union reached by the invading Nazi Wehrmacht during Case Blue, the offensive which led to the Battle of Stalingrad. Light armoured forces of German Army Group A made brief scouting missions as close as 100 kilometres to Astrakhan before withdrawing. In the same period, elements of both the Luftwaffe's KG 4 and KG 100 bomber wings attacked Astrakhan, flying several air raids and bombing the city's oil terminals and harbour installations.

Present-day Astrakhan is a large industrial centre of the Volga country with a population of 100,000. Starting nearly 400 years ago and continuing to the present day, Astrakhan has been Russia's main centre of fish processing. The market for fish is a large component of the economy in this city.

Astrakhan is well known for many things but it is the capital of the caviar trade, with 90% of Russian caviar coming from here. My next outing away from the ship onto land was a trip to a fish farm. It was an hour and a half drive south from Astrakhan out into the delta of the Volga where its waters empty into the Caspian Sea. The main river divides and there are a myriad of channels and islands. The land is flat and sandy, with well-drained but thin soils. The area has poor soils but a good climate and plenty of water so there are many greenhouses growing fruits, vegetables and flowers.

The road delved deeper into the delta and the number of farms thinned until it was low-lying marshland with just a few trees. A sign at the side of the road pointed to the Astrakhan Organic Fish Farm and Restaurant.

Sturgeon and beluga are protected in the wild so cannot be caught for their eggs or their meat. All modern production comes from fish farms. This particular farm uses tethered floating cages along the shore of one of the many channels crossing the delta. The process starts in April and May when eggs are harvested from the female fish. They are gently massaged and the fish roe floods out and the fish is returned to their cage. A single fish can produce eggs that can amount to between 10% and 20% of its body weight. The beluga can live for a hundred years and the largest beluga ever caught was 7.2 metres long and weighed just over one and a half tons but these sizes are impractical for fish farms.

About 90% of production is for selling as caviar, but 10% is retained to maintain a population of healthy fish. Male fish are milked for their sperm and the eggs are fertilised. After just over a week, the eggs hatch and the small fry are kept in tanks on land. They grow to about four centimetres in four months and are then transferred to the floating cages. They are periodically separated by size and age to ensure no overcrowding and that the farm retains the nest specimens.

They will be kept here for several years until they mature, between 3 and 10 years depending on the breed. Sexing fish is difficult so ultrasound is used to accurately determine the sex of the fish. A few large healthy and lucky males are kept for breeding and the rest are sold as meat.

There is a lot of investment in the fish before they produce eggs and hence the high prices. In addition, conditions have to be just right for the fish to produce eggs and some farms, especially those further north have to keep their fish in tanks on land and heat the water. Even so, some breeds don't produce every year but every 2–3 years and hence even with mature fish, there may be a shortage in any 1 year. Beluga caviar is the most prized but other sturgeon fish are farmed and sterlet is also prized and claimed to be the best source of caviar. Other fish can be used to produce roe but the flavours and textures are not the same quality that can be found in Caspian sturgeon.

Then it was time to visit the restaurant. It is on a floating platform overlooking some of the cages where the fish are kept. Regrettably, caviar was not on the menu, only different types of meat but the gift shop sold several types of processed caviar, both pasteurised and non-pasteurised and despite buying directly from the producer, the prices were still steep. After all, it is a luxury product and takes a lot of time and effort to produce just a spoonful of roe.

I had some spare time to walk around the farm through some of the buildings and exhibits on site before the long drive back to Astrakhan to re-board the ship. I got back with only minutes to spare before the gangplank was pulled up and we set sail back up the river to Volgograd.

The journey back up the river would take longer than the journey down the river. The ship had to battle against both the current and the wind which was blowing a cold gale from the north. Looking out at the marker buoys, there was a distinct wake downstream of each buoy which I hadn't noticed on the journey down to Astrakhan. The wind combined with the current to push water past the buoys and some of them were pulling at their anchors and tilted downstream from the pressure.

Astrakhan lies at 28 metres below sea level and Volgograd river port lies at 65 metres above sea level. The distance between the two is about 420 kilometres, ignoring some of the longer twists and turns of the river, so it falls 93 metres over that distance which is about 22 centimetres every kilometre (roughly a foot every mile), so it ought to be gentle river flow but judging by the tug of the river flow, it seemed to be faster than that.

There was little to see on a full day of steaming upstream. There were several fishermen in small boats and inflatables, hoping for that big catch or just passing time and relaxing. There were some sandbanks to avoid but little in the way of human habitation. There were settlements and roads somewhere off to the west and a major road according to the map but I couldn't see anything from the ship. In places, the banks rose high above the water level with just a few footpaths to get down to the water's edge.

The main attraction was passing near Kapustin Yar which was a rocket firing range set up in 1947. It developed into a scientific research centre and became a closed city. It fired several rockets and space rockets and Sputnik 1 and 2 were launched from here. It was used for several low-yield atmospheric atomic tests

1957–1961 and tested hundreds of military missiles. Its use decreased with the development of Baikonur Cosmodrome in Kazakhstan for space flights.

We moored just off the main navigation channel for the night and resumed our journey upstream at dawn. We arrived in Volgograd during breakfast, moored and those of us who wanted another taste of the city were allowed off the ship for a few hours.

We set off from the passenger terminal in Volgograd and made a large U-turn to head downstream again. The entrance to the Volga-Don Canal is at a sharp angle to the Volga River. Shipping wishing to enter it coming from the north has to sail past the opening, turn in the main river and then approach the canal heading upstream.

Chapter 15
Volga-Don Canal to Rostov-on-Don

Near the start of the canal is a giant statue of Lenin overlooking the canal standing high up on the bank with his characteristic pose with his arm stretched out. It is a fitting statue as the full name of the canal is the Lenin Volga-Don Shipping Canal and it connects the Volga River and the Don River at their closest points. It was opened in 1952. The waterway is 101 kilometres long with 45 kilometres through rivers and reservoirs, and the rest had to be dug.

There are nine locks some in close proximity to each other over a distance of 20 kilometres to lift ships from the Volga to the highest point on the Volga-Don Canal at an elevation of 73.5 metres. Here there is a flat section for 26 kilometres before the first set of down locks, four over a distance of 47 kilometres to the Zimljansker See. This is a long reservoir before the final two sets of locks and we would join the Don River. This part of the river has a dam across it downstream at Volgodonsk.

The canal forms a part of the Unified Deep-Water System of European Russia. Together with the Lower Volga and the lower Don, the Volga-Don Canal provides the most direct navigable connection between the Caspian Sea and the world's oceans via the Sea of Azov and the Black Sea. With the construction of the Volga-Don Shipping Canal in 1952, Rostov-on-Don has become known as a port with access to five seas, the Black Sea, the Sea of Azov, the Caspian Sea, the White Sea and the Baltic Sea.

As the lower course of the Don approaches the lower course of the Volga near Volgograd, the idea of connecting the two rivers by an artificial waterway has a long history ever since Peter the Great captured Azov in 1696.

Peter the Great decided to build a canal to link the two rivers but due to a lack of resources and other problems, the attempt was abandoned in 1701. In the same year, he initiated a second attempt, the so-called Ivanovsky Canal at Yepifan under the administration of Knyaz Matvey Gagarin. Instead of connecting the lower course of the Don with the lower course of the Volga near the present canal, the Ivanovsky Canal connected the upper courses of the Don and Volga in what is now Tula Oblast. Between 1702 and 1707, 24 locks were constructed, and, in 1707, about 300 ships passed through the canal under remarkably difficult navigation conditions. In 1709 due to financial difficulties caused by the Great Northern War, the project was mothballed.

In 1711, under terms of the Treaty of the Pruth, signed on the River Pruth between Russia and the Ottoman Empire ending the Russo-Turkish War, Russia withdrew from Azov and Peter the Great lost all interest in the canal, which was abandoned and fell into ruin. Over time, other projects for connecting the two rivers were proposed, but none was attempted.

The actual construction of today's Volga-Don Canal began prior to the Great Patriotic War, which interrupted the project. Construction work recommenced in 1948 and lasted until 1952. Navigation was officially opened on 1st June 1952. The canal and its facilities were built by about 900,000 workers including some 100,000 German POWs and 100,000 Gulag prisoners. A day spent on the construction site was counted as three days in prison, which spurred prisoners to work.

The canal starts at the Sarepta backwater on the Volga River in the southern suburbs of Volgograd with Lock No. 1 and ends in the Tsimlyansk Reservoir of the Don River at the town of Kalach-na-Donu. The canal has nine single chamber canal locks on the Volga slope that can raise ships 88 metres, and four canal locks on the Don slope that can lower ships 44 metres.

The overall dimensions of the canal locks are smaller than those on the Volga River, however, they can pass ships of up to 5,000 tonnes cargo capacity. The smallest locks are 145 metres long, 17 metres wide, and 3.6 metres deep. Maximum allowed vessel size is 140 metres long, 16.6 metres wide and a draft of 3.5 metres which is sometimes referred to as the Volgo-Don Max Class. The Volga-Don Canal is filled from the Don River. Three powerful pumping stations maintain water levels in the highest central section.

Types of cargo transported from the Don region to the Volga region include coal from Donetsk, Ukraine, minerals, building materials, and grain. Cargoes from the Volga to the Don include lumber, pyrites, and petroleum products carried mostly by Volgotanker boats. Tourist ships travel in both directions.

More than 8.05 million tonnes of cargo was transported through the canal in total in 2006. Most of the cargo was moved from the east to the west, namely, 7.20 million tonnes were transported through the canal from the Volga/Caspian basin to the Don/Sea of Azov/Black Sea basin, and only 0.85 million tonnes were carried in the opposite direction. Just over half of all cargo was oil or oil products (4.14 million tonnes), predominantly shipped from the Caspian region.

It was reported in 2007 that in the first 55 years of the canal's operations, 450,000 vessels had passed through carrying 336 million tonnes of cargo. Recent cargo volume stood at 12 million tonnes a year.

It was going to be another day cruising and would only arrive in Rostov after lunch. Or rather that is what the schedule advised. In reality, the ship slowed and dropped its anchor 4 hours early. We had moored to one side of the main shipping channel. A few boats went past but there was also a railway line between the shore and the steep slope which lined the river bank. There was an almost constant rattle of trains as 12 and 15-carriage-long passenger trains came and went, interspersed with long freight trains.

I counted all the wagons as they rolled past. One train had five locomotives pulling a mixture of wagons, open freight cars, grain carriers and oil tankers. There were 89 wagons but that was a long way short of the longest train that I have ever seen. Had we arrived and moored early I might have gone off to do my own thing. Not far away is the open-air Museum of Railway Equipment which is just up my street. But there is always something to come back to see so if there is another time, I will pre-book a taxi and go straight there.

An hour before we were due to go on our city tour, the main engines started the anchor was pulled up and we headed off downriver to reach the river port. We circumnavigated an island in the river to approach the berth against the current.

The captain stopped the ship just upstream of our intended berth and dropped the anchor. Our berth was between two other ships, a passenger ship downstream of us and a floating restaurant upstream. It was a tight fit but angling the ship against the current, using his engines and slowly letting out the anchor chain, the ship moved sideways and with an almost imperceptible little bump, we were moored.

We walked up the embankment to find our coaches and guides waiting and we set off for our city tour. It was the usual mix of the largest square in the city opposite the railway station with an eternal flame next to the war memorial consisting of a very tall slender metal tower with a statue at the top covered in gold leaf, with all the names of the fallen around the base.

From ancient times, the area around the mouth of the Don River has held cultural and commercial importance. Ancient indigenous inhabitants included the Scythian, Sarmat, and Savromat tribes. It was the site of Tanais, an ancient Greek colony, Fort Tana, controlled by the Genoese and Fort Azak in the time of the Ottoman Empire.

In 1749, a custom house was established on the Temernik River, a tributary of the Don, by the edict of Empress Elizabeth, the daughter of Peter the Great, in order to control trade with Turkey. It was co-located with a fortress named for Dimitry of Rostov, a metropolitan bishop of the old northern town of Rostov the Great. Azov, a town closer to the Sea of Azov on the Don, gradually lost its commercial importance in the region to the new fortress.

In 1756, the Russian commercial and trading company called Constantinople was founded at the merchants' settlement on the high banks of the Don. Towards the end of the eighteenth century, with the incorporation of previously Ottoman Black Sea territories into the Russian empire, the settlement lost much of its militarily strategic importance as a frontier post. The Russo-Turkish War of 1768–1774 was a major armed conflict that saw Russian armies largely victorious against the Ottoman Empire.

Russia's victory brought Kabardia, part of Moldavia, the Yedisan between the rivers Bug and Dnieper, and Crimea into the Russian sphere of influence. Though a series of victories accrued by the Russian empire led to substantial territorial conquests, including direct conquest over much of the Pontic-Caspian steppe, less Ottoman territory was directly annexed than might otherwise be expected due to a complex struggle within the European diplomatic system to maintain a balance of power that was acceptable to other European states and avoided direct Russian hegemony over Eastern Europe.

Nonetheless, Russia was able to take advantage of the weakened Ottoman Empire, the end of the Seven Years' War, and the withdrawal of France from Polish affairs to assert itself as one of the continent's primary military powers. The war left the Russian empire in a strengthened position to expand its territory and maintain hegemony over the Polish-Lithuanian Commonwealth, eventually leading to the First Partition of Poland. Turkish losses included diplomatic defeats that saw its decline as a threat to Christian Europe and the beginning of European bickering over the Eastern Question that would feature in European diplomacy until the collapse of the Ottoman Empire in the aftermath of the First World War.

In 1796, the settlement was chartered and in 1797, it became the seat of Rostovsky Uyezd within the Novorossiysk Governorate. In 1806, it was officially renamed Rostov-on-Don. During the 19th century, due to its river connections with Russia's interior, Rostov developed into a major trade centre and communications hub. A railway connection with Kharkiv was completed in 1870, with further links following in 1871 to Voronezh and in 1875 to Vladikavkaz.

Concurrent with improvements in communications, heavy industry developed. Coal from the Donets Basin and iron ore from Krivoy Rog supported the establishment of an iron foundry in 1846. In 1859, the production of pumps and steam boilers began. Industrial growth was accompanied by a rapid increase in population, with 119,500 residents registered in Rostov by the end of the nineteenth century along with approximately 140 industrial businesses. The harbour was one of the largest trade hubs in southern Russia, especially for the export of wheat, timber, and iron ore.

In 1779, Rostov-on-Don became associated with a settlement of Armenian refugees from the Crimea at Nakhichevan-on-Don. The two settlements were separated by just a few fields and with continued expansion, the two towns merged in 1928 to become the third-largest city in Russia.

During the Russian Civil War, the White and the Red Armies contested Rostov-on-Don, then the most heavily industrialised city of South Russia. In the Soviet years, the Bolsheviks demolished two of Rostov-on-Don's principal landmarks, St Alexander Nevsky Cathedral built in 1908 and the St George Cathedral built between 1783 and 1807.

During the First World War, Germany and Austria-Hungarian forces captured Rostov-on-Don in 1917. During the Great Patriotic War, Nazi forces occupied Rostov-on-Don from November to December 1941, and then again for seven months from July 1942. The town was of strategic importance as a railway junction and a river port accessing the Caucasus, a region rich in oil and minerals. It took 10 years to restore the city from the damage during the war.

Between 1942 and 1943, 27,000 Jews were massacred by the Nazis at a site called Zmievskaya Balka by the SS Einsatzgruppe D during the Holocaust in Russia. It is considered to be the largest single mass murder site of Jews on Russian territory during the Second World War. The name means 'the ravine of the snakes'. Einsatzkommando 10a, commanded by Heinrich Seetzen and Geheime Feldpolizei initially arrested some 700 people on the grounds that they were Soviet partisans and party functionaries and executed about 400 by 2nd August 1942.

Although many Jews had fled from Rostov when the city was under the control of the Red Army, about 2,000 remained and the Einsatzkommando began registering them, demanding that they gather at collecting points on 11th August 1942. Over the next three days, the Jewish men of Rostov were marched to Zmievskaya Balka, where they were shot by the Einsatzkommando. The women, children and elderly were gassed in trucks, and their bodies buried in the same ravine.

After the initial massacres, until February 1943, the SS continued to bring thousands of Jews to be killed at the Zmievskaya Balka ravine, and between 15,000 and 18,000 Jews were murdered in further mass shootings. Communists and Red Army soldiers were also killed and buried there, along with their families.

The Don River is a major shipping lane connecting the Black Sea via southwestern Russia with the north. Rostov-on-Don was a trading port for Russian, Italian, Greek and Turkish merchants selling, for example, wool, wheat and oil. It is also an important river port for passengers. The Rostov-on-Don agricultural region produces one-third of Russia's vegetable oil from sunflowers.

We had a walk around the main theatre followed by a visit to an Armenian church, and noticeably different when compared with Russian Orthodox churches as it was a lot plainer.

We were driven past some beautiful buildings along a main road which survived the war and have been carefully restored and the nearby main cathedral. Then we had some spare time to go shopping and a chance to get some souvenirs. If I actually went souvenir shopping every time, I was given the opportunity, there would be no space left in my luggage for any clothes but it seems that every guide and tour made sure we had every opportunity to spend money on tourist trinkets made in China.

In modern times, Rostov-on-Don has experienced significant economic growth. Numerous start-up companies have established headquarters in the city, the median income is increasing, and the city is being transformed into a modern, industrial and technology hub.

Rostov-on-Don has been home to many famous people, many of them writers such as Mikhail Sholokhov, novelist and winner of the 1965 Nobel Prize in Literature. He is known for writing about the life and fate of Don Cossacks during the Russian Revolution, the civil war and the period of collectivisation, primarily in his most famous novel, And Quiet Flows the Don.

A monument to Anton Chekhov who was born in the city was erected in 2010 a bronze statue of the writer standing next to a balustrade atop of a red granite plinth erected in 2010 to commemorate the 150th anniversary of his birth.

Others include Mikhail Kalinin, Bolshevik revolutionary and Soviet politician after whom Kaliningrad is named, Alexander Pushkin, poet, playwright, and novelist of the Romantic era. Maxim Gorky, writer and political activist, Aleksey Nikolayevich Tolstoy, Alexander Solzhenitsyn and Yuri Zhdanov, chemistry professor, rector of the University of Rostov, son of Soviet politician Andrei Zhdanov and former husband of Joseph Stalin's daughter, Svetlana Alliluyeva are also connected with the city. A monument to Aleksandr Solzhenitsyn, who lived in the city for 18 years and studied mathematics at Rostov University, is being planned by city authorities.

Some of the other passengers had left the evening before and some had early flights and had left before dawn. It was much quieter in the restaurant on my last morning on the ship. I lingered over my coffee until it was time for my pick-up. I had left my luggage outside my door at 7.15 am as instructed. It had been carried off the boat and stacked with other bags on the embankment.

I looked out from the restaurant and noticed that my bag and all the others had gone. I was ready to go so I went to find my bag. It had been moved up to the pavement next to the road where several coaches were waiting to take people to the airport. There were people milling about, saying their goodbyes before getting on to whichever coach they had been allocated. Before getting on, they identified their luggage and a member of the ship's crew would load it onto the coach. My bag had been mixed up with another group so I rescued it and walked up and down the pavement, waiting for my lift to the coach station to appear.

The allotted time for the transfer came and went and I was still standing on the pavement, waiting for a car. My instruction was that I would be met by my driver who would be holding a sign with my name on it. I approached every car that came along the road and stopped but no one got out with a sign. I was getting concerned as I had an hour to find my coach to Krasnodar at the bus station and with this delay I now had only half an hour. I knew it was only a 5-minute drive to the coach station but I don't like to be late.

My driver eventually found me, he had parked some distance away and was making his way through the crowd asking for me by name but without any sign. He drove me to the coach station and made sure that I was in the right queue for the right coach.

The dispatcher checked each passenger's tickets as they got on but mine was not in order and my name did not appear on the manifest. I was asked to wait whilst everybody else got on the bus. Then she re-read my documents and asked me to follow her to the office. There was some problem and I had no idea what it might be but she read and re-read my documents as did her colleague, her supervisor and what I assumed was the most senior manager on duty, they all had uniforms on but his had the most braid and six golden pips on his shoulder epaulettes.

I was concerned as the coach should have departed a quarter of an hour ago and from my position in the office, I couldn't tell whether the coach had left without me and I had no idea whether there was another coach that day.

To my relief, after several phone calls, they decided that my email was a valid ticket and the dispatcher escorted me back to the coach which thankfully was still there. I had spent some of the time waiting for officialdom to work its way through the cogs of power by reading the timetables posted on the walls of the office. The next coach was midday, 3 hours away.

I went to put my bag into the baggage compartment under the coach but the driver asked for my ticket. I showed it to him but he frowned and handed it back to me. Unbeknown to me, I should have bought a separate ticket for my baggage if I had to put it into the hold. I would have to nurse my bag on my lap for the next 5 hours. I climbed aboard and apologised to the other passengers for the delay as I boarded. And we were away to Krasnodar.

Chapter 16
Krasnodar

We drove out of the bus station next to the railway station, through a security checkpoint and onto the main road. We crossed the Don and soon we were driving at speed down the main A134 road southwards. After just 20 minutes of driving, the driver pulled over at a motorway service station and announced that we would have a 5-minute break. A few passengers got off and a few new faces got on.

The journey was 280 kilometres between the two cities but scheduled to take more than 5 hours. That is an average speed of 56 kmph. Then I realised my mistake as the bus would stop at all sorts of small places to drop off and pick up passengers and wait a while, hence the slow average speed. I had purposefully booked a ticket to travel during daylight hours so that I could see some of the countryside but had not checked the detailed timetable as in my ignorance, I had thought that it would be a direct service.

The 5-minute break took more like 15 minutes. There were toilets, a café and a grocery shop. I had a bag of sandwiches and a few cans of drink as I was not sure what facilities might be on hand. I also took the chance to buy a ticket for my baggage as I didn't want it on my lap for the whole journey and it was too big to squeeze under the seat.

I had a window seat and spent most of the journey staring out of the window. There were several more stops at roundabouts, motorway service stations and bus stations. The scenery was interesting but it wasn't spectacular. In the early afternoon, the coach pulled into the bus station in Krasnodar. I checked the timetables and got a local bus into the town centre to find my hotel for a couple of days.

Krasnador is the administrative centre of Krasnodar Krai, located on the Kuban River. It is a growing city with a million people making it Russia's 16th largest city. It was founded on 12th January 1794 as per the Gregorian calendar as Yekaterinodar although there is a large red granite block near the cathedral with 1793 on it but that would be based on the Julian calendar. The block is there to mark the site of a fort built within a bend in the river so that it was surrounded on three sides by the river and swamps so that it was a good defensive position.

The original name meant 'Katherine's Gift', recognising both Katherine the Great's grant of land in the Kuban region to the Black Sea Cossacks and Saint Katherine of Alexandria, who is considered to be the patron of the city.

On 7th December 1920, as a result of the October Revolution, Yekaterinodar was renamed Krasnodar meaning 'Gift of the Reds'. The new name consists of Krasno meaning 'red', i.e. Communist, but also the archaic and poetic form of 'beautiful' and dar meaning 'gift'. The coat of arms of Yekaterinodar was introduced in 1841 by the Cossack yesaul Ivan Chernik. The royal letter 'E' in the middle is for Ekaterina II (Russian for Katherine II). It also depicts the date the city was founded, the Imperial double-headed eagle symbolising the tsar's patronage of the Black Sea Cossacks, a bulawa or baton indicating power of a Cossack Ataman, Yekaterinodar fortress, and flags with letters 'E', 'P', 'A' and 'H' standing for Katherine II, Paul I, Alexander I and Nicholas I.

The city originated in 1793 as a military camp, then a fortress was built by the Cossacks to defend themselves and the Imperial borders and to assert Russian dominion over Circassia, a claim that Ottoman Turkey contested. In the first half of the 19th century, Yekaterinodar grew into a busy centre of the Kuban Cossacks, gaining official city status in 1867. By 1888 about 45,000 people lived in the city, which had become a vital trade centre for southern Russia. In 1897, an obelisk commemorating the 200-year history of the Kuban Cossacks was erected in Yekaterinodar.

During the Russian Civil War 1917–1922, the city changed hands several times, coming successively under the control of the Red Army and the Volunteer Army. Many Kuban Cossacks, as committed anti-Bolsheviks, supported the White Army under the command of General von Denikin. Lavr Kornilov, a White general, captured the city on 10th April 1918, only to be killed a week later when a Bolshevik artillery shell blew up the farmhouse where he had set up his headquarters.

During the Great Patriotic War, units of the German Army occupied Krasnodar between 12th August 1942 and 12th February 1943. The city sustained heavy damage in the fighting. There is a large war memorial in the park near the cathedral consisting of a plinth of polished red granite and a statue of a Soviet soldier, twice life-size. Flanking him are limestone walls to commemorate those lost during the fight for the city, to the left are the carvings of soldiers and to the right are carvings of citizens who died caught up in the fighting and bombing.

Nazi forces, including Gestapo and mobile SS execution squads, killed thousands of Jews, Communists, and supposed Communist partisans by shooting, hanging, burning, and even gas vans were used.

In the summer of 1943, after the liberation of the city, the Soviets began trials for collusion with the Nazis and for participation in war crimes. The first such trial took place at Krasnodar from 14th to 17th July 1943. The Krasnodar tribunal pronounced eight death sentences, which were summarily carried out in the city square in front of a crowd of about thirty thousand people.

Krasnodar is home to the steel lattice hyperboloid tower built by the Russian engineer and scientist Vladimir Grigorievich Shukhov in 1928 which is located near Krasnodar Circus.

Other attractions along the road include St Katherine's Cathedral, the State Arts Museum, a park, a theatre named after Maxim Gorky, the beautiful concert hall of the Krasnodar Philharmonic Society, which is considered to have some of the best acoustics in southern Russia, the State Cossack Choir, the Krasnodar Circus, the Aurora cinema and the Triumphal Arch.

At one end of Krasnaya Street, which translates as 'Red, or Beautiful Street' is the Nevsky Cathedral. Just to the left of the entrance is a column and sitting on top at head height is the bust of the legendary Alexander Nevsky 1221–1263 who ruled from 1236 until his death.

There is a park in front of the cathedral and off to the right is a large statue of Katherine on a plinth. Running down the front of the plinth is a scroll that represents the treaty granting the gift of land to the Kuban Cossacks. Around the plinth stand several nobles and advisors. She is looking across the park where there are government offices. In her direct line of sight between the two is an empty plinth. A statue of Lenin used to stand here staring back at Katherine but since the fall of communism, his statue has been removed. All through the park and streets, the street furniture has the first letter of Katherine's name in Cyrillic picked out in gold, it looks like a capital 'E' with curves or a figure '3' but facing in the opposite direction.

The road leading away from the cathedral is a busy thoroughfare during the week but from 8 pm on Friday night, it is blocked off and becomes a pedestrianised area. Further along the street, standing in front of the Pushkin Library is a statue of Pushkin. He had been exiled from St Petersburg for expressing some of his more extreme views and lived here in Ykaterinodar. On the plinth is a sentence revealing what he thought about the city.

On one corner is an architecturally interesting building of a Muslim merchant. It has since been converted into the Modern Arts Museum. During the war, the curators managed to pack away and either hide or ship exhibits to safer areas of the country although they didn't have time to rescue the avante garde collection of treasures. The Nazis captured the city and stole the items that they thought were valuable but had no taste for avante garde and so they didn't steal them and neither did they destroy it, so it survived and can still be seen today.

Theatre Square is home to the largest splash fountain in Europe. This fountain was officially inaugurated on 25th September 2011 along with an official ceremony to celebrate City Day in Krasnodar. There are some other interesting buildings that either survived the war or have been rebuilt in the traditional style. However, many of the buildings are more modern.

On a corner where a side street crosses the main road, there is an unusual bronze statue of a dog. It was inspired by Vladimir Mayakovsky, a well-known Russian poet and installed in 1970. He was visiting the city in 1926 and was surprised by the number of pedigree dogs walking the streets. Their wealthy owners had fled the city taking the valuables that they could carry but had left their dogs. Local tradition has it that you can stroke the statue and make a wish and that it will come true.

Krasnodar is the economic centre of southern Russia. For several years, Forbes magazine named Krasnodar the best city for business in Russia. The industrial sector of the city has more than 130 large and medium-sized enterprises with two-thirds of the economy centred on agriculture, food processing, energy, fuel and tourism which comprises a large part of Krasnodar's economy. The city has several major museums more than eight theatres, a state circus and its own Philharmonic Orchestra plus plenty of retail opportunities.

Per capita, Krasnodar has the highest number of malls in Russia and boasts the largest shopping mall in the south of Russia, the Oz Mall. This mall is a giant modern retail and leisure complex overlooking the dam across the Kuban River. It is distinctive due to its wavy roof line and it is lit up at night in changing colours. Therefore it is not surprising that retail trade is booming and despite the economic turndown seen in other cities, Krasnodar continued to grow. The city has the lowest unemployment rate among the cities of the Southern Federal

District at 0.3% of the total working-age population. In addition, Krasnodar holds the first place in terms of the highest average salary.

Growth comes from the many people who relocate here from other areas of Russia as there are good job prospects, the housing can be cheaper and the weather is much more benign than in areas further to the north.

A short walk up Ulitsa Krasnaya, there is a park with tall trees providing shade in summer and on one side is the State Museum. It is housed in a beautiful and carefully restored merchant's house (and he owned the equally attractive buildings on either side so he owned the whole block facing the street). Inside are various exhibits including the original parchment giving the Kuban Cossacks the gift of land.

The items that I had come to see were the Kuban Cossack treasures that had been returned to their rightful place. They had been removed for safety, firstly to Serbia and later to America. They would only be returned on three conditions. Namely that the cathedral be rebuilt, which had been destroyed by the Bolsheviks has been completed. It is not in its original position as that was further along the street but the city had expanded and there was not enough room for it in its original position. Therefore, it was rebuilt at the nearest point to the original site of the old fortress possible which was at the start of Krasnaya Street.

The second condition was that the Gate that was at the fortress was to be rebuilt. Like the cathedral, it had been demolished by the Bolsheviks and the city had expanded and it could not be rebuilt on the original site. Therefore it was built further along Ulitsa Krasnaya where the road widens into a dual carriageway.

The third condition was that the city should be renamed Ykaterinodar. There was broad support for this but public support fell away as the cost was prohibitive to reprint maps and change all the street names and road signs but the memory of Katherine lives on with the first letter of her name in Russian emblazoned on railings and street furniture. Not all three conditions were strictly met but it was close enough so the treasures were returned.

Then my guide and I caught a bus to what is nicknamed the Colosseum. In actual fact the Colosseum is the modern stadium of the Krasnodar Football team owned by Sergey Galitsky. He is a wealthy oligarch having created Magnet, a major supermarket chain seen throughout Russia which started from their base in Krasnodar and spread throughout the country, firstly opening in small towns and cities to build presence but therefore underrepresented in Moscow and St

Petersburg. The word in Russian is pronounced as Magneat, but I have used the Latin spelling.

Sergey Galitsky sold out of Magnet but now he concentrates his energy on his football team that he owns in Krasnodar. He has also donated a huge park to the city around the stadium on what was previously waste ground and has bought up adjacent tracts of land to expand the park. There are sports zones where you can play basketball or football, children's zones where they can play in the water or in the sand pits, interactive music zones where you can play zylophones, open-air cinema areas and formal gardens. It is a fascinating place, so clean, no litter anywhere and no graffiti and a popular place to visit.

Then it was back to the city and we rejoined Krasnaya Street at the opposite end from the site of the fort and the cathedral. We passed a large brick arch with plenty of decorative red brickwork. This was the recreation of the city's Gate to the fortress and the second condition for the return of the treasures. The city is also known as the City of Moving Monuments.

The cathedral used to be sited further up the street but it was destroyed by the Bolsheviks. When it came to be rebuilt, it was built in a different place. The original arch had suffered a similar fate so when it came to be rebuilt, modern traffic could not get through the arch so it wasn't rebuilt in the centre but further up the road on a wide boulevard on a roundabout so traffic could see it but it is not an obstruction.

There is an island in the Kuban River which hosts a funfair and has a submarine pulled up on the shore that people can visit and visitors can walk around and imagine and feel the claustrophobia of the small spaces in a noisy machine underwater. The island is connected to the mainland by the Love Bridge. This is where lovers attach padlocks as a sign of love, however, when I visited, the bridge needed repainting and all of the locks had been removed except for one that had been attached after all the others had been cut off by workmen.

We had to get back to the centre and the Stan restaurant for the end of the city tour. This was one of the better restaurants, newly built but in a traditional style overlooking the river. Stan was a place where soldiers might stay or where wandering peasants might stay. The insides are full of traditional decorations, furniture and hangings. I had the borscht followed by pelmeni and vareniki, both are similar to ravioli but the difference is that pelmeni is without meat, and vareniki is with meat.

I went back to my hotel to collect my luggage and caught a local bus to the bus station. Travelling overnight is never my preferred option as I prefer to sleep in a bed than a seat in an upright position. Also if I am travelling, I suffer from FOMO so I like to see the countryside as I may only come to this one once.

Saving the price of a hotel room was one issue. Another issue and a persuading factor was that there was only one road into Sochi. It is a mountainous area and there is no direct route through the mountains. In order to get to Sochi, travellers need to go south to Tuapse and then it is still nearly 120 kilometres and 3 hours on the coach southeast along the coast road to Sochi. And I would be travelling back up it in daylight when I left Sochi so I wouldn't suffer from FOMO and I would save the cost of a hotel room for the night.

I hadn't done a long overnight trip on a coach for a while and I was soon reminded why I travel during the day and sleep in a hotel overnight. The country is large and there is a network of routes criss-crossing the whole country. Most bus stations are therefore open 24 hours and the larger ones have shops that are also open 24 hours. But in my opinion, long coach journeys are uncomfortable and although the frequent stops mean that you are not caught short, there are frequent interruptions to any sleep that you might get. In the dark, there is nothing to see and every stop is the same…tired people milling about under the glare of bright lights, eating fatty foods and drinking indifferent coffee for want of anything else to do.

The overnight bus from Krasnodar arrived a few minutes early but outside the station was my local driver, holding up a board with my name on it. He introduced himself as Max and he drove me to my hotel. We stopped outside of the Dolphin Hotel, not the Barkhanye Sozeny Russky Dom as per my itinerary. He assured me that this was a much better hotel and that he had changed it and had forgotten to change my itinerary.

It was a modern building but built in a traditional style. It was smart, clean and had a giant room with tall ceilings, a table with four chairs and a bed big enough for three. It was also near the centre and on the seafront rather than tucked away near the Olympic Park. Murmansk had snow on the ground and ice in the rivers. Moscow had been cold but Rostov-on-Don was pleasant. But this far south and later in the spring, the temperatures were in the low twenties; hence, its appeal as a holiday destination along with most of the Black Sea coast.

I had an hour to shower, shave and unpack after my overnight coach trip. I was waiting in reception when Max returned to start my tour. In the back of the car was my local guide who Max introduced as Svetlana. Max drove out of town towards my first stop in Krasnaya Polyana whilst Svetlana kept up a running commentary.

Krasnaya Polyana lies about 40 kilometres due east from Sochi but to get there, the road goes south-east along the coast before turning inland. Sochi is the longest city in Russia stretching more than 100 kilometres along the coast, although the guide in Volgograd still claimed that their city was bigger and derided Sochi for including suburbs in its claim. Sochi is a long and thin city as the hills inland have prevented further development from spreading away from the coast, only along it. The road from Sochi to Adler, a suburb of Sochi is congested as there is little other space to build a road. A new road was built further inland as part of the planning for the Olympics using tunnels and viaducts to overcome the difficult terrain but the roads are still congested.

When trains were developed, the engineers didn't have the finance to build tunnels and viaducts so the track was squeezed into what little space was left between the road and the beach between Sochi Central and Adler before turning inland at Adler where there is more space to climb into the hills to reach Krasnaya Polyana.

The road reaches the delta of the Mzymta River that rises in the mountains behind Adler. Over millennia, it has washed down millions of tons of stones and sand to create the large flat wasteland swamp on which the area of Adler and the Olympic Games destinations were created. Some 40,000 tons of material is washed down and deposited on the coast every year.

We drove around the site and Svetana pointed out many of the buildings. The buildings are not open to the public unless a specific event is being staged. There were some events planned and barriers had been erected to marshal people and vehicles in certain directions such as signs pointing to a musical event and an ice hockey match to be played later in the day. Other areas were reserved for parking and some areas were closed off so navigating through the network of roads and paths was difficult.

Added to this, the area is also host to the Sochi Grand Prix Race Track. The first Grand Prix in Russia was held in 1913 near St Petersburg. There had been various people expressing a desire to see a Russian Grand Prix race in the late 20th century including Vladimir Putin and Bernie Eccleston.

When Vitaly Petron joined Renault and became Russia's first Formula One World Championship driver in 2010, he added further momentum to the project.

After several decades of attempting to re-establish the race in Russia, the new Russian Grand Prix was officially announced on 14th October 2010 for a debut in 2014, running through to 2020. The race is held in the resort city of Sochi, the host city of the 2014 Winter Olympics, at the Sochi Autodrom, a 5.9-kilometre street circuit which passes around the venues of Sochi's Olympic Park.

The circuit was, designed by German architect Hermann Tilke and has the start grid on the northern edge of the Olympic Park next to the railway station. The circuit then heads southwest towards the Black Sea coast and runs along the outer edge of the central Sochi Medals Plaza, the podium for Olympic medal ceremonies, then circles the plaza counterclockwise and makes three turns around the Bolshoy Ice Dome. Then it follows a series of tight corners before turning north where the track skirts the edge of the Olympic Park past the main Olympic Village and the Adler Arena Skating Centre before passing the skating and curling centres, before funnelling up behind the pit paddock towards the train station and completing a circuit with two ninety-degree right turns. It seemed that if we wanted to go anywhere by foot there were several footbridges to climb up and over to get to where you wanted to go as the track weaves its way around some of the stadiums.

We went past the media centre, the athletics centre, the curling venue and several skating rinks. The area is huge with plenty of open spaces between the venues and hotels. There were already plenty of people there, sometimes just to relax, to enjoy the spring sun, to exercise or to just fill in time. In the centre of the area is the Olympic Medal Plaza. There is a tall slender Olympic flame made of concrete.

On one side is a modest monument to all the medal winners. It is a steel hollow mesh globe with the continents picked out in solid metal. On each side are sloping struts that support the globe. The strut's other ends are embedded in two walls that flank the globe which carry all the names of the medal winners and under their names, the country that they represented and the sport for which they won the medal. Gold winners are nearest the centre followed by silver and bronze towards the edges. A challenge is to find all your country's representatives. Since the UK is good with some winter sports such as snowboarding and curling, it was easy to find some of our winners.

Chapter 17
Circassian Genocide

The Sochi Olympic Park is a sprawling confusing site but Max found his way out and then it was a short road journey of 68 kilometres along the Mzymta River up into the hills. This is the home to the new Rosa Khutor and the alpine ski resort of Krasnaya Polyana, with a base elevation of 560 metres. The lift system starts above the town centre and rises up to the summit at 2,320 metres giving a vertical drop of 1,760 metres. There are usually good snow conditions in winter due to the high snowfall in the area and the height so it is generally snow-assured but the snow can get slushy towards the end of the season.

The resort hosted the World Cup Alpine events in February 2012 and the Alpine and Nordic events of the 2014 Winter Olympics. The resort also hosts the ashes of where Canadian skier Sarah Burke was spread. She was a Canadian freestyle skier and pioneer of the superpipe event. She was a five-time gold medallist and was a favourite to continue her medal successes in Sochi but was killed in a training accident.

At the top of the resort is an ethnological attraction with various buildings in traditional styles. Before the decision to make Sochi the destination for the Winter Olympics in 2014, there were just a few modest houses there. The whole resort was built from scratch.

The name literally means Red Glade and it is alleged that it was given that name because of the thick overgrowth of ferns, the leaves of which had a reddish-brown colour in the autumn. However, Walter Richmond, director of Russian Studies at Occidental College, Los Angeles and a historian of the Circassian Genocide claims that Krasnaya Polyana was named after the last stand by the Circassian Ubykhs, of whom many died there in 1864.

The Ubykh tribe used to inhabit this area which was called Circassia, centred around their capital of Sache, present-day Sochi meaning in their language 'seaside'. They were semi-nomadic horsemen and had a finely differentiated vocabulary related to horses and tack. Some Ubykh also practised favomancy, a form of divination that involves throwing beans on the ground and interpreting the patterns into which the beans fall. Other groups are said to have practised scapulimancy, the practice of divination by the use of scapulae or shoulder blades, using the bones and the pattern that they made to divine meanings.

The Russo-Circassian War had been continuing for decades as Russia sought to expand its empire and consolidate control over new areas where Russians were settling to expand trade and colonise new areas. The war had been fought since 1763 but it was mainly a series of localised conflicts and raids with intermittent periods of relative peace, and only completed with the expulsion of the Ubykh in 1864.

In 1857, Count Dmitry Milyutin, who was a soldier who fought in the Caucasus War 1839–45, was wounded and returned to the military academy as a professor. He emphasised science in the military and studied the causes of the defeat in the Crimea War and was Minister of War from 1861 to 81, and was responsible for sweeping military reforms that changed the face of the Russian army in the 1860s and 1870s. Further, he was instrumental in creating the framework for the Circassian Genocide and he was the first to voice the idea of resolving the issue of unrest between Russian settlers and nomadic herdsmen by the mass expulsions of Circassian natives.

Milyutin argued that the goal was not to simply move them so that their land could be settled by productive farmers, but rather that 'eliminating the Circassians was to be an end in itself', to cleanse the land of hostile elements. The decision was made at a meeting in Vladikazkaz in October 1860. The motion was formerly proposed by General Yevdokimov, supported by Baryatinsky and endorsed by Tsar Alexander II. Milyutin became the minister of war in 1861 to oversee the policy of expulsions which began occurring in the Caucasus, first in the northeast and then in the northwest. The tribes were to be given the choice of emigrating to the Ottoman Empire or settling further north in the Kuban area. In practice, most were simply driven to the coast to be expelled.

General Yevdokimov was tasked with enforcing the policy, using mobile columns of Russian riflemen and Cossack cavalry. In a series of sweeping military campaigns lasting from 1860 to 1864, the northwest Caucasus and the Black Sea coast were virtually emptied of local and Muslim villagers. Columns of the displaced were marched either to the Kuban River plains or toward the coast for transport to the Ottoman Empire. One after another, entire Circassian tribal groups were dispersed, resettled, or killed én masse.

Such tactics had been in use for a number of years. Count Leo Tolstoy, the future author of War and Peace, saw action in the war in 1850–51. He described how 'It had been the custom to rush the auls (mountain villages) by night, when, taken by surprise, the women and children had no time to escape, and the horrors that ensued under the cover of darkness when the Russian soldiers made their way by twos and threes into the houses were such as no official narrator dared describe'.

Similar atrocities committed in the final campaign of 1859–1864 were recorded by other contemporary observers. A British consul named Dickson recounted in an 1864 dispatch: 'a Russian detachment having captured the village of Toobah on the Soobashi river, inhabited by about a hundred Abadzekh, a minor tribe of Circassians. After these had surrendered, they were all massacred by the Russian troops. The detachment in question belonged to Count Evdokimoff's Army and is said to have advanced from the Pshish valley. As the Russian troops gain ground on the Black Sea coast, the natives are not allowed to remain there on any terms, but are compelled either to transfer themselves to the plains of the Kuban or emigrate to Turkey.'

The explosions seem to have started in 1861–62. Some wealthy Circassians had already left in 1860 and 10,000 Kabardians had left in 1861. In April 1862, 15,000 Temirgoys were driven to the coast and in May, the Natukhajs were the subject of mass marches. In May 1862, a commission was formed to organise the deportation. Each deported family was to be given 10 roubles. The number of people expelled was several hundred thousand, with a large percentage dying on the march, waiting on the beach, on overloaded boats or of disease such as plague after arrival on the Turkish shore. The future Kuban Oblast lost 94% of its native population.

A historian, Richmond, estimated population changes in the northwest Caucasus between 1835 and 1882, that Circassians had fallen from 571,000 to 36,000, non-Circassian Abazas, from 70,000 to 10,000 and Karachays, down from 24,000 to 17,000. However, Russians and Ukrainians increased from 110,000 to 926,000.

The last battle of the war occurred at Qbaada Meadow near Sochi on 27th May 1864 when the Russians defeated a group of Ubyks. On 2nd June, Evdokimov declared the war over and held a victory parade. In 1869, the place was settled by Russians and named Krasnaya Polyana. Some of the first inhabitants came from Estonia and the name of another resort reflects this connection.

These expulsions, along with the actions of the Russian military in acquiring Circassian land, have given rise to a movement among descendants of the expelled ethnicities for international recognition that genocide was perpetrated. Some sources state that hundreds of thousands of others died during the exodus. Several historians use the term 'Circassian massacres' for the consequences of Russian actions in the region.

Circassian historians cite casualty figures that lie near the four million mark, whilst official Russian figures are only 300,000. The Russian census of 1897 records only 150,000 Circassians, a fraction of the original number, still remaining in the now-conquered region. In reference to the actions of the Russian army during the conflict, Russian President Boris Yeltsin stated in May 1994 that resistance to the tsarist forces was legitimate. However, he did not recognise 'the guilt of the tsarist government for the genocide'.

Circassians have attempted to attract global media attention to the Circassian Genocide and its relation to the city of Sochi where the Olympics were held in 2014, on the official anniversary of the genocide by holding mass protests in Vancouver, Istanbul and in New York during the 2010 Vancouver Winter Olympics.

In October 2006, Circassian organisations of many countries in North America, Europe and the Middle East sent a letter to the president of the European Parliament requesting recognition of the genocide. On 20th March 2010, a Circassian Genocide Congress was held in Tbilisi, Georgia. The congress passed a resolution, urging Georgia to recognise the Circassian Genocide.

Some sources state that three million Circassians were evicted from Circassia in a period lasting until 1911. Other sources cite upwards of two million Circassian refugees fleeing Circassia by 1914 and entering nations and regions such as the Balkans, Turkey, what was the Ottoman Empire in what was known as the Muhajir, Iran, Syria, Lebanon, what is now Jordan, Kosovo, and Egypt. There is a link with Egypt as Circassians had been recruited as part of the Mamluk armies since the Middle Ages. Some also went to Palestine, now Israel in the villages of Kfar Kama and Rikhaniya, since 1880 and as far afield as upstate New York and New Jersey.

Some 90% of people of Circassian descent now live in other countries, primarily in Turkey, with only a few hundred thousand remaining in what is now

Russia. The depopulated Circassian lands were resettled by numerous ethnic groups, including Russians, Ukrainians and Georgians. Friction developed between the latter group and the remaining indigenous people in Abkhazia, a factor that later contributed to friction between the two ethnic groups and the resulting war in Abkhazia.

By 1864, during the reign of Tsar Alexander II, the Russian conquest of the Northwestern Caucasus was being consolidated. Other tribes such as the Abkhaz were decimated, and the Abaza had largely been driven out of the Caucasus.

Faced with the threat of subjugation by the Russian army, the Ubykh looked for a solution. The Ottoman Empire offered to harbour the Circassians who did not wish to accept the rule of a Christian monarch, and many emigrated to Anatolia, the heart of the Ottoman territory. Various Russian, Caucasus, and Western historians agree on the figure of circa 500,000 inhabitants of the highland Caucasus being deported by Russia in the 1860s. A large proportion of them died in transit from disease or attacks by the Russian army on the stragglers and the rearguard of the Ubykh irregular fighters.

The Ubykhs as well as other Muslim peoples of Caucasus, left their homeland én masse beginning on 6th March 1864. By 21st May, the vast majority of the Ubykh nation had departed from the Caucasus. They initially settled in a number of villages in western Turkey around the municipality of Manyas but later spread throughout the Middle East.

Today, the Ubykh diaspora has been scattered about Turkey and to a much lesser extent, Jordan. The Ubykh nation per se no longer exists, although those who are of Ubykh ancestry are proud to call themselves Ubykh, and a few villages are still found in Turkey where the vast majority of the population is Ubykh by descent.

In order to avoid discrimination, the Ubykh elders encouraged their people to assimilate into Turkish culture. Having abandoned their traditional nomadic culture, they became a nation of farmers. The Ubykh language and other Circassian dialects were rapidly displaced by Turkish and the last native speaker of Ubykh, Tevfik Esenç, died in 1992.

Chapter 18
Sochi

I took one of the ski lifts with Svetlana up to the top of the mountain, changing at the halfway station. The winter was finishing but summer hadn't arrived. At these altitudes, there can be extremes of weather in early spring. The trees were bare, the bushes void of leaves and where the grass wasn't covered by snow, it was faded and had not yet got the warmth of the spring sunshine to turn green and sprout new growth.

The mountains here form part of the Caucasus National Park which is the largest and oldest specially protected natural area in the Caucasus, having been created in 1924 as the Caucasian Bison Reserve. In 1979, the site was named a UNESCO Biosphere Reserve, and in 1999 included as a UNESCO World Heritage Site. In 2008, it was officially renamed after Khachatur (Christopher) G. Shaposhnikova, the biologist who founded the reserve. The area is situated in the Mostovsky District of Krasnodar Krai, covering an area of 280,335 hectares. It is bounded on the south by Sochi National Park and the ridge of the Caucasus running along the Georgia-Abkhazia border.

Altitudes range from 260 metres to 3,360 metres. The plant life of the reserve is characterised by high biodiversity, reflecting the position of the site at the meeting point of several different zones such as temperate and sub-tropical and with a wide range of altitude zones from forested river valleys to mountaintop tundra. The reserve has recorded 1,500 species of plants, of which 20% are endemic to the Caucasus. Most of the territory is forested, with sub-alpine and alpine meadows at the higher elevations. The coniferous yew trees in the Khosta sector can reach an age of over 2,000 years. The typical trees of the lower elevations are oak and alder. The upper forest levels are typically fir and spruce.

The animal life of the reserve is noteworthy for the large number of species, particularly of large mammals. Scientists on the reserve have recorded 89 species of mammals, 15 species of reptiles, 9 of amphibians, 21 of fish, over 100 species of molluscs and more than 10,000 species of insects. Bird life is also prolific, with 248 species of birds, including 112 that nest within the borders of the Caucasus reserve.

As a strict nature reserve, the Caucasus reserve is mostly closed to the general public, although scientists and those with 'environmental educational' purposes can make arrangements with park management for visits. There are several 'ecotourist' routes in the reserve that are open to the public but require permits to be obtained in advance.

For pedestrians, the top of the summit was cold, windswept and not inviting. There are meant to be good views but there was low cloud and little to see. The halfway station was at about base cloud level so there were some views but continually obscured by low clouds blowing past but by the time I got to the top station, it was continual cloud.

I wasn't in ski gear, not that there was enough snow to ski but without the insulation and protection of some serious winter clothing, just after a short while, I was heading back into the warmth and comfort of the restaurant at the top station for a coffee to warm up before descending.

Next, it was just a short drive back down the road to see a small spring. The water comes out of the mountain but its mineral composition includes arsenic, boron and lithium. I was initially put off trying it but I was assured that the amounts were miniscule. It wasn't on the itinerary but I wanted to go and have a look. Max drove in and despite a large car park, there was no one else there. It is only a modest entry fee, so most tourist coaches stop here. I had said that I only wanted to be poisoned if I didn't have to queue so since there weren't any other visitors, I got to drink poison.

Funnily, and against expectation, it was a pleasant taste and I filled my empty plastic water bottle before heading off to a local restaurant. It was built like a castle but behind the stone facade, it was all neat reinforced concrete. There was a public area, several different-sized private dining rooms and a function room.

Lunch consisted of several local dishes. Svetlana translated the menu and whenever it said that it was a traditional local delicacy, then that was what I was going to have. Therefore I had, lavash, trout in pastry, salad and kompost, which is a drink made from crushed fruit sometimes with added sugar, feijoa, also called pineapple guava and khachapuri. Khachapuri is a traditional Georgian dish of cheese-filled flatbread. The bread is leavened and allowed to rise and in the middle, there is the filling which contains cheese and eggs. The edge or crust of the bread is torn off and used to dip into the filling.

Then it was a climb back towards the mountains to visit the Sky Park. This is the original sky-high adventure park for bungy jumping and is situated in the picturesque Ahshtyrskaya Valley and high across the road to Krasnaya Polyana. On site, you can find one of the longest suspended pedestrian bridges in the world at 439 metres long and 207 metres high and includes adventure activities from AJ Hackett Bungy International named after Alan John Hackett, a New Zealand entrepreneur who popularised the extreme sport of bungy jumping after he jumped from the Eiffel Tower in 1987 and founded the first commercial bungy site in 1988.

On offer is a drop of 207 metres a shorter 69-metre drop or a giant swing, dropping 170 metres. There is also a high zip-wire dive across the valley. At 439 metres it is the sixth longest pedestrian footbridge in the world after the number one being at Wanjiazhai Dam, China at 500 metres. But the second and third longest are not far behind Charles Kunonen, Switzerland at 494 metres and the Kushma Bungy, Nepal at 490 metres.

There are also ancillary adventures which may be more attractive to the less foolhardy or brave, whichever end of the scale you prefer to call yourself but after you have done some of the big drops on a bungy, some of these will look rather a second rate or at least unappealing and unchallenging such as the Rope Adventure Park and Via Ferrata.

You can see some stunning panoramic views of the Caucasus Mountains and the Black Sea coast in the distance. From the rides atop the valley rim or from the central dip in the pedestrian bridge, there is a clear view of the Adler Fish Farm at the bottom of the valley below.

I love to eat fish and it was too good an opportunity to miss. I was taken around the farm and had everything explained. The farm covers 82 hectares, the first basin contained 4-year-old trout that were bigger than my forearm. They were the usual grey colour but there were also plenty of golden fish plus blue and white fish. They are called rainbow trout as they come in several different colours. They are predators and when you throw feed into the basin, they rive and thrash about to get the pellets.

This farm specialises in the standard grey-backed trout and golden trout. The golden trout tastes better, have less of a strong fish taste and have softer flesh, so commands a higher price. On the other hand, the blue and white adults are very unusual but they are infertile and cannot produce offspring. They are also not sold commercially. Only one in 10,000 eggs produce a white or blue fish so they are rare and they are kept as a tourist attraction as they are so interesting to see. They also breed beluga and sturgeon fish for their roe to make into caviar. Larger ponds downstream hold fish for anglers to catch.

Max met me at reception with Svetlana for a tour of the city. Max dropped us off outside the Sochi railway station. The site for the construction of the railway terminal was defined in 1913, next to the fairgrounds in front of the city cemetery which is now the Zavokzalny memorial complex.

The present railway station was designed by Alexey Dushkin. It was constructed between 1950 and 1952. Its architectural style is a mixture of classical and Communist. It is built of carved limestone polished marble and granite. The building is 145 metres long, up to 50 metres wide and the clock tower is 55 metres tall and features a clock of five metres diameter.

The clock face is a representation of the signs of the zodiac. However, on closer inspection, they are not in the correct order and he arbitrarily replaced some of the correct symbols with others such as a snake and a swan for an inexplicable reason and no one dared to question the decision. He reused the same plans to build a copycat station in Simferopol in 1951.

Much of the building is classical but under the frieze, there is a Soviet-style worker carved into the wall and there is the red star and the hammer and sickle symbols. After Stalin's death, he was much criticised for the cost of the project.

Opposite the railway station is the main shopping street running down to the port. Shade is provided by many trees including a long line of palm trees which is a sight that I never thought I would see in Russia as these are tropical and sub-tropical plants and I associated the country with cold, snow and ice. Just to the right of the main thoroughfare is a hill overlooking the harbour where the first fortress, originally made of wood but later replaced with stone was built in 1838 and garrisoned by the Navginsky regiment.

When the Ottoman supported by French and British troops attacked the Crimea, in 1854, the regiment was posted to the Crimea but before they left they demolished the fortress to stop it from being used by the Ottomans should they attack the area. Only one short section of the low wall remains.

In 1898, the Orthodox cathedral dedicated to the Archangel St Michael was built on the top of the hill, re-using some of the stone from the fortress. It is an ornate typical-style Russian church with domes and although new, it was built in the traditional style.

Down in the port is the main passenger terminal, a giant building topped with a red star on a tall spire standing on top of a stepped tower. Around the tops of the steps of the main tower are the statues of four seasons, 12 dolphins and several traditionally dressed representatives of nations from throughout the Russian empire to welcome all nations, neatly sidestepping the issue of the Circassian Genocide.

In front of the main building on the landward side, there is an ornamental fountain on a plinth supported by more dolphins depicting the goddess of navigation holding a ship and a map in one hand with the right hand outstretched, palm down to calm the waves.

Just a 15-minute walk along the promenade is the winter theatre with its tall broad colonnades and opposite it, the Pearl Hotel, which did a roaring trade in providing accommodation to visiting artists. It was called the winter theatre to distinguish it from the summer theatre which had a roof but no walls although walls have now been added and it can be used all year round.

A little way along the coast and setback, high up in the mountains, is one of several dachas throughout the country that were for the use of the senior party figures but dubbed Stalin's dacha. This building was formerly owned by a wealthy merchant although it has been extended. It is not a big property, but it does have most of the required facilities. There is an indoor swimming pool, a large dining room to entertain guests, a study that doubles as a cinema and a billiards room. Apparently, Stalin wasn't very good at billiards but he often played with one of his security detail who whether he was good or not, probably thought it was worth his while to let his boss win more times than he did.

Then it was time to start our journey up the coast. The next stop on the itinerary was the town of Dagomys, just 12 kilometres up the coast from Sochi. It is known for its resorts, hotels and tea plantations. It was developed as a resort before the Russian Revolution when a botanical garden was founded by the order of Tsar Nicholas II. The word 'Dagomys' is literally translated from Adyghe language as a cool, shady place. A modern hotel complex was opened there in 1982.

Adjacent to Dagomys is the Bocharov Ruchey, a dacha built in the 1950s for Kliment Voroshilov who was a prominent Soviet military officer and politician during the Stalin era. He was one of the original five Marshals of the Soviet Union, the highest military rank of the Soviet Union, along with Chief of the General Staff of the Red Army, Alexander Yegorov, and three senior commanders, Vasily Blyukher, Semyon Budyonny, and Mikhail Tukhachevsky. After his death in 1969, the dacha was upgraded into the summer country residence of the President of Russia, where he normally spends his vacations and confers with leaders of other states.

During the Circassian Wars, a military outpost was built here and a village sprung up around it, settled by many retired soldiers. By the start of the 20th century, there were about 300 people living here. They were joined in later years by Armenians fleeing the Armenian Genocide and Orthodox Christians, fleeing Ottoman repression.

The most valuable land near the sea was purchased by government officials, ministers, prominent landowners and bankers. A plot of 2,500 hectares and a cattle breeding farm at the mouth of the river Dagomys was owned by Tsar Nicholas II of Russia. This royal settlement was managed by Prince Uspensky. The farm was profitable as it was selling part of its production at the market of Sochi, and the citizens considered it an honour to buy the tsar's produce.

Some settlers attempted to grow tea, which was then an expensive item yet the most popular non-alcoholic beverage in Russia. The early attempts in the 1870s and 1880s failed because of the cold winters, and the first successes were only achieved in the early 1900s by the Ukrainian farmer Judas Antonovich Koshman (1838–1935). Koshman previously worked for a tea factory in Adjara, a town south of Sochi on the Black Sea coast. That tea was known in Russia but its taste was unpopular.

In 1901, Koshman brought seeds of tea plants from Adjara to Solokhaul, a village near Dagomys and developed a brand which was not only resistant to cold but also had a rich taste. The first successful plantation is dated to 1905. This new tea later became the distinct brand of Krasnodarsky Tea, which is the most prominent Russian-grown tea and is the northernmost-grown tea in the world. Koshman's house still stands in Solokhaul along with the tea bushes planted with his own hands.

In 1930, an intensive development of resorts was started in Sochi and along the coast. In Dagomys, there were two tourist camps and several small sanatoriums. Prominent buildings appeared there only in the 1970s when the Yugoslav firm 'Mavrovo' built two hotels, 'Dagomys' and 'Olympic'. These hotels soon became popular tourist destinations and the location for conferences, such as the 38th Pugwash Conference on Science and World Affairs led by Andrei Sakharov.

The 27-storey recreational complex seen today is the most prominent building in Dagomys and was built in 1982. It then belonged to the Intourist travel agency and thus was restricted to foreign visitors. With the dissolution of the Soviet Union in the 1990s, the complex became empty. The complex can accommodate up to two thousand guests and up to ten parallel events and has a staff of 1,600. It was expanded in preparation for the 2014 Winter Olympic Games. We left Dagomys behind and climbed into the hills around tight turns and up steep gradients.

Set high on the crest of a ridge overlooking the town and the seashore far below is the tea house that we were going to visit. Had I been asked, I would have happily passed it by and gone on to the next item on the schedule as I am not a tea drinker and I had no idea what to expect but I was so glad that I didn't pass it by.

The car park is set some way back along the track that leads to the tea house so that you have to leave the car and walk through some forest before reaching the tea house itself.

The premises are quite large, two storeys high but with rooms off a large central hall complete with a gallery and a large balcony area overlooking the coast. It was built by a father and his two sons who considering the size of the building must have worked very long and hard or had a lot of help.

The whole building is made of wood, large rounds of timber for the walls, rough planed wood for floors and ceilings and allegedly using no nails. I had a tour of the building before reaching the balcony where the table was set for tea with a choice of two types of tea, two types of bread, honey, several types of jam and as much hot water as you want from the large samovar sitting on another table.

But that wasn't all as I was also going to have a musical recital. This had been laid on especially for me but the other guests benefitted from the display. There was just one musician but had an array of musical instruments, largely wind but with a few percussion instruments and a balalaika. He was playing the harmonium as we walked in and settled down for our tea.

He then explained the development of each type of instrument and played a few tunes on each. He took us through some of the history of the development of music from simple wind instruments of two notes and penny whistles to more sophisticated flutes and clarinets. With the help of a backing tape, he used all the instruments to play several popular traditional tunes and finished with the balalaika.

A few more instruments were handed out for some audience participation, doing a few simple dance moves and playing some of the instruments. I thoroughly enjoyed the experience which was so much more than I would have anticipated. I also had an interest in musical instruments as one of my brothers used to collect stringed musical instruments and I learnt how to play them all.

On the walk along the ridge back to the car park, we took a diversion through some of the trees to see one of the tea gardens. There were a few holes in the rows of bushes and having visited tea gardens in Turkey, India and Kenya, these bushes didn't look like they were in the best of health and needed some attention.

After tea, it was time to move along the coast. I said goodbye to Svetlana and she got off next to a bus stop to get home to Sochi. Then Max set out on the long drive of 147 kilometres from Dogamys to Gelendzhik.

Chapter 19
Hero City Novorossiysk

We travelled along the only road out of Sochi. We passed through several other towns along the coast that I had passed through a few days earlier on my overnight coach trip to get to Sochi. It was a busy road that went through mountains with steep gradients, hairpin bends and a lot of slow traffic made slower by road works and accidents.

We stopped at a garage and I bought a Kvass and a Baikal which is a Soviet-era imitation of Coca-Cola. We passed through Tuapse. It didn't matter whether you had the window up or down as the smell of petroleum permeated everything. The Soviets developed Tuapse as an oil terminal and depot. An oil pipeline from Grozny via Maykop was in operation by 1928, designed by Vladimir Shukhov and an oil refinery was built here at the same time.

Tuapse was originally a Greek colony known by the name of both Topsida and later as Nicopsis. It was integrated into the kingdom of Abkhazia and subsequently into the kingdom of Georgia in the eleventh century. With the chaos of the sixteenth century, Georgia lost Nicopsia to the Circassians. The name of the town in Adyghe literally means 'two waters'.

The area became part of the Russian empire in 1829 during the rule of Tsar Alexander II under the terms of the Treaty of Adrianople that concluded the Russo-Turkish War of 1828–29. The current settlement dates from 1838, when the Russians built the fort of Velyaminovsky. During the Crimean War, the Ottomans seized the fort and held it for 2 years 1857–59. The village of Velyaminovskoye was established here in 1864 and it had grown into Tuapse and became a town in 1896.

It was more than another 2 hours of driving to get to Gelendzhik. We stopped for 20 minutes short of the city to view the Sail Rock on the shore of the Black Sea. It is 25 metres tall and 20 metres wide but only one metre thick, an unusual vertical slab of sandstone rock. The unique nature of the rock is enhanced by a square hole towards the landward side of the slab.

We reached Gelendzhik, a small town located on a bay just along the coast. In antiquity, the Gelendzhik Bay was the site of a minor Greek outpost, mentioned as Torikos in the Periplus of Pseudo-Scylax. It was later abandoned but reappeared in Roman records under the name of Pagrae in 64 BC although this settlement was wiped out by the invading Huns.

The bay and its sheltered harbour were a pull and later during the Middle Ages, the bay was of some mercantile importance to the Genoese traders who referred to the settlement as Maurolaca.

Before Russia secured the coast by the Treaty of Adrianople, there was a brisk slave trade carried on between the local settlers and the Ottoman Empire. Since the Circassian beauties were usually traded for gold and other valuable commodities before being taken to Turkish seraglios, the marketplace became known as Gelendzhik from the Turkish 'gelincik', meaning literally, 'little bride'. In 1831, one of the first forts of the Black Sea Coastal Line to secure the new lands for the Russian empire was set up at Gelendzhik.

At the outbreak of the Crimean War, the fort was blown up and abandoned, but it was resettled by Cossacks in 1864, at the conclusion of the Russian-Circassian War, and became known as the stanitsa of Gelendzhiksaya.

During the Soviet period, Gelendzhik was developed as a spa town. It possessed sandy beaches and today has three waterparks, two aerial tramway lines which rise from the shore up to the cliffs overlooking the bay and two Orthodox churches dating from 1909 and 1913. The environs of Gelendzhik are noted for a chain of waterfalls, several dolmens and ancient pine and juniper groves.

The city is known for its annual hydroaviasalon held here since 1996. Hydroaviasalon or its correct name, the International Exhibition and Scientific Conference on Hydroaviation is an international airshow on hydroaviation. It has been held every even year since 1996 and the event alternates with the MAKS Airshow on general aviation, which is held in odd years.

The air show draws special attention to amphibious aircraft and seaplanes, ship-based aircraft, fire-fighting aviation, missiles and sea-based space systems, search-and-rescue aviation, sea ecological monitoring aviation, navigation equipment, small ships, launches and yachts.

We passed the turn-off to the coastal village of Arkhipo-Osipovka. This is where the Blue Stream gas pipeline leaves Russia and crosses the Black Sea at times up to 2.2 kilometres deep to deliver gas supplies from Russia to Turkey and avoid crossing third countries. It is a joint venture between Russian Gazprom and Italian Eni. The Turkish land section is owned and operated by the Turkish energy company BOTAŞ. The pipeline is 1,213 kilometres long and delivers up to 16 billion cubic metres per year to Ankara.

We stopped at a particularly well-recommended small café for an evening meal with a 4.8 score on Trip Advisor called U Diany. I ordered some soup, a shrimp Caesar salad and khachapuri. This khatchapuri was different from the one I had near Sochi a few days earlier as this was a pizza-style base, stuffed with cheese with more cheese melted on top. To wash it down, I ordered a homemade lemonade which when it was served incorporated a red liquid made from dogwood berries, served with a sprig of spearmint with some stoned cherries in the bottom. I queried the colour and additional ingredients and learnt that lemonade in Russia is not always made from lemons which do not grow in the country so other fruits are used but it is still called lemonade.

Max picked me up from my hotel and introduced me to my next local guide, Olga, and we headed off for the first stop of the day which was a trip back up the road towards Sochi but we would be going barely a handful of kilometres before we turned off to see some dolmens. These megalithic single chamber tombs comprise several vertical megaliths supporting a single slab for the roof. They date from around the Neolithic era, 4000–3000 BC. Sometimes they are covered with earth or smaller stones to form a tumulus. They are common throughout Europe.

We parked outside and Olga and I worked our way through the main visitor reception area which was a gravel-covered open space surrounded by covered wooden stalls. Only a few traders were open and the majority of the site looked abandoned but it was both early in the day and early in the season. After the main visitor area, it was a gentle walk up the valley lined with stunted trees, across a small stream and up a gravel track to see some dolmens.

There were several people camping there, despite the cold. These were believers who were in tune with the mystics of ancient times, the power of natural forces and lay lines. It is claimed that if you link up all the original sites of dolmens, they point west. Some of the dolmens here have been moved here from other sites to preserve them and make for a better visitor experience.

The first two were high-value dolmens of the late era, well carved, with small, round entrances chiselled into the rock, so small that I couldn't get my shoulders through but the people were smaller in those days. These dolmens together with the surrounding rocks had been transported here and carefully recreated so as to be as authentic as possible.

We wandered through the site and saw some more dolmens. There were others on site but they were a long walk away and we didn't have a lot of time. There was also a waterfall, but given the low water levels in the stream, I doubted that it would be very interesting so we went back to Max and he drove through Novorossiysk to Abrau Durso.

The area of Novorossiysk is one of Russia's main wine-growing regions. The wineries of Abrau Durso, established by Tsar Alexander II in 1870, produce table and sparkling wines for domestic consumption. It is one of the most famous wineries and its products are widely available throughout the country. The winery was established in 1870 by the decree of Tsar Alexander II to provide his court with local wines. Now, it not only produces sparkling wines, it also operates a hotel, spa, and restaurant. Abrau Durso is described as owning one of the best wine regions in Russia, with a majority shareholding owned by Boris Yurievich Titov, born 24th December 1960, a Russian politician, businessman, and Presidential Commissioner for Entrepreneurs' Rights. He has led the Party of Growth previously known as Just Cause.

The winery looks like a grand French champagne house transplanted to Russia. The buildings are located on the shores of Lake Abrau, a short distance west of Novorossiysk on Russia's Black Sea coast, in the Krasnodar Krai region. It was established in 1870 but it only produced its first wines in 1877. The wines were such a success that a large wine-making plant was built that was finished in 1891 and although expanded considerably since, the original buildings can still be seen today.

Prince Lev Golitsyn, an important figure in Russian wine, brought in a team of French specialists to help make sparkling wine, and by the turn of the 20th century, the newly dug underground tunnels were full of the Russian version of champagne. The tunnels were later expanded by the same company that excavated the tunnels for the London Underground Metropolitan Line.

The French assistance continued until the revolution in 1917 when they left, but the Russians they had trained carried on making sparkling wine, which until very recently was known as Sovetskoye Shampanskoye.

Now the winery is organised as a commercial operation named Abrau Durso, with shares held jointly by the government and a group of companies headed by successful businessman Boris Titov who since 2006, has owned a 58% share.

Recently Titov has been looking to expand by raising capital to increase production. The company floated on the stock exchange in April 2012, and some of the capital raised was used to develop a luxury hotel and spa facility on the site. Currently, there is a very attractive 40-room Imperial Hotel near the winery, offering campaign baths but the accommodation is not considered big enough and there are further expansion plans.

Dug into the hills behind the winery are some 5.5 kilometres of tunnels, with the potential for storing 10 million bottles. Annual production is now some 34 million bottles. There is both sparkling wine production using modern methods but there is still a significant high-end or collectable range that uses the traditional Champagne style but more labour-intensive methods of production.

I was waiting in the shade of the inner courtyard when Chris came over and introduced himself. I left Olga and Max sitting in the sun and had a personal tour of the facility by one of the English-speaking guides and everything was explained and my curious questions answered. Sometimes my question would be answered straight away and sometimes, I was advised that I would discover the answer later on the tour.

There is a lot of technical detail in making champagne, but broadly, standard wine is produced but the fizzy element is produced by a secondary fermentation. A little extra sugar and yeast is added to the wine and it is corked in a strong bottle. The yeast converts the sugar to alcohol and carbon dioxide, which can't escape and it is absorbed into the liquid. There are accidents as the measures may be wrong or particularly powerful yeasts may overreact with the sugars. Losses are often low, something over 3% but massive losses up to nearly half have occurred when the process has broken out of its normal parameters.

The filled bottle is stored and then rotated and turned upside down over weeks and the sediment from the fermentation collects at the neck of the bottle. The shoulder of the bottle is frozen and it forms a plug. The bottle is opened and a small amount of liquid and the sediment is removed whilst the frozen wine in the neck of the bottle holds the contents in. Some liquid from the same batch is added back to ensure that the bottle is 'full' and a proper cork and wire cover are added.

The process is not without hazards so the freshly corked bottle is left to stand for two weeks before shipment. Losses here again are minimal but explosions occur in individual bottles so it is best to be safe than sorry, hence the two-week delay before packing into boxes for dispatch.

I went through the area between the long-term storage and the labelling and dispatch area. There's an interesting mechanical system running through the tunnels for transporting bottles in metal cradles, upside down, four at a time from the storage areas to the area where the temporary 'cork' is removed, the sediment extracted, and some extra liquid from the same batch is added. This system dates back to the 1950s.

Bottles ready for labelling and sale are transported to the labelling plant. Firstly the dust of months that has collected on the outside is cleaned off. The bottles are sent through the labelling plant. Duds and broken bottles are removed and bottles with poor label alignment are pulled out, stripped of the poor label and returned to the start of the process.

This winery is quite a tourist draw and 150,000 visitors come here annually. Production currently stands at about 15% being made by the traditional Champagne method, the remainder is by modern methods. The company currently owns 560 hectares of vineyards. Only a few years ago there was a project to grow production to 30 million bottles but that had been exceeded easily by 2018 when production passed 34 million bottles.

The product range consists of a number of tiers. The cheapest wines, produced by modern methods, have a 16-day short second fermentation in pressure tanks. The next tier, what was until recently called Sovetskoye Shampanskoye, spends at least 26 days in the pressure tanks.

The rest of the range is traditional method Champagne-style wine. Some imported grapes are still used, but higher up in the range it is all Russian wine from Russian grapes. At the top of the tree is the Imperial group of three wines, which is where Hervé Jestin helps as a consultant. Hervé is renowned as one of the most talented oenologists in Champagne, having been Chef de Caves at Duval Leroy for 20 years and now acts as a consultant throughout the world and is considered to be one of the world's leading specialists in biodynamic sparkling wine-making.

After my tour of the winery, we headed back to Novorossiysk for a tour of the city. The city was granted the title Hero City Novorossiysk in May 1973. The first cities to receive the title due to their successful struggle in defeating the Nazi invaders during the Great Patriotic War were Leningrad, Stalingrad, Sevastopol and Odesa. Stalin made those awards on 1st May 1945. Later, other cities received the honour such as Murmansk, Moscow, Tula, Smolensk, Minsk, Kiev and Kersk.

The city of Novorossiysk lies on the eastern coast of the Black Sea and was a stronghold against the German summer offensive of 1942. Intense fighting in and around the city lasted from August until it was captured by the Germans in mid-September 1942. The Soviets however retained possession of the eastern part of the bay, which prevented the Germans from using the port for supply shipments. It is a major port on the Black Sea and the leading Russian port for exporting grain. Even in Greek and Roman times, it was important until the 11th century when it was overrun by nomads from the Eurasian steppes. In the 15th century, Genoese merchants from the Ghisolfi family maintained a trade outpost in the area. Archaeological investigation of related sites is in its infancy, but some interesting items have already been uncovered.

From 1722, the bay was controlled by an Ottoman fortress named Sujuk (also transliterated as Sudzhuk, Sudschuk and Soğucak). This name may be derived from Susaco and, as late as 1769, the area was sometimes named in European maps as Suzako.

The coastline was ceded to Russia in 1829 as a result of the Russo-Turkish War. After this, admirals Mikhail Lazarev and Nikolay Raevsky founded an eastern base for the Black Sea fleet on the shore in 1838. Named after the province of Novorossiya, the port formed a vital link in the chain of forts known as the Black Sea Coastal Line, which stretched south to Sochi.

During the rest of the 19th century, Novorossiysk developed rapidly. It was granted city status in 1866 and became the capital of the Black Sea Governorate, the smallest in the Russian empire, in 1896. In December 1905, the city was the seat of the short-lived Novorossiysk Republic. From 26th August 1918 until 27th March 1920, Novorossiysk was the principal centre of Denikin's White Army. Denikin's South Russian Government was moved to Crimea and many Whites escaped from Novorossiysk to Constantinople during the Evacuation of Novorossiysk in 1920 before it fell to the Red Army.

During the Great Patriotic War, most of the city was attacked by the German and Romanian Armies on 10th September 1942. A small unit of Soviet sailors defended one part of the town, known as Malaya Zemlya, for 225 days beginning on 4th February 1943. The city was finally liberated by the Red Army on 6th September 1943. The heroic defence of the port by the sailors allowed the Soviets to retain possession of the city's bay, which prevented the Axis Powers from using the port for supply shipments.

The front line has been left as it was at the end of the fighting. On this stretch of ground is a selection of restored period military vehicles, tanks and guns. By the seashore is a brutalist monument of concrete, an angled monolith with giant metal figures representing the soldiers and sailors that fought here. At the top of the site is a more modest monument with an inscription to commemorate the fallen in the revolution. Lenin had ordered the Black Sea fleet destroyed to stop it from falling into General von Denikin's hands during the civil war and so using it against the Bolsheviks but it had never recovered its former strength.

The communists have always created dramatic and eye-catching monuments. On the other side of the bay are two more monuments. One is a burnt-out railway wagon, to commemorate the railway workers who were so important in saving factories and delivering supplies. This ammunition wagon caught fire and the workers rescued most of the ammunition except a few boxes which ultimately exploded and blew out a few struts of the wagon car. On the other side of the road is the shell of a concrete factory with shell holes and bullet holes. In front of it is a plinth with a restored T34 tank on it.

In 1960, the town was commemorated in Dmitri Shostakovich's work Novorossiysk Chimes, the Flame of Eternal Glory (Opus 111b). In 2003, President Vladimir Putin signed a decree setting up a naval base for the Black Sea fleet in Novorossiysk. Russia had allocated 12.3 billion roubles (about USD480 million) for the construction of the new base between 2007 and 2012. The construction of other facilities and infrastructure at the base, including units for coastal troops, aviation and logistics, would continue beyond 2012.

The Russian lease on port facilities in Sevastopol, which, though the main base of Russia's Black Sea Fleet, is part of Ukraine, was set to expire in 2017. Ukraine was reported to be planning to not renew the lease. However, in April 2010 the Russian and Ukrainian presidents signed an agreement to extend the lease by 25 years, with an option of further extension of 5 years after the new term expires. However, in 2014, Crimea was annexed by the Russian Federation during the 2014 Crimean crisis and as such the question of renewing the lease does not immediately arise whilst Crimea remains de facto part of the territory of the Russian Federation.

The Novorossiysk Commercial Sea Port serves Russian sea trade with regions of Asia, the Middle East, Africa, the Mediterranean, and South America. It is the busiest oil port in the Black Sea and the terminus of the pipeline from the Tengiz Field, developed by the Caspian Pipeline Consortium. The Tengiz

Field is an oil field located in northwestern Kazakhstan's low-lying wetlands along the northeast shores of the Caspian Sea. It covers a 2,500 square kilometres project licence area which also includes the smaller Korolev field as well as several exploratory prospects.

Sizewise, the Tengiz reservoir is 19 kilometres wide and 21 kilometres long. Discovered in 1979, the oil field is one of the largest discoveries in recent history. The city of Atyrau, 350 kilometres north of Tengiz, is the main transport hub for Tengiz oil. Many nations are involved in a large geopolitical competition to secure access to this source of oil.

Tengiz is operated by Tengizchevroil, a 40-year partnership planning to produce billions of barrels of oil from the field. The Tengizchevroil consortium has developed the Tengiz Field since its founding in April 1993. The partners in Tengizchevroil are Chevron 50%, Exxon Mobil 25%, the Kazakhstan government through Kazakhstan Petroleum 20% and Lukoil 5%.

In 2001, the partners opened the USD2.7 billion, 1,505 kilometres Caspian Pipeline Consortium pipeline to export oil from Tengiz to the Black Sea port of Novorossiysk in Russia. The pipeline which was inaugurated in March 2001 and loaded its first tanker in October 2001 carried 600,000 barrels per day with planned output to increase to 700,000 barrels per day for 2010 and an eventual maximum output of 1.5 million barrels per day.

The Kashagan oilfield is located approximately 130 kilometres west of Tengiz and is the world's largest discovery in the last 30 years, and the area will be a major competitor with the 22 billion barrels of US oil reserves. Given that Kazakhstan has considerable reserves, it is considering building new export routes such as a Trans-Caspian Oil Pipeline through Azerbaijan, Georgia, Turkey or Iran to reduce dependence on Russia.

Novorossiysk is also an industrial city with an economy built on steel, food processing, and the production of metal goods and other manufactures. Extensive limestone quarries supply important cement factories in and around the city.

One of the tourist sights on offer is the Soviet-era light cruiser Mikhail Kutuzov. It was commissioned in 1954 and joined the Black Sea fleet in 1955. She was decommissioned and became a museum ship open to the public in 2002. There are guided tours around much of the ship and it was fascinating to wander along corridors and see the officer's mess, the bridge, the working insides of the ship and of course, the guns.

On the way out of the city back along the main coast road on a headland standing high above the road is the massive Soviet red granite Monument to the Sailors of the Revolution. There is a giant plinth with surrounding walls which could be described as having a passing resemblance to a submarine and its conning tower, and on top is a giant size statue of a sailor looking out across the bay.

Chapter 20
Russian Wineries

Max and Olga met me outside of my hotel and we set out on the road back through Novorossiysk and along the coast road towards the northeast tip of the Caucasus. Our next stop was due to be the Ethnographic Village Ataman. The far west portion of the Caucasus is called the Taman Peninsula and is a land where people have lived for thousands of years. The history of the Kuban Krai began here when the first Black Sea Cossacks crossed the Sea of Azoz and settled on the shores of the Caucasus more than 200 years ago.

The Cossacks were not a race but were a mixture of people from other areas. They were free peasants, largely from Ukraine but didn't want to be under the control of the early tsars and they migrated outside the control of the tsars to the Don Basin and the Caucasus. They prided themselves on their horsemanship skills and were regarded as fierce fighters and they often hired themselves out as mercenaries. It was a dangerous job but if you survived you would have been paid well and there was always a good chance of either promotion or further riches or at least some plunder.

Katherine the Great had a long-standing problem with expanding the rule of the tsars just as the Imperial urge to expand the empire became front of the stage and came up against the Cossacks who would happily work for the enemy if they were prepared to pay. However, her plan was to offer them the land which they had settled in return for obedience and protection from the Imperial forces which they accepted.

We passed through the city of Taman after which the peninsular on which it sits is named. At the end of the peninsular and visible from Taman is the Crimean Bridge. This is a pair of parallel bridges constructed by the Russian Federation to span the Strait of Kerch between the Taman Peninsula of Krasnodar Krai and the Kerch Peninsula of Crimea. The bridges are in parallel and provide four-lane road traffic and two rail lines. The rail bridge has a length of 18.1 kilometres, and it is the longest bridge in both Russia and Europe. The road bridge is 16.9

kilometres long. The longest single span is 227 metres with a 35 metres clearance for shipping and the bridge stands in up to 30 metres of water.

There is a tectonic fault running up the strait so the towers stand on top of piles driven up to 91 metres into the rock, some of them at an angle to provide support during an earthquake. Many unexploded bombs were found and several wrecks of aircraft were found during the clearance operations to allow the builders to start work. The greater portion of the length of the bridge is a long causeway on the Taman Peninsula side mostly running along the Tuzla Spit.

The bridge was christened the Crimean Bridge after an online vote in December 2017, whilst 'Kerch Bridge' and 'Reunification Bridge' were the second and third most popular choices. The road bridge was opened in October 2018 but the railway bridge opening was delayed beyond its scheduled December 2019 opening.

The first bridge was considered by the British as a railway link to India in 1870 but was considered too expensive. Tsar Nicholas II considered a rail link in 1903 but the Russo-Japanese War of 1904 and later the First World War distracted attention from progressing the project. During the Great Patriotic War, the Nazis built a cableway across the strait and later a combined road and rail bridge. When the fortunes of war turned against the Nazis and the Red Army turned the tides of war at Stalingrad and went onto the offensive, the Nazis retreated and blew up the completed sections of the bridge in September 1943. The Russian Red Army liberated Crimea and used the materials left behind by the Nazis to build a bridge but this was washed away by floating ice the next winter.

An agreement between Russia and Ukraine was signed in 2010 to build a bridge. However, the annexation of Crimea in March 2014 side-lined the agreement and in January 2015, the contract for the construction of the bridge was awarded to the SGM (Stroygazmontazh) Group, whose owner Arkady Rotenberg is reportedly a close personal friend of Putin. Sanctions were imposed in response to the Russian military involvement in Ukraine. SGM typically constructs pipelines and had no experience building bridges but the project went ahead and was underwritten by a small Crimean insurance company.

Some way between the start of the bridge and Taman is the tourist attraction of the Cossack village of Ataman where you can learn about their way of life in times gone by. There are several shades and at least one from each different area of Krasnodar Krai. My guide didn't use the Russian word for house, 'dom' but 'hada'. Just like 'dacha', English doesn't have a single word for this sort of dwelling, but it is typically old, small as in cramped, run-down with age and rural something like a farm labourer's cottage of just two rooms. It can also be used as a derogatory term such as when someone has built a large and modern but ugly house, and you might say that 'He has a nice hada'.

There are several cottages all furnished as they would have been used as dwellings with beds, chests for clothes, spinning wheels and traditional ovens in the kitchen area. There are also outbuildings, barns and cellars, not built under the house but underground in the garden with a door and steps leading down to the storage area.

Various trades that would have been found in a village are represented such as saddlery, shoemaking, a barber and the blacksmith with all the necessary tools on show. Staff were dressed in period costumes and the forge was hot with the blacksmith making horseshoes. One of the members of staff was making charcoal and using the smoke to smoke fish and cheese which he let me try.

The village Ataman or headman's house was near the school but to me, it looked indistinguishable from the other buildings. There was a school, a lookout tower used in times of trouble and curiously, a tower with a clock at the top and a bell at the bottom, rung on the hour. I could have stayed all day but we were pushed for time as it was a long drive to reach here and we had a winery to visit.

We moved on to Sennoy, a little further up the coast to visit the Fanagoria winery. The name comes from the ancient Greek settlement of Phanagoria, founded here on the Black Sea coast in 542 BC. Until around 200 BC, Phanagoria was a major trade centre, and there is ample archaeological evidence of wine-making occurring during this time. Much later, there was a revival of wine-making in this region during the 19th century, and by the beginning of the 20th Century, Kuban, the old name for the Krasnodar region, became one of the key Russian wine-growing areas.

Fanagoria is now one of Russia's largest wine producers, and makes a wide range of wines, sparkling wines and brandies. They produce 25 million bottles of wine a year, as well as tetrapak and bag-in-box products. This year they also launched their own cooperage. "Big wineries are supposed not to make good wine," says marketing director Vladimyr Pukish, "but we do our utmost to prove that this is wrong, but it is much more difficult to make a good wine in a big winery."

Fanagoria is currently aiming to improve the quality and quantity of its wines by expanding its vineyard holdings. Six years ago they had 900 hectares of vineyard, but now this has risen to 2,500 hectares. They still make some low-end wines that are not made exclusively from Russian grapes but are moving away from this practice. The wines that I tasted here were all from Russian grapes.

Fanagoria's history is quite interesting. It was founded in 1957 for grape juice production. The natural grape juice was chilled, pasteurised and bottled here. Their natural grape juices featured heavily in the 1980 Olympics, held in Russia.

In 1990, things all changed. The facility decided to stop making juice and start making wine and a bit of vodka and cognac too. They got the licence to sell cognac in 2006, and are currently they are the third-largest cognac producer in Russia.

The latitude here is 45 North, and it's quite risky for wine production because of the winters. Once every 3–7 years temperatures will drop to -30 °C, and not every year is guaranteed to give a good crop. John Worontschak, an Australian-born winemaker who has worked throughout the world improving production and is an important influence in the English wine production business has worked here as a consultant winemaker. I visited the vineyards and the cooperage with the Fanagoria team and then toured the extensive winery, followed by a tasting. This tasting here was restricted to the two higher-level labels, NR and Cru Lermont. Both were great to taste but it was time to move on.

We had a long transfer by car to Slavyansk na Kubani. Max usually takes his guests to Krasnadar but I had already been there so I had changed the itinerary and arbitrarily opted for the small market town of Slavyansk na Kubani.

Slavyansk originated in the Middle Ages as Copa or Coparia, a Genoese trade outpost controlled by the Ghisolfi family. After the fading of Genoese power, the site was abandoned until 1747 when the Crimean Khanate erected a small fort, known in Russian sources as Kopyl.

After the conquest of the Taman Peninsula by the Russian empire, the Tatar fort was occupied by General Suvorov to defend the southern borders of Russia. In 1865, it was renamed after the Slavyansky regiment that had been quartered there under Katherine the Great. In 1958, it was renamed Slavyansk na Kubani in order to distinguish it from the eponymous city of the same name in Ukraine. During the Second World War, this town was occupied by the Germans from 1942 until it was liberated by the Red Army in 1943.

I had a four-star hotel overlooking the river so on paper it seemed quite good but the reality was very different. If I were to rate it on TripAdvisor, I would give it a zero. I was the only guest for the two nights that I was there. I had to let the water run for 10 minutes before it became warm. There was no internet in the hotel, only in the café next door which was part of the hotel but only accessed by venturing outside into the rain and cold and only opened at lunchtime. There were only Russian-language TV channels so the internet would have been a lifeline but what four-star hotel doesn't have internet?

The front of house staff when I arrived only spoke Russian and what I think was Polish so although I signed in alright in Russian, my knowledge and vocabulary weren't good enough for some of the other difficulties so they found a kitchen porter who spoke enough English to assist and explain about the internet.

The hotel was built next to the river but sideways so none of the rooms had a view across the river. The local teenagers gathered in the car park behind the hotel with their car radio ghetto blasters turned up to maximum volume as background music as they demonstrated doughnuts to their screeching and giggling girlfriends for what seemed like most of the night, but never in one go. There would be a series of screeching tyres and the smell of rubber drifting up to the bedrooms and then they would go away to annoy another neighbourhood for a while before coming back and giving it another go just outside my window.

And it was expensive yet there was no complimentary coffee in the rooms nor even a kettle just in case you had your own supply of tea or coffee. Another little niggling issue was that there was no bedside light and no light switches next to the bed so I had to feel my way around the room in the dark, banging my shins or stubbing my toes on furniture.

In the mornings, I had breakfast by myself in a cavernous dining room. It was a huge function room with a dance floor, glitter ball and stage at one end and a dozen circular tables each with seating for ten and space to erect more tables. It was just a bit intimidating to eat by myself in an echoing hall whilst the waitress pretended to be busy but was on hand in case I needed anything.

Although the town is a small market town with little to add to the history of the country, it does have its own charms. Near the hotel is the Monument to Taman participant's march of the Red Army. It has an inscription near the base of a tall obelisk. On each side are a pair of cannons pointing outwards. In front of it is an eternal flame, a burner with burn marks around the edge of the hole but oddly, it was not lit and the whole edifice was surrounded by builders' metal mesh fencing. Given its location next to the doughnut-driving teenager's car park, I guess that it was too often a scene of less reverence than should have been shown to the monument.

Even this small town of less than 70,000 people in the middle of nowhere had an eternal flame in a park next to the main road where it crosses the river. There were 16 panels with the names of those from the town who had died during the war, and each panel had 200 names engraved so there was a significant loss of life for this small community. Many were men but there was also a significant proportion of women. Even today there is a great gender imbalance as the country's population has 79 million females but only 68 million males.

Some of the street furniture included outlines of a piano, a cello and a gift-wrapped box, all made of metal wire and draped with white fairy lights and lit up at night. There is a large green space near the centre with a lake. Overlooking the lake is a large hotel and in the summer there is a large fountain in the lake. However, the fountain is removed at the end of the summer and put into storage so that it isn't damaged by the freezing winter. And to continue the theme, there is a model of a sailing ship made from metal wire and it too is draped with white fairy lights and lit up at night. And for some unknown reason, there is a life-sized model of a crocodile lurking in the reeds nearby.

There might not be a Kremlin but the town does have an interesting church complete with golden domes known as the Dormition Cathedral. Behind it is a large graveyard which I spent some time wandering through looking at the funeral architecture.

Whilst I was staying in Slavyansk na Kubani, Max drove me out to the Lefkadia Valley winery. This is a modern, purpose-built winery with recently planted vines, but mature enough to produce good grapes but without the history of the Abrau Durso Winery. The logo of the winery is half the face of Adonis in white and half the face of a centaur on the right in brown, to represent the pleasure of drinking and of overindulgence.

Lefkadia is a proud producer of premium quality wines produced from grapes harvested in the Lefkadia Valley. The area has some clay soils with traces of marl and everything is harvested by hand. In contrast, the winery has state-of-the-art equipment and gravity-flow technology, carefully handled ageing casks and an unreserved aspiration to produce wines that fully express the terroir's unique aspects.

They are proud of their association with the world-class grandmaster of wine-making, Patrick Léon, one of the most experienced and admired vignerons, a renowned oenology consultant who has worked side by side with such 20th-century viticulturists as Baron Philippe de Rothschild, Alexis Lichine and Robert Mondavi. From the day Lefkadia Valley Wine Estate was established, Patrick was investing his expertise into the wines.

Annual production is two million bottles. It sounds a lot but compared with the 34 million that Abrau Dorso produce, it is small. But the advantage is that all the grapes grown locally can be transferred to the winery in under 15 minutes meaning that the grapes can be processed before any oxidation can occur between harvesting and the start of the wine-making process.

Wine makers usually decide when to pick using their judgement but here, there is a large laboratory that takes the juice from one hundred grapes and runs various tests on the juice. Then in conjunction with the wine makers, they collectively decide when to harvest.

The grapes are crushed to extract the juice and either the skins are left in the mixture for red wine or removed if the final product is to be a white wine. Several different types of grapes are grown and more than ten types of wine are produced. The juice is fermented in enclosed steel vats that are the size of a pallet. The temperature is carefully controlled with red wines fermented at a slightly higher temperature.

After fermentation, the traditional process of storing in oak barrels is used. Brand new barrels are used but not more than three times before they are sold for a fifth of the original price to cognac producers. The wine isn't bottled on this site but is transported to their sister winery just down the road.

They also do quite a bit of experimentation and research. They ferment some batches in Georgian qvaris, some held in frames above ground and some in qvaris buried in the ground in the traditional Georgian manner with just their tops above the level of the ground. In another room were several egg-shaped vats made from concrete each standing in its own steel frame. These are so heavy that they were made on site and the rest of the building was erected around them.

There was also a pair of novel vats made of steel with ten sides, each a pentagon, welded together. The guide said ten-sided but with the top and bottom, there are in fact 12 sides. The winemaker and wine taster said that this was the ideal shape and produced a better wine than the control batch made in their usual manner.

Then it was the most important part of any tour of a winery, the tasting room. I had the opportunity to taste five wines, a Riesling, a rose, two reds and a premium red, accompanied by five cheeses. The Riesling was completely different to the north European Rieslings with more body due to the climate and local soil conditions. The premium red was great and a lot better than the average plonk from a supermarket, but it had been left open for too long and it had passed its best.

The next day Max drove me back towards the Crimea Bridge. En route, we passed through several road works where the road to Crimea is being upgraded. When Russia annexed Crimea from Ukraine, Crimea could only be reached by ferry from the Russian mainland, hence the need for a fixed link. The Russian motorway network does not yet reach Crimea but it is under construction. Similarly, the rail network is not connected and a new double line is being built through the Taman peninsular, across the Straits of Kerch and will be connected to the rail network in Crimea.

Other problems arose as Crimea's electrical system had to be connected to the main Russian network and there were power shortages until the connections were sufficient to provide enough power. Wages had been lower in Crimea when it had been part of Ukraine. When it was annexed, civil servants, soldiers, police and anyone employed by the state got pay rises to bring them into line with Russian levels. However, prices are higher in Russia so prices went up and non-state employees suffered from inflation but their wages did not increase.

The majority of the Crimean population is ethnically Russian and Russian speaking and felt that they were welcomed back. However, the individual's view of annexation depends on where the individual is on the economic spectrum. There are other costs associated with changing road signs and street names, reprinting maps and changing Ukrainian signs to Russian. A different legislative environment was imposed so the labelling of products had to change.

Max was going to drop me off to catch a coach to cross the bridge by public transport. I wanted to cross the new bridge connecting the Russian mainland to Crimea in daylight; however, I had a choice of just one coach in the late afternoon. Max dropped me at a petrol station in the middle of nowhere. I might have been worried about this being a bus stop but I had travelled from Rostov-on-Don to Krasnodar to Sochi by coach so I was used to long-distance coach stops being at unusual places.

I said goodbye to Max and bought my two tickets, one for me and one for my baggage. The coach arrived and tired people got off to stretch their legs or to get something to eat or drink. At the due departure time, I joined the queue to get on the coach, showing my two tickets to the dispatcher.

At last, I was crossing the Crimea Bridge. Ever since it was announced that it was to be built, I was queueing up to cross it. I had viewed it from the shore next to the Cossack village yet it seems odd that you see very little of it if you are on the structure. It is a similar experience to me like sitting on a carriage pulled by a steam engine in that you are on the train but have no idea of what is actually powering you along the track, only that you could stand next to the engine in the station but then get on board and not see it doing its stuff. The best views are from the air or a perpendicular view, watching the train being pulled by its steam engine, huffing and puffing along the line.

It was late afternoon as I crossed but at least I had seen it and had been over it and I resisted the temptation to take a photo due to security issues. Then it was a long journey through dusk to reach Simferopol. It was late when I arrived and I had little time to explore the city as I was intent on finding my hotel just off the main square. I remember little of the city other than the main railway station, an impressive building lit up at night. I didn't see much of the city in the morning as I left before the sun had risen.

Chapter 21
Crimea

I had arrived in Simferopol in the dark and I was leaving it in the dark. The city was originally named Simferopolis by Greek settlers but was renamed Simferopol in 1784 after the annexation of the Crimean Khanate to the Russian empire by Katherine II and literally means 'the city of usefulness'.

The city has featured in several military conflicts. It was a major Russian base during the Crimea War and more than 30,000 soldiers are buried there. At the end of the Russian Civil War, the headquarters of General Pyotr Wrangel, leader of the anti-Bolshevik White Army, were located there until 13th November 1920 when the Red Army captured the city. In the Great Patriotic War, the city was occupied by the Nazis from November 1941 to April 1944 where in one atrocity, on 9th December 1941, the Einsatzgruppen D under Otto Ohlendorf's command killed an estimated 14,300 Simferopol residents and most of them were Jews. When the city was liberated by the Red Army on 18th May 1944, the Crimean Tatar population of the city was forcibly deported to Central Asia in a form of collective punishment.

I wasn't spending any time in Simferopol but just moving through. It has the longest trolleybus line in the world with a total length of originally 86 kilometres but after annexation, it was extended to 96 kilometres connecting Simferopol to Yalta.

My ultimate destination in Crimea was Sevastopol but I was making a diversion to take in Balaklava and Yalta én route and despite the trolley bus option, I was taking the 2-hour coach to reach Yalta on the Black Sea coast.

This small beach resort nestling between the shore and the towering limestone cliffs behind it was made famous throughout the world as the meeting place in February 1945 when the allied leaders Stalin, Churchill and Roosevelt, met for a weeklong conference to decide how to re-order the world after the impending defeat of the Nazis in Europe and to discuss what it would take to persuade the Russians to join in the fighting against the Japanese whose defeat was not yet obvious. Stalin didn't like flying and travelled everywhere on his own armoured train so Churchill and Eisenhower had to make the perilous journeys by plane, ship and submarine halfway around the world to speak to Stalin in person.

I wanted to visit the actual site where the meeting took place and where that iconic photograph of the three was taken. The actual site is just a little west along the coast and is called the Livadia Palace. It was a summer retreat of the last Russian tsar, Nicholas II, and his family. It housed the American delegation and where all the negotiations would take place whilst the Russian delegation was housed in the Yusupov Palace and the British delegation was housed in the Vorontsov Palace some eight kilometres away.

It was further than I had time to walk so I left my bag in a locker at the bus station and got a local bus. I got to the right place but was devastated as the structure was undergoing refurbishment. It was surrounded by scaffolding and wrapped in plastic and however much I peered through the fence and pushed branches aside, I could see very little from the perimeter fence.

I spent more time waiting at the bus stop for the return ride back to the main bus station. I rechecked the times of buses from here to Balaklava and onward to Sevastopol and was reassured that there were plenty so I didn't have to make sure I was back at a certain time so I didn't need to buy a ticket and book a seat straight away.

Yalta is a well-known summer resort on the Black Sea offering warmth, sunshine and relaxation and a place in the sun to Russians who live in remote or in the bleak far north. Even this early in the season, the temperatures were mild but there were still a few tourists braving the beaches; however, it had the air of a summer paradise shut down for the winter and it was empty.

And despite the reputation of a popular resort, the beach is not sand but stony. But there are plenty of attractions on offer for families such as parks, zoos, aquariums, a cable car ride to the top of the mountain behind the town and numerous restaurants, cafes and bars. And of course, the chance to catch up with some rays. The town has expanded along the thin strip of coast in both directions and up the valley into the hills behind. The main road along the coast is inland, in the hills and the bus station is near the main road. It was a long walk down towards the beach.

I had tried to find a tourist office for a map of the town but I couldn't find one and not even a small map in any of the shops. Besides the promenade, the other big attraction for me was to visit Cherkov's house. I had studied the town layout on my laptop in the hotel the night before just in case I couldn't find a map locally as I like to prepare and know maps aren't always easy to find.

I was confident that I was in the right area but my confidence levels fell as I wandered the streets without any result. I asked a couple of people but they just shrugged their shoulders or said that they didn't know. It looked easy on the map but somehow reality was more difficult than I expected and I gave up the search. I was lost after having turned so many corners and losing my sense of direction so my only solution was to head downhill. I would eventually get to the seashore, and it would be easy to find the main street and up and away from the sea back to the bus station.

The promenade stretches a long way along the seafront and is a series of open public spaces and parks lined with statues and trees or palms for shade. It would be heaving in summer with temperatures hitting 40C but this early in the season, the visitors had yet to arrive in force and many businesses had shut for the winter and had yet to reopen. I would hate it at the height of summer, far too hot and too many people so this was a good time of year to visit for me.

Walking along the front back towards the centre I came across a distinctive seafront cafe and restaurant. It was built on a pier, pointing out to sea on stilts and took the form of a Greek galley or a quinquereme but with only one row of oars sticking out of its sides. I looked at the prices and my suspicions were confirmed that the unique architecture also meant a little extra on the prices for the novelty value.

Along the front in a park, I found a statue of Chekhov. He was a Russian playwright and short-story writer, who is considered to be among the greatest writers of short fiction in history. His career as a playwright produced four classics, and his best short stories are held in high esteem by both critics and other writers. He bought a plot of land in Yalta in 1898 and built a villa. It was a niggling reminder that his home was somewhere behind me but I had missed it.

One well-known symbol associated with the city is the lady with a dog statue in bronze, one of Chekhov's well-known characters. I walked past the end of the road leading back to the bus station to walk a little further along the promenade. A few shops were open and a few bars plus a wine bar offering tastes of local wines. Its particular advertising point was having a mannequin of Vincent van Gogh sitting at one of its tables. I fancied a selfie of him and me but I was horrified at the high prices of the wines so I quickly moved on and back towards the bus station for the journey to Balaklava.

The coach worked its way along the coast road through the limestone hills that line the coast. The road weaves its way through the hills so I only got occasional glimpses of the sea. The driver turned off the main road and followed a road down a valley to reach our next stop in Balaklava located on the southern coast of the Crimea.

This is where it all happened, made famous by Alfred Lord Tennyson's poem about the Charge of the Light Brigade. In it, he said 600 but there were actually 670 but that didn't rhyme and hence the inaccuracy. Actually, 110 were killed and 160 wounded, a casualty ratio of 38% and they lost 375 horses.

The town is spread thinly along the small strip of land between the harbour that takes up most of the space at the bottom of the valley and the steep valley sides. Further development has taken place further up the valley where the hillside is not so steep. The site of the battle of Balaclava and the Charge of the Light Brigade is further inland but new development has encroached on the battlefield.

I had climbed the hill to the west of the harbour but the valley sides were so steep that I soon lost the view of both the harbour and the town on the far side. I tried to make my way around the hillside to the site of the battle but found my way blocked by a large hole in the ground. This is all limestone country, and it is quarried extensively for cutting into building blocks, aggregate and making into cement.

I returned down the hill the way I had come and made my way to the submarine pen built underground on the western side of the harbour. Outside the entrance was a research submarine and a bathysphere. I bought a timed ticket and then had some time to kill before my tour group would be allowed in.

At the entrance was a plan of the underground facility built into the mountain and some photographs of both when it was operational and how badly it had decayed before repair work was undertaken and it was opened as a tourist attraction.

The entrance to the harbour is difficult as it requires boats to take a hard right and then a hard left turn to enter the harbour so it is only suitable for small boats and leisure craft. The submarine pen has two entrances, one facing the open sea so avoids the problem of the dog leg entrance and the other entrance is into the inner harbour.

The harbour entrance to the submarine pen has a massive blast door so that it can be sealed against a nuclear attack. The door weighs 150 tons, it is 14 metres high and 9 metres wide to close the entrance and to make it bomb-proof. Our guide started her spiel as we walked through the entrance and into the shelter.

There was a bit about how it was constructed and a long history of submarines. There were models and pictures of just about every submarine type ever built and I lost interest in some of the detail. The submarines could be refuelled and rearmed underground, with mines, torpedoes or rockets.

There was even a dry dock underground where damaged submarines could be worked on. There were several small submarines on show within the repair area. The walls of the dock area were lined with old tyres to protect the submarines from hitting the reinforced concrete walls of the tunnels.

There were display areas with uniforms, models, a mock-up of sections within a submarine and an area dedicated to submarine warfare. There was also a large segment dedicated to the Kursk submarine disaster. Another area was dedicated to the nuclear attacks on Japan and their effects. We passed the facility's own atomic reactor to power all the lights, doors, lifts, hoists and its own blast doors to protect the submarine area from the reactor area and vice versa. We exited the facility through the land-based entrance to the facility which had its own set of blast doors.

I walked back up the road, around the head of the harbour and through the town area next to the harbour with its promenade, cafes and restaurants and of course its numerous souvenir stands. There was a museum somewhere and I even had the address but it was elusive as it was hidden up an alley. It was supposedly a museum on the history of Balaklava and it had had several good reviews. However, it turned out to be more of a cafe with bric a-brac around the walls and hanging from the ceiling so it wasn't quite what I expected.

I walked to the seaward entrance of the harbour and looking back, I saw the seaward entrance to the submarine pen. There are some older buildings here, largely ruins, from the medieval defences and high up on the top of the cliff were more towers and ruins for those feeling fit enough to climb up a long flight of steps. I had time but there wasn't much to see so I made my way back to the bus station for the hour bus ride to Sevastopol.

The original name of the settlement was Sevastopolis, chosen in the same etymological trend as other cities in the Crimean peninsula as it was intended to express its ancient Greek origins. It is a compound of two Greek words meaning 'venerable' and 'city'.

Despite its Greek origin, the name is not from ancient Greek times. The city was founded as Sevastopol in 1783 and Katherine II visited the city in 1787, accompanied by Joseph II, the Emperor of Austria, and other foreign dignitaries.

In the west of the city, there are some well-preserved ruins of the ancient Greek port city of Chersonesos, founded in the 5th or 4th century BC by settlers from Heraclea Pontica. This name means 'peninsula', reflecting its immediate location.

The Greek city of Chersonesus existed for almost 2000 years, first as an independent democracy and later as part of the Bosporan Kingdom. In the 13th and 14th centuries, it was sacked by the Golden Horde several times and was finally totally abandoned. The modern-day city of Sevastopol has no connection to the ancient and medieval Greek city, but the ruins are a popular tourist attraction located on the outskirts of the city.

Modern Sevastopol was founded in June 1783 as a base for a naval squadron under the name Akhtiar meaning White Cliff due to the limestone cliffs by Rear Admiral Thomas MacKenzie, also known as Foma Fomich Makenzi who was a native Scot in the Russian service after Russia annexed the Crimean Khanate. Five years earlier, in 1778, General Alexander Suvorov ordered that earthworks be erected along the harbour and garrisoned by Russian troops.

In February 1784, Katherine the Great ordered Grigory Potemkin to build a fortress there. The realisation of the initial building plans fell to Captain Fyodor Ushakov who in 1788 was named commander of the port and of the Black Sea squadron. It became an important naval base and later a commercial seaport. In 1797, under an edict issued by Emperor Paul I, the military stronghold was again renamed Akhtiar. Finally, on 29th April 1826, the city was renamed Sevastopol.

One of the most notable events involving the city is the Siege of Sevastopol 1854–55 carried out by the British, French, Sardinian, and Turkish troops during the Crimean War, which lasted for 11 months. Despite its efforts, the Russian army had to leave its stronghold and evacuate over a pontoon bridge to the north shore of the inlet. The Russians chose to sink their entire fleet to prevent it from falling into the hands of the enemy and at the same time to block the entrance of enemy ships into the inlet. When the enemy troops entered Sevastopol, they were faced with the ruins of a formerly glorious city.

During the Great Patriotic War, Sevastopol withstood intensive bombardment by the Germans in 1941–42, supported by their Italian and Romanian allies during the Battle of Sevastopol. German forces used railway artillery, including history's largest-ever calibre railway artillery piece in battle, the 80 centimetres calibre Schwerer Gustav and specialised mobile heavy mortars to destroy Sevastopol's extremely strong fortifications, such as the Maxim Gorky Fortress.

After fierce fighting, which lasted for 250 days, the supposedly untakable fortress city finally fell to Axis forces in July 1942. It was intended to be renamed Theoderichshafen about Theoderic the Great and the fact that the Crimea had been home to Germanic Goths from the 18th century. It was liberated by the Red Army on 9th May 1944 and was awarded the Hero City title a year later.

During the Soviet era, Sevastopol became a closed city. This meant that any non-residents had to apply to the authorities for a temporary permit to visit the city. In 1954, under Nikita Khrushchev, both Sevastopol and the remainder of the Crimean peninsula were administratively transferred from being territories within Russia to being territories administered by the Ukraine.

In 1992, the commander of the joint Russian-Ukrainian Black Sea fleet, Eduard Baltin, accused Ukraine of converting some of his fleet and conducting an armed assault on his personnel and threatened to take countermeasures by placing the fleet on alert. In June, Russian President Boris Yeltsin and Ukrainian President Leonid Kravchuk had agreed to divide the former-Soviet Black Sea fleet between Russia and Ukraine. Eduard Baltin had been appointed commander of the Black Sea fleet by Yeltsin and Kravchuk on 15th January 1993.

In May 1997, Russia and Ukraine signed the Peace and Friendship Treaty, ruling out Moscow's territorial claims to Ukraine. A separate agreement established the terms of a long-term lease of land, facilities, and resources in Sevastopol and the Crimea by Russia.

The ex-Soviet Black Sea fleet and its facilities were divided between Russia's Black Sea Fleet and the Ukrainian Naval Forces. The two navies co-used some of the city's harbours and piers, whilst others were demilitarised. Sevastopol remained the location of the Russian Black Sea fleet headquarters with the Ukrainian Naval Forces Headquarters also in the city. A judicial row periodically continued over the naval infrastructure both in Sevastopol and on the Crimean coast especially lighthouses historically maintained by the Soviet or Russian Navy and also used for civil navigation support.

As in the rest of the Crimea, Russian remained the predominant language of the city, although following the independence of Ukraine there were some attempts at Ukrainisation with very little success. Russian society in general and even some outspoken government representatives never accepted the loss of Sevastopol and tended to regard it as temporarily separated from the homeland.

On 27th April 2010, Russia and Ukraine ratified the Russian-Ukrainian Naval Base for Gas treaty, extending the Russian Navy's lease of Crimean facilities for 25 years from 2017 to 2042 with an option to prolong the lease in 5-year extensions. The ratification process in the Ukrainian parliament encountered stiff opposition and erupted into a brawl in the parliament chamber. Eventually, the treaty was ratified by just a 52% majority vote. The Russian Duma ratified the treaty by a 98% majority.

On 20th February 2014, Russian armed forces seized control of the Crimean peninsula. The city council of Sevastopol reportedly unilaterally declared that it wished to join the Russian Federation as a federal subject. The city council on 11th March released a joint resolution with the Supreme Council of Crimea to unite as an independent republic between the potential passing of the referendum and union with Russia. Ukrainian authorities and the international community strongly criticised the referendum decision. The actions of the Russian Federation were qualified by the international community as aggression against Ukraine, and occupation of its territory.

The controversial referendum on leaving Ukraine resulted in a 95.6% vote in favour though these results are contested, but a later survey showed that 83% of Crimeans felt that the results of the referendum correctly reflected the views of most people there. Sevastopol is ethnically 72% Russian and 22% Ukrainian.

Whilst Russia and ten other UN member states recognised the Crimean peninsula as part of the Russian Federation, Ukraine continues to claim Crimea and Sevastopol as an integral part of its territory, supported by most foreign governments and United Nations General Assembly Resolution 68/262.

Sevastopol maintains a large port facility in the Bay of Sevastopol and smaller bays around the Heracles peninsula. The port handles both local passengers and cruise passengers, cargo, and commercial fishing. The port infrastructure is fully integrated with the city of Sevastopol and the naval bases of the Black Sea fleet. Sevastopol Shipyard has facilities that repair, modernise, and re-equip Russian Naval ships and submarines. The Sevastopol International Airport is used as a military aerodrome at the moment and is being reconstructed to be used by international airlines so flights have been diverted to Simferopol International Airport.

After the devastation of the Second World War, Sevastopol was entirely rebuilt. Many top architects and civil engineers from Moscow, Leningrad, Kyiv and other cities and thousands of workers from all parts of the USSR took part in the rebuilding process which was mostly finished by the mid-1950s. The downtown core situated on a peninsula between two narrow inlets, South Bay and Artillery Bay, features mostly Mediterranean-style, three-story residential buildings with columned balconies and Venetian-style arches, with retail and commercial spaces occupying the ground level. Some carefully restored landmarks date back to the early 20th century to preserve the sense of traditional architecture of the time.

Due to its military history, most streets in the city are named after Russian and Soviet military heroes. There are dozens of monuments and plaques in various parts of Sevastopol commemorating its military past.

I was delighted with my hotel accommodation after the disaster of the hotel in Slavyansk na Kubani. It was a modern purpose-built hotel up a quiet street just away from the main centre. The staff all spoke excellent English and the internet worked. I was going to be here for several nights as there is a lot to see. Had the hotel not been adequate, there were plenty of others and I would have moved but it fitted my requirements perfectly.

My first day's tour was to Inkerman, a suburb of Sevastopol to the northeast which was the scene of a battle during the Crimea campaign and there is a medieval fortress sitting on top of some cliffs with the Monastery of St Clements with some of its chapels and rooms in caves dug into the limestone cliffs. For good measure, the village also hosts a large winery whose brand name is Inkerman and produces several different types of quality wines.

I caught the 92 bus from the centre of the city and despite being just on the outskirts to the north, the bus headed off southwards through the suburbs and made a large swing around the eastern suburbs before making its way down a dry valley to reach Inkerman. It was two sides of a triangle rather than a direct bus and I think that I could have walked it faster than the convoluted route that the bus took.

The monastery was a lot smaller than I had expected but it had its charms. There was just a modest entry price and visitors can wander through the various chapels at will. This is the site of a medieval Byzantine monastery probably founded in the 8th century where the relics of St Clement were supposedly kept before their removal to San Clemente by Saints Cyril and Methodius. The caves were looted by British soldiers during the Crimea War. The current range of buildings of the monastery was built in 1850.

The main two churches were added later. One church was built in 1905 to commemorate the 50th anniversary of the Crimea War. The other church was added after the Borki Incident in 1895. There was a train disaster on 29th October 1888 near Borki, Ukraine, 295 kilometres south of Kursk, when the Imperial train carrying Tsar Alexander III of Russia and his family from Crimea to St Petersburg derailed at high speed. Twenty-one people were killed and many others were injured. According to the official version of events, Alexander, who was known as a well-built man, held the collapsed roof of the royal carriage on his shoulders whilst his family escaped the crashed carriage uninjured. The story of the miraculous escape became part of contemporary lore and government propaganda.

What is immediately noticeable about the site is that there is a railway line just metres from the main buildings and the cliff face. The Bolsheviks had closed many churches or had used them for other purposes in a direct and sustained attack on the church and what it represented as the old order. Therefore despite the fact that the railway could have been built a little further away and lower down the slope, this was deliberately placed here to cause maximum disruption. Just the other side of the railway to add to the disruption is a steel fabrication yard, a cement plant and some quarry buildings.

In the hills just behind the monastery and the medieval fortress on the top of the cliff are the now disused quarry workings with lakes in the bottom for fisherman to try their hand at catching something. But the noise even on the weekend that I visited would have made a mockery of any attempt at functioning as a monastery but it was exactly what the Bolsheviks intended.

From the car park, a path winds its way up the slope to the fortress. There are views down to the monastery on one side and long drops down vertical walls of limestone to the quarry workings on the other side. The fortress is just a number of ruined towers and a few walls but in its heyday, it would have been quite a sizeable site and enclosed a large area. There is a direct path that links the monastery to the fortress but not open to the public.

Across the estuary of the small river that enters the sea here are the hills on which the Battle of Inkerman was fought on 5th November 1854. Troops had landed in Crimea in September 1854 and had first engaged the Russians at the Battle of Alma, on the road between Sevastopol and Simferopol and drove them back. The allies had set up a supply base at Balaklava and although the Charge of the Light Brigade was a disaster, the numerically superior Russian force was repulsed but they had captured some cannons which were proudly displayed in Sevastopol.

A siege was being prepared to capture Sevastopol but the British, French and Ottomans didn't have enough troops to be fully effective. The Russian commander Prince Menshikov saw an opportunity and advanced from Sevastopol towards Inkerman. The smooth-bore muskets of the Russian troops were no match for the rifled Minié balls of the British troops and the early morning fog caused problems.

The Russians lost twice as many troops as the allies and they retreated to Sevastopol and the siege started. Had the Russians had better intelligence, one more attack would have defeated the allies before their reinforcements could have been deployed but then that is the fog of war. The Russians retreated and would not engage the enemy in the field again for the rest of the war.

I walked up the road to the Inkerman Winery only to find that it was shut but then of course I should have checked the opening times but I had seen plenty of other wineries so I didn't feel that I was missing out…except for the chance of a few free tastings and the opportunity to buy some bottles at less than the prices in the shops. I waited at the bus stop for the bus to take me on another convoluted tour of the Sevastopol suburbs before dropping me off near my hotel in the city centre.

Chapter 22
Sevastopol

I took the ferry to the far side of the harbour, passing the Monument to the Sunken Ships. It is a double-headed Imperial Eagle standing on top of a column. It was erected in 1905 as part of the 50th-anniversary celebrations of the Siege of Sevastopol during the Crimean Wars to remember the dozen or so ships that the Russians lost from their Black Sea fleet in the harbour.

I walked along the shoreline towards the Konstantinovskaya Battery at the mouth of the harbour. I could see the outer walls of the battery from the ferry but it was a distant view. It sits on the end of a long spit of land closing the mouth of the harbour and there was nowhere on land from which to take a decent photo. I was also aware that there is a military base nearby and I didn't get the camera out as I didn't want to get a free trip to the Siberian Salt mines for 20 years.

The battery has recently been lovingly restored and it is in pristine condition. There are two levels from which heavy calibre guns cover the approaches to the inner harbour. The guns were housed on one side of the central aisle and their crews lived in the chamber opposite. One of the chambers had been set up as it would have been in the mid-nineteenth century, with a gun being manned by its crew and the living quarters opposite. Other chambers had photographs and exhibits. Between each chamber was a giant circular metal oven to warm the space, a metre in diameter and two and a half metres high. If they were all in use at the same time, this place would be roasting.

The bridge of land connecting the renovated battery to the mainland was only lightly protected during the Crimea War but was heavily built up with concrete gun emplacements by the Russians in preparation for the German offensive during 1941 and suffered badly. Then they were upgraded by the Nazis only to be destroyed again by the Russians as they liberated the Crimea from the Nazis. It has yet to receive any extensive renovation but there is some work taking place so it will be different in years to come.

Just a little further into the harbour on the same side as the Konstantinovskaya Battery is another massive, supporting gun emplacement, the

Mikhailovska Battery, with a similar array of double-stacked firing positions for heavy calibre artillery. This gun emplacement has yet to receive the same kind of renovation that the Konstantinovskaya Battery has received. One corner is crumbling away, there is a large crack in one of the walls and the landward outer wall of the battery has a lot of shrapnel marks and some stones missing.

And as with most wartime historical sites, there are a few artefacts on show from the Great Patriotic War such as several anti-aircraft guns, some rockets, a plane and a tank.

Inside, one of the chambers has been set up to show how it might have looked in the mid-nineteenth century, and very similar to the reproduction in the Konstantinovskaya Battery. Many of the other chambers have guns on show, uniforms, flags and photographs and again those large cylindrical, vertical, metal ovens.

I took the ferry back to the other side of the harbour and walked up the main road past the theatre to Nakhimova Square. On one side of the road is some brutalist Communist architecture, a massive slab of rock with some statuary at one end to represent an idealised Soviet soldier as a monument to the fallen, the names of those who died battling for the city and an eternal flame.

Opposite this on the other side of the road is a statue of Admiral Pavel Nakhimov, commander of naval and land forces during the Siege of Sevastopol during the Crimea War. He was a brilliant commander and earlier in his career had defeated a Turkish fleet at Sinope with a much inferior force in 1853 and became the overall commander of the defences in Sevastopol against a numerically superior foe. He held out from October 1854 fighting several memorable battles until killed by a sniper in July 1855. The city fell just a few weeks later to allied forces in September 1855.

There is a square here and some steps down to the waterfront. These are the Sevastopol Sea Station Steps which led down to the water at Grafskaya Quay, or Count's Jetty where local ferries stop to take passengers across the harbour. And I like connections and this was one. John Upton was born and lived in Petworth, West Sussex not far from my home town. He became an engineer and amongst his other creations, he designed this quay, redesigned the road layout of the city and planned the city's water mains system.

Following the main road along the coast is the Museum of the History of the Black Sea Fleet. It is an interesting building architecturally and although modest, I found it fascinating. The exhibits aren't so numerous that there are hall after hall of repeated items but they all document the history of the navy. There are displays of models, photographs, uniforms, guns, paraphernalia, gifts, medals and the like, all of which are great if you like that thing and also not so large in case you don't like that stuff but I was more fascinated with the architecture.

Just a short walk away is an underground museum, a former bomb shelter dug into the cliffs and just one of several but at this one, I was barred entry. There was no sign but one policeman in uniform and a lot of young, muscled men with short haircuts wearing curly plastic earpieces and small microphones. Someone important was visiting or about to visit and the place was closed to the public. There were no signs and no barriers but if you walked too close, the policeman would shout at you and two of the beefsteaks would move towards you. I backed off and would come back another time.

Set high up on a cliff overlooking an arm of the inner harbour is The Panorama Museum of the Defence of the City of Sevastopol, a great ornate circular building. A panorama of the siege was created by Franz Roubaud, a Russian painter who created some of the largest and best-known panoramic paintings. After its destruction in 1942 during the Great Patriotic War, it was restored and is currently housed in a specially constructed circular building in the city. It portrays the situation at the height of the siege, on 18th June 1855.

They claim to be the biggest panorama but my guide in Volgograd had claimed that it was the largest just a couple of weeks before which I would imagine would have a greater claim as it is much newer and they would have been aware of the size of the Sevastopol panorama. I didn't realise that there were so many claims to something that I had never really been that interested in!

I had a timed ticket so I had to wait a while. Next to the panorama building in the park surrounding it according to my map were a statue of Tolstoy, the site of the 4th Battery, the memorial to the Warriors of the 4th Battery, the actual 38th Battery and some other sights. I went to investigate but was stopped by some red and white plastic tape and a mass of builders' paraphernalia, piles of sand, pallets of paving slabs, torn-up paths, piles of rubble and so on. It was undergoing refurbishment. There didn't seem to one anyone about so I ducked under the plastic tape and turned a corner to come face to face with a security guard. I was ushered off the site so I returned to the panorama to sit in the sun until it was time to go in.

I am not a great fan of panoramas but it was realistic and very well done. It did look like a battle scene with the foreground bunkers, mannequins and artefacts blending in well with the painted scenes on the walls further away. Add in a few sounds of battle and it is very convincing. The guide told several stories of heroism and pieces of the battle that were depicted.

I walked across the city to reach Malakov Kurgan. This is a prominent hill to the north of the city and was vital to the defences of the city. From here, visitors can gaze out across the city and to the north are the hills where the Battle of Inkerman was fought. To the south, there is a panoramic view of the city and the harbour, the entrance to the harbour and both the Konstantinovskaya and Mikhailovska Battery.

The British forces had attacked this point since January to no effect. It was a French assault that finally captured the position in August. The Russians had to retreat from the position, and given its strategic position, it dominated the section of the city nearby which the Russians also had to withdraw from and it was only weeks later that the siege ended when the attacking forces captured the whole city.

A memorial was created in 1905 to commemorate the 50th anniversary of the start of the siege but the area was badly damaged during the defence of the city during the Great Patriotic War and it was only re-established as a memorial site in the 1960s. It is a favourite park for locals and groups of school children who come to visit from all over the city so I was heading there first thing in the morning before it became too crowded.

There are monuments here to both the Crimea War and the Great Patriotic War. After passing through the entrance arch, there are a series of steps leading up towards the top. The first monument is to the Warriors of the 8th Air Army and opposite it is a Memorial to the French and Russian Warriors of 1855.

Further up on the left is the No. 2 Artillery Gun of Lieutenant Commander A P Matyukhin Battery No 111, 1941-42 and beyond it is the No. 1 Artillery Gun and between them and slightly in front is his headquarters, down half a flight of steps to a small bunker. Both of these guns were rescued from his ship which had been sunk in the harbour but it sat on the bottom of the harbour seabed and the superstructure was above the water line, one of many ships that had been sunk in the harbour and remembered by another monument standing in the water. The two guns and their ammunition were removed and added to the defences surrounding the city.

A large monument of a gentleman leaning against a rock with his right arm raised whilst to one side of the rock, a sailor is loading a cannonball into a cannon is a tribute to Vice Admiral V A Kornilov. In 1827, he fought in the Battle of Navarino as a midshipman aboard the fleet's flagship Azov, when a joint Russian, French and British naval force supporting Greek independence attacked the Ottoman fleet in Navarino Bay. This was the last time that a major sea battle was fought by sailing ships. During the Crimean War, Kornilov was responsible for the defence of Sevastopol but he was killed early in the siege and eventually was buried in the Admirals' Burial Vault on the top of Malakov Kurgan.

Between this statue and the squat tower at the very top of the hill is an array of mid-19th century artillery pieces and a mock-up of a gun emplacement complete with a cannon and gabions as it might have been during the siege.

The squat tower and surrounding stone emplacements are a reproduction as it was damaged in the original assault and was not strong enough to withstand the modern weapons of the Nazis during the Great Patriotic War. On the ridge nearby is a plaque recording the spot where Admiral P S Nakhimov was fatally wounded by a sniper.

I walked into the city centre and found a Number 95 bus. It stopped at the end of the line in a small village called Bazan. A short walk past the few houses found me standing on the cliff edge overlooking the Black Sea. This is the most westerly point of the Crimea and was the symbolic end of my journey through Russia.

I had gone from the far north, the Arctic Ocean and the White Sea via Moscow and the Volga to the Black Sea admittedly with some doubling back on myself such as northwards to Murmansk and Norway before heading south again, along the Moscow Canal twice and steaming along the Volga between Volgograd and Astrakhan twice. I had covered more than 8,500 kilometres, nearly a fifth of the way around the world all in one country ignoring the side trip to Norway. This was the end of another chapter of my journey around the world.

Recipes

Russia is not known for its culinary skills probably due to its harsh climate in the north making the choice of ingredients limited and whilst trade could increase the range of ingredients, the vast expanses of the empire made transport expensive and hence out of reach of the ordinary peasant.

However, there are several traditional dishes and knowledge of some of its dishes is widespread. Here are just a few of those dishes whose details I picked up when I was travelling through the area.

Borscht

This is a dish that originated in Ukraine but it spread throughout the area and is found in some form in every Slavic culture. There are both simple recipes and complicated artistic forms. I suspect that it originated as a soup based on a local root vegetable that would grow in the harsh climate and that anything left over from other meals could be thrown in to make it a little different.

I have been back to the same restaurant and found that the borscht the next day was different from the borscht the day before. It is said that there are as many recipes for borscht as there are housewives. Prospective husbands and grooms would also want to test the quality of their prospective wife's cooking ability by tasting the borscht that her mother made, hence getting the right mix is important and mothers would swear daughters to secrecy about what went into their borscht.

Ingredients

- 500 grams stewing beef
- 2 large uncooked beetroots
- 4 tablespoons olive oil
- 1 tablespoon vinegar
- 1 tablespoon sugar
- 2 tablespoons of tomato paste concentrate

a knob of butter
1 onion, finely diced
2 carrots, grated
2 large potatoes sliced or diced
half a small cabbage, sliced
2 tomatoes, peeled and diced
2 bay leaves
pepper and salt to taste
1/4 cup chopped parsley
2 cloves of garlic, finely chopped
sour cream
fresh dill for garnish

Method

1. Cut the meat into one-centimetre cubes and place in a large saucepan, add three litres of water and salt. As soon as it boils, remove the surface foam and reduce to a simmer for 45 minutes. Periodically remove any additional foam.
2. Grate the beetroots and sauté in olive oil and vinegar for 5 minutes, reduce the heat and stir in sugar and tomato paste. Continue to sauté, stirring occasionally until the beetroot begins to soften. Remove from the pan and set aside.
3. Add butter to the frying pan (no need to wash it) and sauté the onion to soften; add carrots and sauté for another 5 minutes.
4. After the meat has cooked for at least 45 minutes, add the potatoes to the simmering meat for 10 minutes.
5. Add cabbage, the sautéed beetroot, the tomatoes, the onion/carrot mix and chopped tomatoes and cook until the potatoes are soft but still firm enough to hold together.
6. Add bay leaves, parsley, garlic, salt and pepper, cover and remove from the heat and leave for 20 minutes for the flavours to mix.
7. Serve with a dollop of sour cream and several sprigs of dill.
8. For a vegetarian and vegan alternative, simply leave out the meat and butter.

Alternatives include serving with a freshly broken egg stirred just once into the bowl. There is also a 'green borscht', leaving out the beetroot and adding lots of sorrel but to my mind borscht is beetroot and it is rather like having a vegetarian dish without vegetables and shouldn't exist. If you really want a name for a soup with almost the same ingredients, it should be called Sorrel Soup.

Blini

These are so important to Russian culture and they are a pearl of Russian cuisine. It is a fundamental part of Russian culture and is associated with Maslenitsa, an ancient Slavic festival to mark the end of winter and occurs at the start of Lent 8 weeks before Easter.

The pancake is representative of the sun and is eaten to welcome the sun and spring after a long, cold winter. Everyone makes pancakes and offers them to everyone else. Other activities include a party where a large bonfire is lit and upon which a large straw effigy is burnt which represents winter. So the festival represents a point in the calendar which throws off winter and welcomes the coming of spring and summer.

Ingredients

400 grams wheat flour
1/2 teaspoon salt
1/4 teaspoon baking soda
3 tablespoons sugar
2 eggs
800 ml milk
100 ml cream
5 tablespoons butter
sunflower oil

Method

1. Mix flour, salt and baking soda in a bowl and set aside.
2. Mix sugar and eggs thoroughly together and gently add in the milk and cream.

3. Gradually add in the flour mixture and blend until smooth.
4. Melt the butter and blend into the mixture.
5. Pour some sunflower oil into a frying pan over high heat and pour in some of the mixture to form a thin circular pancake. When that side is cooked, flip it over and cook the other side and it is ready to eat.
6. Serve plain or offer jam, jelly or honey as desired.

Pelmeni

Ingredients for dough

2/3 cups buttermilk
1 tablespoon sour cream
2 large eggs
2 cups warm water
1 teaspoon salt
1 kilo unbleached all-purpose flour
Ingredients for Pelmeni filling
1 tablespoon olive oil
1 medium onion, finely diced
3 garlic cloves, finely chopped
1 kilo of minced meat whatever your preference may be such as turkey, chicken, pork or beef
Salt and pepper to taste
1 teaspoon hot sauce (optional)
Butter, sour cream and dill, finely diced for the topping

Method to make the dough

1. Put the buttermilk, sour cream, eggs, water and salt into a bowl and whisk until well blended.
2. Add half the flour and knead. Slowly add the remaining flour, one handful at a time. Knead until it no longer sticks to the bowl and turn out and leave on a lightly floured surface.

Method to make the filling

1. Lightly sauté the onions in oil until golden and add garlic and sauté for two more minutes.
2. Add meat, salt and pepper, mix and remove from heat.

Making the Pelmeni

Roll the dough flat.

1. Use a circular pastry cutter to form rounds of dough about 4 centimetres across. Fill the centre with the filling.
2. Fold the dough over to make a semicircle and crimp the edges together. Then fold the ends over and crimp together.
3. Place the pelmeni on a lightly floured board and place in the freezer. When they are frozen, they can be used straight away or saved for later.

Cooking pelmeni

Bring a pot of salted water to the boil. Add the frozen pelmeni and bring back to the boil. The pelmeni should float to the top. Boil for another 3 minutes or until the meat is cooked. Drain, toss with butter and sprinkle with dill and serve with sour cream, vinegar or any sauce you may prefer such as ketchup.

Stroganov

There are both beef and mushroom versions and vegetarian or vegan-friendly versions. Stroganov recipes and the evolution of the dish have been mentioned earlier and even the beef version has mushrooms in the sauce. It has become so popular that there are many different versions of the recipe. I will describe how to make the sauce and it is the chefs' choice with a bit of intuition on how to create his own version of this classical dish.

Ingredients

1 tablespoon vegetable oil
1 large chopped onion
4 cloves of chopped or crushed garlic
500 grams sliced mushrooms (finely chopped and less for the beef version)
2 heaped teaspoons Dijon mustard (coarse or smooth)
1 heaped teaspoon paprika
2 tablespoons flour
1 cup of beef cube stock or a vegetable cube for a vegetarian/vegan-friendly version
1 tablespoon Worcestershire sauce
Salt and pepper to taste
1 cup light sour cream
Freshly chopped parsley to garnish

Method

1. Lightly fry the onions and garlic until soft.
2. Add the mushrooms and cook until the mushrooms are tender and then add in the mustard and paprika.
3. Mix the flour slowly into the stock, add the Worcestershire sauce and blend into a broth, adding extra water as necessary.
4. Add the onion and mushrooms to the broth.
5. Add 500 g sautéed beef, cubes or slices or sliced mushrooms and season.
6. Serve with a scoop of sour cream and parsley plus rice, pasta or noodles.

Russian Tea

Russians drink mostly black, fermented tea. To prepare this kind of tea, leaves are harvested, crumpled and twisted to squeeze out some juice, which accelerates fermentation. Today, tea factories use special machines to twist leaves, but early in the 20th century, the Koshmans did it manually, with their bare hands.

Leaves that have been wrung out in this way were heated in a stove for a short while and then left to dry outdoors under a canopy. When the tea was ready,

Iuda Koshman would carry it on his back all the way down to the market in Sochi on foot along a mountain path for 40 kilometres.

Koshman sent samples of dried leaves to the Russian Academy of Sciences who declared that it was not possible to grow tea trees in the Russian empire and advised the uneducated peasant to keep his fantasies at bay. But Koshman persisted and it was not until the 1920s that he received support from the state and tea plantations started spreading around Solokh-Aul. In the early 1970s, the farm gathered and processed up to 7,000 tons of tea leaves a year.

The tea leaf tips are gathered starting in the spring, as soon as the snow melts in the mountains and the tea bushes start sprouting new leaves. The season is traditionally opened by the head of the company, who picks the first few leaves from a bush near Koshman's grave and picking of the fresh sprouting tips continues every two weeks from April to October. This Russian tea has a mild flavour with a light colour and various aftertastes, which include notes of fruit and a faint flowery scent. Tea is cheap to import so locally produced tea is a premium, novelty product available in local supermarkets.